That's
Easy
FOR YOU *to*
Say

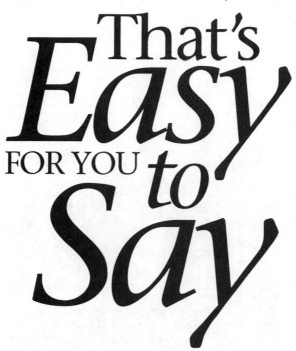

That's Easy FOR YOU to Say

Your Quick Guide to Pronouncing Bible Names

W. Murray Severance

Dr. Terry Eddinger
Compiler of the Bible Name Meanings Section

BROADMAN
& HOLMAN
PUBLISHERS

Nashville, Tennessee

© 1997 BROADMAN & HOLMAN PUBLISHERS
All rights reserved
Printed in the United States of America
1 2 3 4 5 6   03 02 01 00 99 98

ISBN: 1-55819-695-1

Dewey Decimal Classification: 220.3
Subject Heading: BIBLE NAMES
Library of Congress Card Catalog Number: 97–25039

Library of Congress Cataloging-in-Publication Data

Severance, W. Murray.
    That's easy for you to say : a guide to pronouncing Bible names /
W. Murray Severance.
    p.   cm.
    ISBN 1–55819–695–1 (tp)
    1. Names in the Bible—Pronunciation.   I. Title
BS435.S47 1997   97–25039
220.5'2'0014—dc21   CIP

Original Version: 1983
In loving memory of my parents—
Lillian Scarboro Severance
Willard Murray Severance, Sr.

Expanded Edition: 1994
To my wife, Anne Washburn Severance

That's Easy for You to Say: 1997
To my children—
Marc and Marcia
Mark and Deborah

ACKNOWLEDGMENTS

Authors do not work in a vacuum. Support comes from many quarters in the form of research, resources, professional services, management, and personal advice. My special thanks go to the following persons for their help and assistance in creating this book.

In memory of Clifton J. Allen, the instigator, who gave me the concept, helped me see the need, and then encouraged me in the initial work on this idea.

Frank C. Laubach, for his dedication, inspiration, zeal, and expertise in helping others with their own language.

Forrest Jackson, my editor, for his knowledge, experience, and friendly association.

Trent Butler, who assisted in initiating this expanded edition and who continued Dr. Allen's encouragement in this project.

John Joseph Owens, my Hebrew professor, who gave of his expertise in pronouncing many of the difficult Hebraic derivations.

Joel Drinkard, seminary professor, for recommending and pronouncing biblical archaeology names and terms.

Brian Sietsema, pronunciation editor for Merriam Webster, for assistance with phonics.

James McLemore, for submitting names of interest to readers of the *Biblical Illustrator*, of which he is editor.

Mark Davis, Helen McBrayer, and Mary Stanford, computer specialists, for guiding me through the intricacies of developing the manuscript.

Anne Severance, my wife, for her loving support and patience during the months of manuscript preparation.

I also breathe a prayer of thanks to the good Lord for granting me health to persist, patience to endure, and insight to fulfill.

INTRODUCTION

No two scholars in any field agree 100 percent. In fact, no two persons agree totally on any subject. Differences of opinion are a clear indication of individuality. People don't think alike, speak alike, look alike, or do anything else exactly alike. The author of this guide recognizes that distinctiveness. He realizes that all of those seeking to pronounce biblical names or terms will not agree with the conclusions set forth in this book. It is a guide, not the final authority. *Usage* is! Britishers spell the same word differently from Americans. Southerners pronounce words unlike Westerners. Heritage, environment, era, and other factors influence the pronunciation of words in any language.

Pronunciation of Bible names and terms continues to be influenced by the three languages in which the Bible was written. Two dominate—Hebrew and Greek. The third, Aramaic, was used for a number of passages. Hebrew and Aramaic are sister languages. The Koiné Greek, the language of the common person, contains a different number of letters from the Semitic languages and has distinctive rules for accenting and pronouncing. When these three languages are translated into English, other drastic changes appear. Colloquial spellings and pronunciations come as no real surprise, and they do occur. For instance, even the name *Palestine* is pronounced in various ways. The last syllable of the Middle Eastern country rhymes with *tine*, like the prong of a fork. Yet, the last syllable of Palestine, a city in Texas, rhymes with *teen*, a young person! Both are correct.

To a great extent we learn our rules of language and speech from our parents, teachers, and peers. Change may come about slowly, but change is inevitable. Proof of this statement is easily witnessed when a student compares the writings of Shakespeare or Chaucer with the work of modern writers. Even the poorest reader can easily discern the difference.

As a producer of religious audiovisuals for more than thirty years, I have produced literally hundreds of products based on biblical history. Most evangelical filmstrip, motion picture, videotape, and audiocassette narrations include proper Bible names. When dialogue is added to tape or film, "proper" pronunciation of these names gains even more importance. That fact motivated a serious student of the Bible to come by my office many years ago to ask my opinion about pronunciation of a rather obscure Bible name. He was on his way to record some Sunday School lessons for radio. He, like preachers, teachers, and other lecturers, realized that a successful presentation depends as much on how materials are presented as on what is said!

This person, now deceased, was highly respected as a teacher, editor, and writer. For him to come to me was flattering but bewildering! He realized that as a producer I was responsible for total production. After I offered my opinion, it dawned on me that if an educator of his stature needed help, what about others with less training?

For years I have been a follower of Frank C. Laubach and his relentless campaign to educate the illiterate peoples of the world. His slogan was "each one teach one." He developed methods to teach natives how to read in their own language. Where there was no written alphabet, Laubach developed one through interpreters. Charts were constructed, and natives were trained to teach each other. What was his reward?—the satisfaction of helping "each one teach one." Then he would move on to other fields.

Using a method for pronouncing biblical names and terms that parallels Laubach's as well as other existing systems, I produced a CD-ROM version of *That's Easy for You to Say* which can be found in a packet attached to cover page 3 of this book.

In addition, there are hundreds of geographical and personal names listed in Bible atlases, dictionaries, commentaries, handbooks, and other reference materials. For instance, the Middle Eastern cities of Ur, Nineveh, Babylon, and scores of others are mentioned in the text, while Sippar, Nuzi, Persepolis, and many others do not appear in the text but are essential to a more thorough and complete understanding of the history of biblical times. Also added are common terms such as *allegory, canon, codex,* and *monotheism,* cited in alphabetical order in the same listing as names.

2

DIFFERENT TRANSLATIONS

An interesting pattern emerged as the original version of this book was prepared. A comparison of names in the five versions revealed the differences between versions and translations. Compared to the *King James Version*, there are 752 differences in the *New American Standard Bible*, 1,039 in the *New International Version*, 933 in the *Revised Standard Version*, and 1,188 in the *Today's English Version*! Of the 3,492 names, how could up to one-third of the names vary?

All versions began with the texts available at the time of publication. Generally speaking, scholars today know more about the original languages than in 1611 when the KJV first appeared. Like current events versus history, it is generally true that the farther removed an analyst is from an event, conclusions can be more accurate. To date, no known original manuscripts of the Bible have been found, even though great archaeological discoveries like the Dead Sea Scrolls have proven again that later manuscripts are very faithful to earlier ones.

Variations in spelling and pronunciation do occur, however, from one translation to another in the following ways:

1. Doubling letters: Bezaleel vs. Bezalel
2. Substituting letters in transliteration: Chebar vs. Kebar
3. Combining names: Abel Maim vs. Ablemaim
4. Using colloquial spellings: e.g., Judea (American) vs. Judaea (British)
5. Interpreting or translating: Father vs. Abba

These changes have come about as a result of purpose, audience, time of publication, and other factors. Although many versions of the Bible are currently available, the KJV continues to be the traditional favorite. As in pronunciation, one's selection of a preferred translation is a highly personal choice. What appeals to one person leaves another dissatisfied. Therefore, students of the Bible choose different translations for their own purposes.

ALPHABET CHART

Another way of recognizing the problems in translation from one language to another is to study the alphabet chart which includes the Hebrew and Greek with English equivalents. All three start with "a" and "b." Greek points out more graphically where the term "alphabet" (*alpha beta*) originated. From that point on, no two alphabets agree completely, either in number of letters or in the sounds produced. A simple study reveals the difficulty in transliterating any name from one language to another.

To illustrate, in recent years the thrilling story of Masada, beside the Dead Sea, has been reported in archaeological journals, has been novelized, and produced for television. Present-day Israelis mention Masada in a slogan concerning national pride. The "s" in the Hebrew word *Masada* has no direct equivalent in English. A better transliteration of the name to English would be *Metzada* or *Metsada*. Since there were no written vowels in Hebrew until the Massoretes added them in the ninth century A.D., vowel sounds affecting pronunciation changed through the centuries, becoming yet another problem. This fact is graphically demonstrated in the origin of the word *Palestine* being a corruption of Philistine. Harden the "P" by removing the "h," change the vowels, and "Palestine" appears almost magically. (See the note at the bottom of the alphabet chart. Simply by removing the dot from the Hebrew letter "p," the soft sound results). Concerning Masada, the middle consonant of the triconsonantal root is a *tsade*, that, when anglicized, appears as a simple "s" (muh SAHD uh). In Hazor the *tsade* appears as a "z" (HAY zawr).

COMPARISON OF
ENGLISH, HEBREW, AND GREEK ALPHABETS

ENGLISH (EQUIVALENT)	HEBREW CHARACTER	NAME	PRONOUNCIATION	GREEK CHARACTER	NAME	PRONOUNCIATION
a (')	א	aleph	AH leff (glottal stop)	α	alpha	AL fuh
b	ב*	beth	BAYTH	β	beta	BAY tuh
g	ג*	gimel	GHEE mehl	γ	gamma	GAM muh
d	ד*	daleth	DAH lehth	δ	delta	DEHL tuh
e				ε	epsilon	EP sih lahn
h	ה	he	HAY			
v	ו	waw	WAW			
z	ז	zayin	ZA yihn	ζ	zeta	ZAY tuh
h	ח	heth	HAYTH	η	eta	AY tuh
t	ט*	teth	TAYTH	θ	theta	THAY tuh
y	י	yodh	YOHD	ι	iota	ih OH tuh
k	ך,כ*	kaf	KAFF	κ	kappa	KAP puh
l	ל	lamedh	LAH medth	λ	lambda	LAMB duh
m	ם,מ	mem	MAYM	μ	mu	MEW
n	ן,נ	nun	NOON	ν	nu	NEW
s	ס	samekh	SAH mek			
				ξ	xi	ZEE
	ע	ayin	A (a) yihn (rough breath)			
o				ο	omicron	AH mih krahn
p	ף,פ*	pe	PAY	π	pi	PIGH
	ץ,צ	tsade	SAH deh			
	ק	qof	QOHF			
r	ר	resh	RAYSH	ρ	rho	ROH
s, sh	ש,שׁ	sin, shin	SEEN, SHEEN	σ,ς	sigma	SIHG muh
t	ת*	taw	TAW	τ	tau	TAW
u				υ	upsilon	OOP sih lahn
				φ	phi	FIGH
				χ	chi	KIGH
				ψ	psi	puh SIGH
				ω	omega	oh MAY guh

26 letters   22 letters   24 letters

*ב,ג,ד,כ,פ,ת — so-called "beghadkephat" letters. Hard sound with dot in bosom of letter.

Note: A few English letters, such as "c," do not appear—no comparisons.

6

KEY TO PRONUNCIATION

When it comes to language studies, Americans in general are far behind some other nations. Europeans who live in the midst of compacted countries often speak as many as four or five languages fluently. Not so many years ago the "universal" or international language was French. A shift to English has developed.

English continues to be one of the very few languages that can be set without accents, diacritics, or special alphabetic characters. English also uses extensive capitalization. Nevertheless, some method had to be adopted finally which offered a solution to the problem in spite of differences and comparisons.

Criteria for determining the pronunciation of each name and term in this book is based on several factors:

1. Accurately translated
2. Graphically visible
3. Obviously pronounceable
4. Simply expressed
5. Consistently stable, and
6. Currently acceptable

This guide was developed because of a distinct need to present a method of pronouncing names and terms easily. Various opinions are acknowledged and alternate pronunciations often appear. This book presents a respelling system and deals with phonics or audible sounds expressed through a key or code for each sound. Rules are ignored for clarity and visibility. Problems, such as double vowels, or diphthongs, must be eliminated. In English, when a vowel appears, it and/or the consonants around it form a syllable. The key to phonics is to spell a word as it sounds. Spell so as not to be mispronounceable! Some of the spellings will appear unusual at first, but with a little patience and study, the key or code given will be obvious and helpful.

Language experts agree generally that there are at least forty different sounds in English. Some find sixty. Many agree on forty-two. The tiny sound-making muscles, with smacks, clicks, clacks, etc., are capable of making thousands of sounds, but no language requires that many. Since there are only twenty-six letters in the English alphabet, some must do double duty. For example, the letter "a," by itself or in combination (diphthongs), varies more than any other letter. It can be pronounced fourteen different ways! Vowels, not consonants, take care of most of the extra sounds. While that offers a solution, it is also a paradox and thus a problem. The International Phonetic Alphabet was developed so that one symbol stands for one sound, but the system requires extensive learning of new signs. Nevertheless, the IPA is being taught in a number of American colleges and other institutions of higher learning.

Russian and Spanish words are not difficult to spell for those who know the languages. Each letter has a sound to match, and each letter always stands for the same sound. Spelling in English is highly inconsistent with its pronunciation. That's why other symbols, like diacritics, were developed. But, they can be cumbersome, especially for the casual student. English has this one great difficulty—its chaotic spelling. It is perhaps the most irregularly spelled phonic language. A famous American writer once said that he felt sorry for the person who didn't have enough imagination to spell a word more than one way! Coming from so many roots of so many lands, the English language does have the richest language in the world. But the English language is very flexible and confusing. Perhaps you have heard how one witty person used the letters g-h-o-t-i to spell *fish*. Observe:

gh	from *enough*	= f
o	from *women*	= i
ti	from *nation*	= sh
		fish

The genius of the phonic system is that computers today contain all of the symbols:

1. Large caps indicate primary accented syllables.
2. Spaces represent syllable dividers.
3. Lower case letters indicate unaccented syllables.
4. Small caps point out secondary accents.
5. Underlining, used infrequntly, indicates a different sound using the same letters.

A familiar example of the genius of the respelling system is represented in the Hebrew name of Israel's first king, *Saul*. Transliterated from the Hebrew, it appears as "Shaul" with a soft "s" or "sh" sound. The letters "au" make up a diphthong which Webster claims is a "gliding monosyllabic speech sound," treated as a single vowel even though when spoken it "moves from one vowel sound toward the position of another." In Hebrew, however, the name is pronounced "shah OOL," recognizing the two vowel sounds, which in this case means two syllables. This guide acknowledges the problem, but works around it by ignoring the rules for clarification and granting only one way to pronounce. First, the diphthong had to be changed to get rid of the two-syllable possibility. Letter substitutions were considered which would result in an acceptable pronunciation. SAWL, with a "w," substitutes for the second vowel and fulfills all the requirements. But, because of the three distinct "phonic" areas of the United States, SAWL is perhaps more acceptable in the South, whereas the more "national" or midland pronunciation, would be more like SAHL! Both are "correct" according to the cultural pattern of the one speaking. Some New Yorkers may call it SAWRL, but the "r" just isn't there! It's part of their colloquial speech pattern. SAWL appears in all caps as being the accented syllable, but in this case, the only syllable.

Some consonants possess more than one sound possibility. They, too, appear in the code with a more consistent substitute. The letter "c" in *cat* has a "k" sound, whereas in *city* and *cell* it has an "s" sound. Thus, in phonics, the letter "c" is needed only in a "ch" sound in words like *choice, chance, chew,* etc.

Exceptions seem to occur in every situation. Special rules must be made to solve particular problems. The name of the second patriarch, *Isaac,* is a perfect example. No diacritical marks existing can produce the "proper" sound, but phonics or respelling does the job beautifully. The second syllable, "saac" defies all rules, so it must be respelled as it sounds—zik or zihk, with a short "i." The result—IGH (eye) zik.

Several other exceptions to the general rule occur. Because diacritical marks are not used in this expanded edition, a decision had to be made between a long "i" and a short "i." When we come across a short "i," we usually pronounce it as in *hit* or *sit*. The choice of the long "i" in this guide may look strange standing alone, but it is "igh!" Why? When we see this combination in such words as *high, sigh,* and *sight,* the sound is a natural long "i," and pronounced as a capital "I." Applied to Bible names, the last four letters of Israelite, for example, becomes "light." Strangely enough, with two vowels, the "lite" could be pronounced as "lih teh," as already explained. Bible students pronounce "lite" as "light" because the phonics ruling states that the first vowel "does the talking (usually long and predominant), while the second does the walking (usually silent)."

Another exception is the long "e" sound. By itself, the lowercase letter "e" is usually pronounced as in words like *set* or *met*. This guide ordinarily avoids doubling of vowels because of the possibility of doubling syllables. The only way to get a capital "E" sound is to double the "e" as in *keep, sleep,* and *speak* (SPEEK). With grammarians, a diphthong of two vowel letters is considered as a single vowel. But even a name like Saul could be pronounced as SAW ool (anglicized) if the two vowels were considered independently. Strangely enough, the names Saul and Paul derive from two-syllable words in Hebrew, Greek, Latin, and Arabic!

A decision has to be made about two possible pronunciations of "ow," as in *cow, row* (a fight), and *row* (a boat). Since a long "o" is easily sounded by "oh," the sound for "ow" is <u>always</u> pronounced in this guide as in *cow*. "Roh" is used for words like "rowing" a boat—ROH ing. A noisy quarrel or fight would still be a "row" (rhymes with cow)!

The following key or code appears also at the bottom of each double page in the body of this book. Most standard dictionaries follow this same plan. It's the same key or code that appears on page 11, but this chapter contains explanatory remarks.

CODE FOR PRONUNCIATION

CODE	EXAMPLE	CODE	EXAMPLE
a	HAT	oo	LOOK
ah	far, FAHR	<u>oo</u>	boot, B<u>OO</u>T
aw	call, KAWL		
ay	name, NAYM	ow	cow, KOW
b	BAD		out, OWT
ch	CHEW	oy	boil, BOYL
d	DAD	p	PAT
e, eh	met, MEHT	r	RAN
ee	sea, SEE	s	star, STAHR
	ski, SKEE		tsetse, SET see
ew	truth, TREWTH	sh	show, SHOH
f	FOOT		action, AK shuhn
	enough, ee NUHF		mission, MIH shuhn
g	GET		vicious, VIH shuhss
h	HIM	t	tie, TIGH
hw	whether, HWEH thuhr		Thomas, TAH muhss
i, ih	city, SIH tih	th	thin, THIHN, THIN
igh	sign, SIGHN	<u>th</u>	there, <u>TH</u>EHR
	eye, IGH	tw	TWIN
<u>igh</u>	lite, L<u>IGH</u>T	u, uh	tub, TUHB
ih	pin, PIHN, PIN		Joshua JAHSH yew uh
j	jack, JAK		term TUHRM
	germ JUHRM	v	veil, VAYL
k	KISS		of, AHV
	cow, KOW	w	WAY
ks	ox, AHKS		
kw	quail, KWAYL	wh	(whether) see hw
l	live, LIHV, LIGHV	y	year, YEER
m	more, MOHR	z	xerox, ZIHR ahks
n	note, NOHT		ZEE rahks
ng	ring, RING		his, HIHZ, HIZ
oh	go, GOH		zebra, ZEE bruh
	row, ROH (a boat)	zh	version, VUHR zhuhn

Most letters in the alphabet have some variation of sound in particular words. The following are more stable and have little or no variation: b, d, f, j, k, l, m, p, r, and v.

In some words certain letters are considered "silent" and are not pronounced. The following examples are samples: "b" as in *debt*, "c" as in *yacht*, "g" as in *gnat*, "h" as in *hour*, "k" as in *knot*, "p" as in *psalm*, "s" as in *island*, "t" as in *listen*, "u" as in *build*, "w" as in *who*, etc.

A general rule has been followed in order to assure a simple but exact guide. When a foreigner comes to this country, it is expedient that he or she learn English as soon as possible. Naturally the shorter and simpler words are learned first. The code developed for this book reflects such a viewpoint and results in an easy learning process for pronunciation.

This guide will give you both confidence and authority as you speak, teach, or preach by enabling you to pronounce "correctly" the often-difficult Bible names and terms.

In addition to the enclosed CD-ROM, *That's Easy for You to Say* contains a section that provides the meaning of Bible names for which the meaning is known. This section was compiled by Dr. Terry Eddinger.

BOOKS OF THE BIBLE

OLD TESTAMENT

Genesis   *JEN ih siss*

Exodus   *EK suh duhs*

Leviticus   *lih VIT ih kuhs*

Numbers   *NUHM buhrz*

Deuteronomy   *DOO (dew) tuh RAHN uh mih*

Joshua   *JAHSH yoo uh*

Judges   *JUH jihz*

Ruth   *ROOTH (REWTH)*

Samuel   *SAM yoo el*

Kings   *KINGS*

Chronicles   *KRAHN ih kuhls*

Ezra   *EZ ruh*

Nehemiah   *NEE huh MIGH uh*

Esther   *ESS tuhr (thuhr)*

Job   *JOHB*

Psalms   *SAHLMZ*

Proverbs   *PRAHV uhrbs*

Ecclesiastes   *ih KLEE zih ASS teez*

Song of Solomon   *SAHNG (SONG)-ahv-SAHL uh muhn*

Isaiah   *igh (eye) ZAY uh*

Jeremiah   *JER ih MIGH uh*

Lamentations   *LA men TAY shuhnz*

Ezekiel   *ih ZEE kih uhl*

Daniel   *DAN yuhl*

Hosea   *hoh ZAY uh*

Joel   *JOH el*

Amos   *AY muhss*

Obadiah   *OH buh DIGH uh*

Jonah   *JOH nuh*

Micah   *MIGH kuh*

Nahum   *NAY hoom*

Habakkuk   *huh BAK uhk*

Zephaniah   *ZEF uh NIGH uh*

Haggai   *HAG igh (eye)*

Malachi   *MAL uh kigh*

NEW TESTAMENT

Matthew   *MATH yoo*

Mark   *MAHRK*

Luke   *LOOK (LEWK)*

John   *JAHN*

Acts   *AKTS*

Romans   *ROH muhnz*

Corinthians   *koh RIN thih uhns*

Galatians   *guh LAY shuhnz*

Ephesians   *ih FEE zhuhnz*

Philippians   *fih LIP ih uhnz*

Colossians   *kuh LAHSH uhnz*

Thessalonians   *THESS uh LOH nih uhnz*

Timothy   *TIM uh thih*

Titus   *TIGH tuhs*

Philemon   *figh LEE muhn*

Hebrews   *HEE brooz*

James   *JAYMZ*

Peter   *PEE tuhr*

John   *JAHN*

Jude   *JOOD (JEWD)*

Revelation   *REV uh LAY shuhn*

A

Aalar *AY uh luhr*

Aaron *EHR uhn, ER'n*

Aaronic *ehr AHN ik*

Aaronite *EHR uh night*

Abacuc *AB uh kuhk*

Abaddon *uh BAD uhn*

Abadias *AB uh DIGH uhs*

Abagtha *uh BAG thuh*

Abana *AB uh nuh*

Abanah *AB uh nuh*

Abarim *AB uh rim*

Abba *AB buh, AH buh*

Abbas *AH buhs*

Abda *AB duh*

Abdeel *AB dih ehl, AB dee uhl*

Abdenago *ab DEN uh goh*

Abdi *AB digh*

Abdias (Obadiah) *ab DIGH uhs*

Abdiel *AB dih el, AB dee uhl*

Abdon *AB dahn*

Abed-nego *uh BED-nih goh*

Abednego *uh BED-nih goh*

Abel *AY buhl*

Abelbethmaacah *AY buhl-beth-MAY uh kuh*

Abel-beth-maacah *AY buhl-beth-MAY uh kuh*

Abel Bethmaacah *AY buhl-beth-MAY uh kuh*

Abel Beth Maachah *AY buhl-beth-MAY uh kuh*

Abelcheramim *AY buhl-KEHR uh mim*

Abelkeramim *AY buhl-KEHR uh mim*

Abel Keramim *AY buhl-KEHR uh mim*

Abelmaim *AY buhl-MAY im*

Abel-maim *AY buhl-MAY im*

Abel-Maim *AY buhl-MAY im*

Abel-meholah *AY buhl-meh HOH luh*

Abelmeholah *AY buhl-meh HOH luh*

Abel Meholah *AY buhl-meh HOH luh*

Abelmizraim *AY buhl-MIZ ray im*

Abel-mizraim *AY buhl-MIZ ray im*

Abel Mizraim *AY buhl-MIZ ray im*

A

Abel-shittim *AY buhl-SHIT im*

Abelshittim *AY buhl-SHIT im*

Abel Shittim *AY buhl-SHIT im*

Abez *AY bez*

Abi *AY bigh*

Abia *uh BIGH uh*

Abiah *uh BIGH uh*

Abi-albon *ay bigh-AL bahn*

Abialbon *ay bigh-AL bahn*

Abiasaph *uh BIGH uh saf*

Abiathar *uh BIGH uh thahr*

Abib *AY bib*

Abibaal *ay bigh-BAY uhl*

Abida *uh BIGH duh*

Abidah *uh BIGH duh*

Abidan *uh BIGH dan*

Abiel *AY bih el, AY bee uhl*

Abiezer *AY bigh-EE zuhr*

Abi-ezer *AY bigh-EE zuhr*

Abi-ezrite *AY bigh-EZ right*

Abiezrite *AY bigh-EZ right*

Abigail *AB ih gayl*

Abigal *AB ih gal*

Abihail *AB ih hayl*

Abihu *uh BIGH hyoo*

Abihud *uh BIGH huhd*

Abijah *uh BIGH juh*

Abijam *uh BIGH jam, uh BIGH juhm*

Abila *ah BEE lah*

Abilene *ab ih LEE nee, A (a) buh leen*

Abimael *uh BIM ay uhl*

Abimelech *uh BIM uh lek*

Abinadab *uh BIN uh dab*

Abiner *AB uh nuhr*

Abinoam *uh BIN oh uhm*

Abiram *uh BIGH ram, uh BIGH ruhm*

Abisei *ab uh SEE igh (eye)*

Abishag *AB ih shag*

Abishai *uh BISH ay igh (eye), uh BIGH shigh*

Abishalom *uh BISH uh luhm*

Abishua *uh BISH yoo uh*

Abishur *uh BIGH shuhr*

Abisum *uh BIGH suhm*

Abital *AB it tal, uh BIGH tuhl*

Abitub *uh BIGH tuhb*

Abiud *uh BIGH uhd*

Abner *AB nuhr*

Abraham *AY bruh ham*

Abram *AY bruhm*

abrek *AY brek*

---

a-HAT; ah-far FAHR; aw-call KAWL; ay-name NAYM; B-BAD; ch-CHEW; d-DAD; e,eh-met MET; ee-sea SEE; ew-truth TREWTH; f-FOOT, enough ee NUHF; g-GET; h-HIM; hw-whether HWEH thuhr; i, ih-city SI ti, or SIH tih; igh sign SIGHN, eye IGH; igh LIGHT; j-jack JAK, germ JUHRM; k-KISS, chorus KOH ruhss, ks-(for x) ox AHKS; kw-quail KWAYL; l-live LIHV, LIGHV; m-more MOHR; ng-ring RING; oh-go GOH, row ROH (a boat); oo-LOOK; oo-boot BOOT

Abron *AY bruhn*

Abronah *a BROH nuh, uh BROH nuh*

Absalom *AB suh luhm*

Abshai *AB shigh*

Abubus *uh BOO buhs*

Abu Ghosh *AH boo-GOHSH*

Abu Gosh *AH boo-GOHSH*

Abu Simbal *AH boo-SIM buhl*

Abydos *ah BEE duhs*

abyss *uh BISS*

Acacia *uh KAY shuh*

Acacia City *uh KAY shuh-SIH tih*

Acatan *AK uh tan*

Acbor *AK bawr*

Accad *AK ad*

Accadian *uh KAY dih uhn*

Accaron *AK uh ruhn*

Accho *AHK oh, AK oh*

Acco *AH koh, AHK oh*

Accos *AK ahz*

Accoz *AK ahz*

Aceldama *uh SELL duh muh, uh KEL duh muh*

Achab *AY kab*

Achaia *uh KAY yuh*

Achaicus *uh KAY ih kuhs*

Achan *AY kuhn, AY kan*

Achar *AY kahr*

Achaz *AY kaz*

Achbor *AK bawr*

Achiacharus *ak yuh KAY ruhs*

Achias *uh KIGH uhs*

Achim *AY kim*

Achimelech *uh KIM uh lek*

Achior *AY kee awr*

Achish *AY kish*

Achitob *AK uh tahb*

Achmetha *AK mee thuh*

Achor *AY kawr*

Achsa *AK suh*

Achsah *AK suh*

Achshaph *AHK shaf*

Achzib *AK zib, AK zeeb, ahk ZEEB*

Acipha *uh SIGH fuh*

Acitho *ASS uh thoh*

Acraba *AK ruh buh*

Acrabbim *uh KRAB im*

Acre *AH kuhr, AK uhr*

acropolis *uh KRAHP uh liss*

acrostic *uh KRAHS tik*

Acsah *AK suh*

Acshaph *AK shaf*

Actium *AK tih uhm, AK tuhm*

Acts *AKTS*

ow-cow KOW, out OWT; oy-boil BOYL; p-PAT; r-RAN; s-star STAHR, tsetse SET see; sh-show SHOH, action AK shuhn, mission MIH shuhn, vicious VIH shuhss; t-tie TIGH, Thomas TAH muhss; th-thin THIN or THIHN; th-there THEHR; tw-TWIN; u, uh-tub TUB or TUHB, Joshua JAHSH yew uh, term TUHRM; v-veil VAYL, of AHV; w-WAY; wh (whether) see hw; y-year YEER; z-xerox ZIHR ahks, ZEE rahks, his HIZ or HIHZ, zebra ZEE bruh; zh-version VUHR zhuhn

17

A

Acua   *uh KYOO uh*

Acub   *AY kuhb*

Aczib   *AK zib*

Adadah   *AD uh duh*

Adad-nirari   *ay dad-nih RAHR ree*

Adadnirari   *ay dad neer RAHR ih*

Adah   *AY duh*

Adaiah   *uh DIGH uh*

Adalia   *uh DAY lih uh, ad uh LIGH uh*

Adam   *AD uhm*

Adamah   *AD uh muh*

Adami   *AD uh migh*

Adami-nekeb   *ad uh migh–NEE keb*

Adaminekeb   *ad uh migh–NEE keb*

Adami Nekeb   *ad uh migh–NEE keb*

Adana   *AD uh nuh, ah dah NAH*

Adar   *AY dahr*

Adasa   *AD uh suh*

Adbeel   *AD bih el, AD bee uhl*

Addan   *AD uhn*

Addar   *AD ahr*

Addi   *AD igh (eye)*

Addo   *AD oh*

Addon   *AD ahn*

Addus   *AD uhs*

Ader   *AY duhr*

Adhonai   *ad oh NIGH*

Adida   *AD uh duh*

Adiel   *AD ih el*

Adin   *AY din*

Adina   *AD ih nuh*

Adino   *AD uh noh, uh DIGH noh*

Adinus   *uh DIGH nuhs*

Adithaim   *ad ih THAY im*

Adlai   *AD ligh, AD lay igh (eye)*

Admah   *AD muh*

Admatha   *ad MAY thuh*

Admin   *AD min*

Adna   *AD nuh*

Adnah   *AD nuh*

Adonai   *ad oh NIGH*

Adonay   *ad oh NIGH*

Adonibezek   *ad oh NIGH–BEE zek*

Adoni-bezek   *ad oh NIGH–BEE zek*

Adonijah   *ad oh NIGH juh*

Adonikam   *ad oh NIGH kuhm*

Adoniram   *ad oh NIGH ruhm*

---

a-HAT; ah-far FAHR; aw-call KAWL; ay-name NAYM; B-BAD; ch-CHEW; d-DAD; e,eh-met MET; ee-sea SEE; ew-truth TREWTH; f-FOOT, enough ee NUHF; g-GET; h-HIM; hw-whether HWEH thuhr; i, ih-city SI ti, or SIH tih; igh sign SIGHN, eye IGH; igh LIGHT; j-jack JAK, germ JUHRM; k-KISS, chorus KOH ruhss, ks-(for x) ox AHKS; kw-quail KWAYL; l-live LIHV, LIGHV; m-more MOHR; ng-ring RING; oh-go GOH, row ROH (a boat); oo-LOOK; oo-boot BOOT

Adoni-Zedec *ad oh NIGH-ZEE dek*

Adonizedek *ad oh NIGH-ZEE dek*

Adoni-zedek *ad oh NIGH-ZEE dek*

Adora *uh DOH ruh*

Adoraim *ad oh RAY im*

Adoram *uh DOH ruhm*

Adrammelech *uh DRAM uh lek*

Adramyttian *ad ruh MIT ih uhn*

Adramyttium *ad ruh MIT ih uhm*

Adria *AY drih uh*

Adriatic *ay drih A (a) tik*

Adriel *AY drih el*

Aduel *AY dyoo uhl*

Adullam *uh DUHL uhm*

Adullamite *uh DUHL uh might*

Adummim *uh DUHM im*

Aegean *uh JEE uhn*

Aelia Capitolina *AY lih uh-kahp ih tuh LEE nuh*

Aeneas *ih NEE uhs*

Aenon *EE nahn*

Aeolia *ay OH lih uh*

aeon *EE ahn*

Aesora *ih SOH ruh*

aetiological *EE tee uh LAHJ ih kuhl*

aetiology *ee tee AH luh jee*

Afula *ah FOO luh*

Agaba *AG uh buh*

Agabus *AG uh buhs*

Agade *uh GAH dee, ah GAHD*

Agag *AY gag*

Agagite *AY gag ight*

Agai *AY ghee uh*

agape *ah GAH pay*

Agar *AY gahr*

Agee *AY ghee*

Aggaeus *AG ee uhs*

Aggeus (Haggai) *AG ee uhs*

agora *A (a) guh ruh*

Agrippa *uh GRIP uh*

Agur *AY guhr*

Ahab *AY hab*

Aharah *uh HEHR uh*

Aharhel *uh HAHR hel*

Ahasabi *uh HASS uh bigh*

Ahasai *uh HAY sigh*

Ahasbai *uh HAZ bigh*

Ahashtarite *uh HASH tuh right*

---

ow-cow KOW, out OWT; oy-boil BOYL; p-PAT; r-RAN; s-star STAHR, tsetse SET see; sh-show SHOH, action AK shuhn, mission MIH shuhn, vicious VIH shuhss; t-tie TIGH, Thomas TAH muhss; th-thin THIN or THIHN; th-there THEHR; tw-TWIN; u, uh-tub TUB or TUHB, Joshua JAHSH yew uh, term TUHRM; v-veil VAYL, of AHV; w-WAY; wh (whether) see hw; y-year YEER; z-xerox ZIHR ahks, ZEE rahks, his HIZ or HIHZ, zebra ZEE bruh; zh-version VUHR zhuhn

Ahashuerus *uh hash-yoo EHR uhs*

Ahasuerus *uh haz yoo EHR uhs*

Ahava *uh HAY vuh*

Ahaz *AY haz*

Ahaziah *ay huh ZIGH uh*

Ahban *AH ban*

Aher *AY huhr*

Ahi *AY high*

Ahiah *uh HIGH uh*

Ahiam *uh HIGH am*

Ahian *uh HIGH an*

Ahiezer *ay high-EE zuhr*

Ahihud *uh HIGH hudh*

Ahijah *uh HIGH juh*

Ahikam *uh HIGH kam*

Ahikar *uh HIGH kahr*

Ahilud *uh HIGH luhd*

Ahimaaz *uh HIM uh az*

Ahiman *uh HIGH muhn*

Ahimelech *uh HIM uh lek*

Ahimoth *uh HIGH mahth*

Ahinadab *uh HIN uh dab*

Ahinoam *uh HIN oh am*

Ahio *uh HIGH oh*

Ahiqar *uh HIGH kahr*

Ahira *uh HIGH ruh*

Ahiram *uh HIGH ruhm*

Ahiramite *uh HIGH ruhm ight*

Ahisamach *uh HIZ uh mak*

Ahishahar *uh HISH uh hahr*

Ahishar *uh HIGH shahr*

Ahithophel *uh HITH oh fel*

Ahitob *uh HIGH tahb*

Ahitub *uh HIGH tuhb*

Ahlab *AH lab*

Ahlai *AH ligh, AH lay igh*

Ahoah *uh HOH uh*

Ahoh *uh HOH*

Ahohi *uh HOH high*

Ahohite *uh HOH hight*

Ahola *uh HOH luh*

Aholah *uh HOH luh*

Aholiab *uh HOH lih ab*

Aholibah *uh HOH lih buh*

Aholibamah *uh hoh lih BAY muh*

Ahumai *uh HYOO migh*

Ahura-Mazda *uh hoor uh-MAZ duh*

Ahuzam *uh HYOO zam*

Ahuzzam *uh HYOO zam*

Ahuzzath *uh HUH zath*

Ahzai *AH zigh*

Ai *IGH, AY igh (eye)*

---

a-HAT; ah-far FAHR; aw-call KAWL; ay-name NAYM; B-BAD; ch-CHEW; d-DAD; e,eh-met MET; ee-sea SEE; ew-truth TREWTH; f-FOOT, enough ee NUHF; g-GET; h-HIM; hw-whether HWEH thuhr; i, ih-city SI ti, or SIH tih; igh sign SIGHN, eye IGH; igh LIGHT; j-jack JAK, germ JUHRM; k-KISS, chorus KOH ruhss; ks-(for x) ox AHKS; kw-quail KWAYL; l-live LIHV, LIGHV; m-more MOHR; ng-ring RING; oh-go GOH, row ROH (a boat); oo-LOOK; oo-boot BOOT

Aiah   *AY yuh*

Aiath   *AY yath*

Ai-et Tell   *IGH (eye)-et tehl, AY igh*

Aija   *ay IGH juh, AY juh*

Aijalon   *A (a) juh lahn*

Aijeleth   *AY jeh leth*

Aijeleth-shahar   *ay jeh leth-SHAY hahr*

Aijeleth Shahar   *ay jeh leth-SHAY hahr*

Aila   *IGH (eye) lah*

Ailat   *IGH (eye) laht*

ain   *A (a) yin*

Ain Feshka   *ighn-FESH kuh*

Ain Karem   *ighn-KAHR ehm*

Ain Qedeis   *ighn-KEHD esh*

Ain Qudeirat   *ighn-koo duh RAHT*

Ain Rimmon   *ighn-RIM mahn*

Airus   *AY ruhs*

Ajah   *AY juh*

Ajalon   *AJ uh lahn*

Akan   *AY kan*

Akeldama   *uh KEHL duh muh*

Akh-en-aton   *ahk-uh-NAH tahn*

Akhenaton   *ahk uh NAH tahn*

Akhetaten   *ah kit TAH tin*

Akhetaton   *ahk uh TAH tahn*

Akhnaton   *ahk NAH tahn*

Akhziv   *ahk ZEEV*

Akiba   *uh KEE buh*

Akim   *AY kim*

Akkad   *AK ad, ah KAHD*

Akkadian   *uh KAY dih uhn*

Akkub   *AK uhb*

Akrabattene   *ak ruh BAT uh nee*

Akrabbim   *ak RAB rim, uh KRAB im*

Alaca Huyuk   *ah LAH shuh-HOO yook*

Al Aksa Mosque   *ahl-ahk suh-MAHSK*

Alalakh   *ah lah LAHK*

Alameth   *AL ih meth*

Alammelech   *uh LAM uh lek*

Alamoth   *AL uh mahth*

Alashiya   *ah lah SHEE yah*

Alcimus   *AL sih muhs*

Alema   *AL uh muh*

Alemeth   *AL eh meth*

aleph (Hebrew letter)   *AH lef*

Aleppo   *ah LEP oh*

Alexander   *al eg ZAN duhr*

Alexandra   *al eg ZAN druh*

---

ow-cow KOW, out OWT; oy-boil BOYL; p-PAT; r-RAN; s-star STAHR, tsetse SET see; sh-show SHOH, action AK shuhn, mission MIH shuhn, vicious VIH shuhss; t-tie TIGH, Thomas TAH muhss; th-thin THIN or THIHN; th-there THEHR; tw-TWIN; u, uh-tub TUB or TUHB, Joshua JAHSH yew uh, term TUHRM; v-veil VAYL, of AHV; w-WAY; wh (whether) see hw; y-year YEER; z-xerox ZIHR ahks, ZEE rahks, his HIZ or HIHZ, zebra ZEE bruh; zh-version VUHR zhuhn

A

Alexandria   *al eg ZAN drih uh*

Alexandrian   *al eg ZAN drih uhn*

Alexandrinus   *al eg zan DRIGH nuhs*

Alexandrium   *al eg ZAN drih uhm*

algum   *AL guhm*

Aliah   *AL ih uh*

Alian   *AL ih uhn*

Alisar Huyuk   *ah lih sahr-HOO yook*

Alishar   *ah lih SHAHR*

Allammelech   *uh LAM uh lek*

allegorical   *al uh GAHR ih kuhl*

allegory   *A (a) luh gohr rih*

alleluia   *a leh LOO yuh*

Allemeth   *AL eh meth*

Allom   *AL ahm*

Allon   *AL lahn*

Allonbachuth   *al lahn-BAK uhth*

Allon-bachuth   *al lahn-BAK uhth*

Allon Bachuth   *al lahn-BAK uhth*

Allon-bacuth   *al lahn-BAK uhth*

Allon Bakuth   *al lahn-BAK uhth*

alluvial   *ah LOO vih uhl*

alluvium   *ah LOO vih uhm*

Almodad   *al MOH dad*

Almon   *AL mahn*

Almon-diblathaim   *AL mahn-DIB luh THAY im*

Almondiblathaim   *AL mahn-DIB luh THAY im*

Almon Diblathaim   *AL mahn-DIB luh THAY im*

almug   *AL muhg*

Alnathan   *al NAY thuhn*

aloes   *AL ohz*

Aloth   *AY lahth*

alpha (Greek letter)   *AL fuh*

Alphaeus   *al FEE uhs*

Alpheus   *al FEE uhs*

Altaneus   *al tuh NEE uhs*

Al-taschit   *al-TASS kit*

Altashheth   *al TAHSH heth*

Alush   *AY luhsh*

Alvah   *AL vuh*

Alvan   *AL vuhn*

Amad   *AY mad*

Amadatha   *am uh DAY thuh*

Amal   *AY muhl, AY mal*

Amalek   *AM uh lek*

---

a-HAT; ah-far FAHR; aw-call KAWL; ay-name NAYM; B-BAD; ch-CHEW; d-DAD; e,eh-met MET; ee-sea SEE; ew-truth TREWTH; f-FOOT, enough ee NUHF; g-GET; h-HIM; hw-whether HWEH thuhr; i, ih-city SI ti, or SIH tih; igh sign SIGHN, eye IGH; igh LIGHT; j-jack JAK, germ JUHRM; k-KISS, chorus KOH ruhss, ks-(for x) ox AHKS; kw-quail KWAYL; l-live LIHV, LIGHV; m-more MOHR; ng-ring RING; oh-go GOH, row ROH (a boat); oo-LOOK; oo-boot BOOT

Amalekite *uh MAL uh kight*

Amam *AY mam, AY mahm*

Aman *AY man, AY muhn*

Amana *uh MAY nuh*

amanuensis *UH man yoo EN siss*

Amanus *uh MAN uhs*

Amariah *am uh RIGH uh*

Amarias *am uh RIGH uhs*

Amarna, Tell-el *uh MAHR nuh-tel el*

Amasa *uh MAY suh*

Amasai *uh MAY sigh*

Amashai *uh MASH igh (eye)*

Amashsai *uh MASH sigh*

Amasi *uh MAY sigh*

Amasiah *am uh SIGH uh*

Amatheis *am uh THEE uhs (TH as in thin)*

Amathis *AM uh thiss (TH as in thin)*

Amathus *AH muh thoos*

Amaw *AY maw*

Amawite *AY maw ight*

Amaziah *am uh ZIGH uh*

amen *ah MEN*

Amen-em-ope *ah men- EM-oh pih*

Amenhotep *ah men HOH tep*

am ha'ares *ahm-hah AH retz*

Ami *AY migh*

Amiel *AM ih el*

Aminadab *uh MIN uh dab*

Amittai *uh MIT igh (eye)*

Amizabad *uh MIZ uh bad*

Ammah *AM muh*

Amman *ah MAHN, ah MAN*

Ammi *AM igh (eye)*

Ammidian *uh MID ih uhn*

Ammidoi *AM uh doy*

Ammiel *AM ih el*

Ammihud *uh MIGH huhd*

Ammihur *uh MIGH huhr*

Amminadab *uh MIN uh dab*

Amminadib *uh MIN uh dib*

Ammishaddai *am ih SHAD igh (eye)*

Ammizabad *uh MIZ uh bad*

Ammon *AM nahn*

Ammonite *AM uh night*

Ammonitess *AM uh NIGHT ess*

Amnon *AM nahn*

Amok *AY mahk*

Amon *AM uhn*

Amorite *AM uh right*

Amos *AY muhs*

Amoz *AY mahz*

ow-cow KOW, out OWT; oy-boil BOYL; p-PAT; r-RAN; s-star STAHR, tsetse SET see; sh-show SHOH, action AK shuhn, mission MIH shuhn, vicious VIH shuhss; t-tie TIGH, Thomas TAH muhss; th-thin THIN or THIHN; th-there THEHR; tw-TWIN; u, uh-tub TUB or TUHB, Joshua JAHSH yew uh, term TUHRM; v-veil VAYL, of AHV; w-WAY; wh (whether) see hw; y-year YEER; z-xerox ZIHR ahks, ZEE rahks, his HIZ or HIHZ, zebra ZEE bruh; zh-version VUHR zhuhn

23

A

amphictyony *am FIK tee uh nee*

Amphipolis *am FIP uh lihs*

Amplias *AM plih uhs*

Ampliatus *am plih AY tuhs*

Amram *AM ram*

Amramite *AM ram ight*

Amraphel *AM ruh fehl*

Amri *AM righ*

Amuq Valley *ah MOOK-VA lih*

Amurru *ah MOO roo*

Amzi *AM zigh*

Anab *AY nab*

Anael *AN ay uhl*

Anah *AY nuh*

Anaharath *uh NAY huh rath*

Anaiah *uh NAY uh*

Anak *AY nak*

Anakim *AN uh kim*

Anakite *AN uh kight*

Anam *AY nam, AY nuhm*

Anamim *AN uh mim*

Anamite *AN uh might*

Anammelech *uh NAM uh lek*

Anan *AY nan, AY nuhn*

Anani *uh NAY nigh*

Ananiah *an uh NIGH uh*

Ananias *an uh NIGH uhs*

Ananiel *uh NAN ih el*

Anasib *AN uh sib*

Anat *AH nat*

Anath *AY nath*

anathema *uh NATH uh muh*

Anathoth *AN uh thawth*

Anathothite *AN uh thawth thight*

Anatolia *an uh TOH lih uh*

Anatolian *an uh TOH lih uhn*

Ancyra *AHN kuh ruh*

Andrew *AN droo*

Androclus *AN droh kluhs*

Andronicus *an DRAHN ih kuhs*

Anem *AY nem*

Aner *AY nuhr*

Anethothite *AN uh thawth thight*

Anetothite *AN uh toh thight*

angel *AYN juhl*

Aniam *uh NIGH uhm*

Anim *AY nim*

Ankara *ANK kuh ruh*

Anna *AN uh*

Annaas *AN ay uhs*

Annan *AN uhn*

Annas *AN uhs*

---

a-HAT; ah-far FAHR; aw-call KAWL; ay-name NAYM; B-BAD; ch-CHEW; d-DAD; e,eh-met MET; ee-sea SEE; ew-truth TREWTH; f-FOOT, enough ee NUHF; g-GET; h-HIM; hw-whether HWEH thuhr; i, ih-city SI ti, or SIH tih; igh sign SIGHN, eye IGH; igh LIGHT; j-jack JAK, germ JUHRM; k-KISS, chorus KOH ruhss, ks-(for x) ox AHKS; kw-quail KWAYL; l-live LIHV, LIGHV; m-more MOHR; ng-ring RING; oh-go GOH, row ROH (a boat); oo-LOOK; oo-boot BOOT

Annias *uh NIGH uhs*

Anniuth *uh NIGH uhth*

Annunciation *uh nuhn see AY shuhn*

Annunus *AN yoo nuhs*

Annuus *AN yoo uhs*

Anos *AY nahs*

Anshan *AN shan*

Anthothijah *an thoh THIGH juh*

anthropoid *an thruh PAW id*

anthropological *an thruh puh LAHJ ih kuhl*

anthropology *an thruh PAHL uh jee*

anthropomorphic *an thruh puh MAWR fik*

Antichrist *AN tih krighst*

Antigonid *an TIHG uh nid*

Antigonus *an TIHG oh nuhs*

Anti-lebanon *an tih-LEB uh nuhn*

Antilebanon *an tih LEB uh nuhn*

antimony *AN tuh moh nee*

antinomian *an tih NOH mee uhn*

Antioch *AN tih ahk*

Antiocha *an TIGH ah kuh*

Antiochian *an tih AHK ee uhn*

Antiochis *an TIGH ah kiss*

Antiochus *an TIGH ah kuhs*

Antipas *AN tih puhs*

Antipater *an TIP uh tuhr*

Antipatris *an tih PAHT triss*

Antitheses *an TITH uh seez*

Antonia *an TOH nih uh*

Antonius *an TOH nih uhs*

Antothijah *an toh THIGH juh*

Antothite *AN toh thight*

Anub *AY nuhb*

Anus *AY nuhs*

Apame *uh PAY mee*

Apelles *uh PELL ehz, uh PELL eez*

Aphairema *uh FEHR uh muh*

Apharsachite *uh FAHR sak ight*

Apharsathcite *uh FAHR sath kight*

Apharsite *uh FAHR sight*

Aphec *AY fek*

Aphek *AY fek*

Aphekah *uh FEE kuh*

Apherema *uh FEHR uh muh*

ow-cow KOW, out OWT; oy-boil BOYL; p-PAT; r-RAN; s-star STAHR, tsetse SET see; sh-show SHOH, action AK shuhn, mission MIH shuhn, vicious VIH shuhss; t-tie TIGH, Thomas TAH muhss; th-thin THIN or THIHN; th-there THEHR; tw-TWIN; u, uh-tub TUB or TUHB, Joshua JAHSH yew uh, term TUHRM; v-veil VAYL, of AHV; w-WAY; wh (whether) see hw; y-year YEER; z-xerox ZIHR ahks, ZEE rahks, his HIZ or HIHZ, zebra ZEE bruh; zh-version VUHR zhuhn

25

A

Apherra   *uh FEHR uh*

Aphiah   *uh FIGH uh*

Aphik   *AY fik*

aphorism   *AF uh riz uhm*

Aphrah   *AF ruh*

Aphrodite   *af roh D<u>IGH</u> tih*

Aphses   *AF seez*

apiru   *ah PEE r<u>oo</u>*

Apiru   *AH pih r<u>oo</u>*

Apis   *AY piss*

Apocalypse   *uh PAHK up lips*

apocalyptic   *uh pahk uh LIP tik*

Apocrypha   *uh PAHK ruh fuh*

apocryphal   *uh PAHK ruh fuhl*

Apocryphon   *uh PAHK ruh fahn*

apodictic   *ap uh DIK tik*

Apollonia   *ap uh LOH nih uh*

Apollonius   *ap uh LOH nih uhs*

Apollophanes   *ap uh LAHF uh neez*

Apollos   *uh PAHL uhs*

Apollyon   *uh PAHL yuhn*

apology   *uh PAHL uh jee*

apostasy   *uh PAHS tuh see*

apostate   *uh PAHS tayt*

apostle   *uh PAHS uhl*

apostleship   *uh PAHS uhl ship*

apostolic   *ap uh STAH lik*

Apostolicon   *ap uhs STAHL ih kahn*

Appaim   *AP ay im*

Apphia   *AF ih uh*

Apphus   *AF uhs*

Appian   *AP ih uhn*

Appii Forum   *AP ih igh (eye)-FOHR uhm*

Appius   *AP ih uhs*

Aqaba   *A (a) kuh buh*

Aqabah   *A (a) kuh buh*

Aqiba   *uh KEE buh*

aqueduct   *A (a) kwee duht*

Aquila   *AK wih luh, uh KWIL uh*

Ar   *AHR*

Ara   *AY ruh, EHR uh*

Arab   *AR uhb, AY rab*

Arabah   *A (a) ruh bah, AH ruh bah*

Arabattine   *ar uh BAT uh nee*

Arabia   *uh RAY bih uh*

Arabian   *uh RAY bih uhn*

Arabic   *AR uh bik (A as in cat)*

Arabim   *AHR uh bim*

a-HAT; ah-far FAHR; aw-call KAWL; ay-name NAYM; B-BAD; ch-CHEW; d-DAD; e,eh-met MET; ee-sea SEE; ew-truth TREWTH; f-FOOT, enough ee NUHF; g-GET; h-HIM; hw-whether HWEH thuhr; i, ih-city SI ti, or SIH tih; igh sign SIGHN, eye IGH; <u>igh</u> LIGHT; j-jack JAK, germ JUHRM; k-KISS, chorus KOH ruhss, ks-(for x) ox AHKS; kw-quail KWAYL; l-live LIHV, LIGHV; m-more MOHR; ng-ring RING; oh-go GOH, row ROH (a boat); oo-LOOK; <u>oo</u>-boot B<u>OO</u>T

26

Arad *AY rad*

Aradite *AHR uh dight*

Aradus *AHR uh duhs*

Arah *AY ruh*

Aram *A (a) ruhm, AHR uhm*

Aramaean *a ruh MEE uhn*

Aramaic *ar uh MAY ihk*

Aramaism *AR uh may iz uhm (A as in cat)*

Aramean *ar uh MEE uhn*

Aramitess *AHR uh might ess*

Arammaacah *AY ram–MAY uh kuh*

Aram-maacah *AY ram–MAY uh kuh*

Aram Maacah *AY ram–MAY uh kuh*

Aram-naharaim *AY ram–nay huh RAY im*

Aram Naharaim *AY ram–nay huh RAY im*

Aram-Zobah *AY ram–ZOH buh*

Aran *AY ran*

Araq el-Emir *ah RAHK-el-ih MEER*

Ararat *EHR uh rat*

Ararite *EHR uh right*

Aratus *AR uh tuhs*

Araunah *uh ROO nuh*

Aravah *A (a) rah vah*

Arba *AHR buh*

Ar-baal *ahr–BAY uhl*

Arbah *AHR buh*

Arbathite *AHR bath ight, AHR buh thight*

Arbatta *ahr BAT uh*

Arbattis *ahr BAT iss*

Arbela *ahr BEE luh*

Arbite *AHR bight*

Arbonai *ahr BOH nigh*

archangel *AHRK ayn juhl*

Archelais *ark uh LAY uhs*

Archelaus *ahr kuh LAY uhs*

Archevite *AHR kuh vight*

Archi *AHR kigh*

Archimedes *ark kuh MEE deez*

Archippus *ahr KIP uhs, AHR kip uhs*

Archite *AHR kight*

archive *AHR kighv*

arcosolia *ahr kuh SOH lih uh*

Arcturus *ahrk TOO ruhs*

Ard *AHRD*

Ardat *AHR dat*

Ardath *AHR dath*

Ardite *AHR dight*

Ardon *AHR dahn*

---

ow-cow KOW, out OWT; oy-boil BOYL; p-PAT; r-RAN; s-star STAHR, tsetse SET see; sh-show SHOH, action AK shuhn, mission MIH shuhn, vicious VIH shuhss; t-tie TIGH, Thomas TAH muhss; th-thin THIN or THIHN; th-there THEHR; tw-TWIN; u, uh-tub TUB or TUHB, Joshua JAHSH yew uh, term TUHRM; v-veil VAYL, of AHV; w-WAY; wh (whether) see hw; y-year YEER; z-xerox ZIHR ahks, ZEE rahks, his HIZ or HIHZ, zebra ZEE bruh; zh-version VUHR zhuhn

Areli *uh REE ligh*

Arelite *uh REE light*

Areopagite *ehr ih AHP uh gight*

Areopagus *ehr ih AHP uh guhs*

Ares *EHR eez*

Aretas *EHR uh tuhs*

Areus *EHR ee uhs*

Argob *AHR gahb*

Ariarthes *ehr ee AHR theez*

Ariathes *ehr ee AY theez*

Aridai *uh RID ay igh, EHR uh digh*

Aridatha *ar ih DAY thuh*

Arieh *uh RIGH uh, EHR ih uh*

Ariel *EHR ih el*

Arimathaea *AR ih muh THEE uh (TH as in thin)*

Arimathea *AR ih muh THEE uh (TH as in thin)*

Arioch *EHR ih ahk*

Arisai *uh RIZ ay igh, AHR ih sigh*

Aristarchus *ehr iss TAHR kuhs*

Aristeas *ar iss TEE uhs (a as in cat)*

Aristobulus *uh riss toh BYOO luhs*

Aristotelian *ar iss tuh TEEL yuhm (a as in cat)*

Aristotle *AR iss TAHT uhl (A as in cat)*

Arius *EHR ih uhs*

Arkite *AHR kight*

Armageddon *ahr muh GED uhn*

Armenia *ahr MEE nih uh*

Armenian *ahr MEE nih uhn*

Armoni *ahr MOH nigh*

Arna *AHR nuh*

Arnan *AHR nan*

Arni *AHR nigh*

Arnon *AHR nahn*

Arod *AY rahd, EHR ahd*

Arodi *uh ROH digh, EHR uh digh*

Arodite *AY rahd ight, EHR uh dight*

Aroer *uh ROH uhr*

Aroerite *uh ROH uh right*

Arom *EHR uhm*

Arpachshad *ahr PAK shad*

Arpad *AHR pad*

Arpad *AHR pad*

Arphad *AHR fad*

---

a-HAT; ah-far FAHR; aw-call KAWL; ay-name NAYM; B-BAD; ch-CHEW; d-DAD; e,eh-met MET; ee-sea SEE; ew-truth TREWTH; f-FOOT, enough ee NUHF; g-GET; h-HIM; hw-whether HWEH thuhr; i, ih-city SI ti, or SIH tih; igh sign SIGHN, eye IGH; igh LIGHT; j-jack JAK, germ JUHRM; k-KISS, chorus KOH ruhss, ks-(for x) ox AHKS; kw-quail KWAYL; l-live LIHV, LIGHV; m-more MOHR; ng-ring RING; oh-go GOH, row ROH (a boat); oo-LOOK; oo-boot BOOT

Arphaxad   *ahr FAX ad*

Arrad   *ah RAHD, AY rad*

Arsaces   *AHR suh seez*

Arsareth   *AHR suh reth*

Arses   *AHR seez*

Arsinoe   *ahr SIN oh ee*

Arslan Tash   *AHR sluhn-TASH*

Artaxerxes   *ahr tuh ZUHRK seez*

Artemas   *AHR tih muhs*

Artemis   *AHR tih miss*

Arubboth   *uh ROO bohth*

Aruboth   *uh ROO bohth*

Arumah   *uh ROO muh*

Arvad   *AHR vad, AHR vahd*

Arvadite   *AHR vuhd ight*

Arza   *AHR zuh*

Arzareth   *AHR zuh reth*

Asa   *AY suh*

Asadias   *ass uh DIGH uhs*

Asael   *ASS ay el*

Asahel   *ASS uh hel*

Asahiah   *ass uh HIGH uh*

Asaiah   *uh ZAY yuh*

Asaias   *uh ZAY yuhs*

Asana   *uh SAH nuh*

Asaph   *AY saf*

Asaramel   *uh SEHR uh mel*

Asareel   *uh SAY rih el*

Asarel   *uh SAY rehl, ASS uh rel*

Asarelah   *ass uh REE luh*

Ascalon   *ASS kuh lahn*

Ascension   *uh SEN shuhn*

Asclepius   *ass KLEE pee uhs*

Aseas   *ASS ee uhs*

Asebebia   *ass uh BEE bee uh*

Asebia   *uh SEE bee uh*

Asenath   *ASS eh nath*

Aser   *AY suhr*

Aserer   *AY suh ruhr*

Ashan   *AY shuhn*

Asharelah   *ash uh REE luh*

Ashbea   *ash BEE uh*

Ashbel   *ASH bel*

Ashbelite   *ASH bel ight*

Ashchenaz   *ASH kih naz*

Ashdod   *ASH dahd*

Ashdodite   *ASH dahd ight*

Ashdothite   *ASH dah thight*

Ashdoth-pisgah   *ash dahth-PIZ guh*

Asher   *ASH uhr*

Asherah   *uh SHEE ruh*

Asherim   *ASH uh reem*

Asherite   *ASH uh right*

---

ow-cow KOW, out OWT; oy-boil BOYL; p-PAT; r-RAN; s-star STAHR, tsetse SET see; sh-show SHOH, action AK shuhn, mission MIH shuhn, vicious VIH shuhss; t-tie TIGH, Thomas TAH muhss; th-thin THIN or THIHN; th-there THEHR; tw-TWIN; u, uh-tub TUB or TUHB, Joshua JAHSH yew uh, term TUHRM; v-veil VAYL, of AHV; w-WAY; wh (whether) see hw; y-year YEER; z-xerox ZIHR ahks, ZEE rahks, his HIZ or HIHZ, zebra ZEE bruh; zh-version VUHR zhuhn

Asheroth   *ASH ur rahth*

Ashhur   *ASH uhr*

Ashima   *uh SHIGH muh*

Ashimah   *uh SHIGH muh*

Ashkalon   *ASH kih lahn*

Ashkelon   *ASH kih lahn*

Ashkelonite   *ASH kih lahn ight*

Ashkenaz   *ASH kih naz*

ashlar   *ASH lahr*

Ashnah   *ASH nuh*

Ashpenaz   *ASH peh naz*

Ashriel   *ASH rih uhl*

Ashterath   *ASH tuh rahth*

Ashterathite   *ash TEE ruh thight*

Ashteroth   *ASH tuh rahth*

Ashteroth-karnaim   *ash tuh rahth-kahr NAY im*

Ashterothkarnaim   *ash tuh rahth-kahr NAY im*

Ashteroth Karnaim   *ash tuh rahth-kahr NAY im*

Ashtoreth   *ASH tuh reth*

Ashur   *ASH uhr*

Ashurbanipal   *ash uhr BAN ih pal*

Ashuri   *ASH uhr ih*

Ashurite   *ASH uh right*

Ashurnasirpal   *ash uhr NASS uhr pal*

Ashvath   *ASH vath*

Asia   *AY zhuh*

Asia Minor   *AY zhuh-MIGH nuhr*

Asian   *AY zhuhn*

Asiarch   *AY zih ahrk*

Asibias   *ass uh BIGH uhs*

Asidean   *ass uh DEE uhn*

Asiel   *ASS ih uhl*

Asipha   *uh SIF uh*

Askalon   *ASS kuh lahn*

Askelon   *ASS kuh lahn*

Asmodaeus   *az MOH dih uhs*

Asmodeus   *az moh DEE uhs*

Asnah   *ASS nuh*

Asnapper   *ass NAP uhr*

Asom   *AY sahm*

Aspadana   *az puh DAN uh*

Aspalathus   *ass PAL uh thuhs*

Aspatha   *ass PAY thuh*

Asphar   *ASS fahr*

Aspharasus   *ass FEHR uh suhs*

Asriel   *ASS rih el*

Asrielite   *ASS rih uhl ight*

Assabias   *ass uh BIGH uhs*

Assalimoth   *uh SAL uh mahth*

---

a-HAT; ah-far FAHR; aw-call KAWL; ay-name NAYM; B-BAD; ch-CHEW; d-DAD; e,eh-met MET; ee-sea SEE; ew-truth TREWTH; f-FOOT, enough ee NUHF; g-GET; h-HIM; hw-whether HWEH thuhr; i, ih-city SI ti, or SIH tih; igh sign SIGHN, eye IGH; igh LIGHT; j-jack JAK, germ JUHRM; k-KISS, chorus KOH ruhss, ks-(for x) ox AHKS; kw-quail KWAYL; l-live LIHV, LIGHV; m-more MOHR; ng-ring RING; oh-go GOH, row ROH (a boat); oo-LOOK; oo-boot BOOT

Assanias   *ass uh NIGH uhs*

Assassin   *uh SAS uhn*

Asser   *ASS uhr*

Asshur   *ASH uhr*

Asshurim   *ASH uh rim, uh SHOO rim*

Asshurite   *ASH uh right, uh SHOO right*

Assidean   *ass uh DEE uhn*

Assir   *AZ uhr*

Assos   *ASS ahs*

Assur   *ASS uhr*

Assurbanipal   *ass uhr-BAN ih pal*

Assuwa   *ASS yoo uh*

Assyria   *uh SIHR ih uh*

Assyrian   *uh SIHR ih uhn*

Astaroth   *ASS tuh rahth*

Astarte   *ass TAHR tee*

Astartes   *ass TAHR teez*

Astath   *ASS tath*

astragali   *ah STRAH guh lee*

Astyages   *ass TIGH uh jeez*

Asuerus   *AZ yoo EHR uhs*

Asuppim   *a SUHP im*

Asur   *AY suhr*

Aswan   *ass WAHN*

Asyncritus   *uh SIN krih tuhs*

Atad   *AY tad*

Atarah   *AT uh rah*

Atargatis   *uh TAHR guh tiss*

Ataroth   *AT uh rahth*

Ataroth-adar   *AT uh rahth-AD ahr*

Ataroth Adar   *AT uh rahth-AD ahr*

Ataroth-addar   *AT uh rahth-AD ahr*

Atarothaddar   *AT uh rahth-AD ahr*

Ataroth Addar   *AT uh rahth-AD ahr*

Atbash   *AT bash*

Ater   *AY tuhr*

Aterezias   *uh tehr uh ZIGH uhs*

Athach   *AY thak*

Athaiah   *uh THAY yuh, uh THIGH uh*

Athaliah   *ath uh LIGH uh*

Atharias   *ath uh RIGH uhs*

Atharim   *ATH uh rim*

Athbash   *ATH bash*

Athenian   *uh THEE nih uhn*

Athenobius   *ath uh NOH bee uhs*

Athens   *ATH ihnz*

Athlai   *ATH ligh*

Athlit   *ATH lit, AT lit*

---

ow-cow KOW, out OWT; oy-boil BOYL; p-PAT; r-RAN; s-star STAHR, tsetse SET see; sh-show
SHOH, action AK shuhn, mission MIH shuhn, vicious VIH shuhss; t-tie TIGH, Thomas TAH muhss;
th-thin THIN or THIHN; th-there THEHR; tw-TWIN; u, uh-tub TUB or TUHB, Joshua JAHSH yew
uh, term TUHRM; v-veil VAYL, of AHV; w-WAY; wh (whether) see hw; y-year YEER; z-xerox ZIHR
ahks, ZEE rahks, his HIZ or HIHZ, zebra ZEE bruh; zh-version VUHR zhuhn

Atipha   *uh TIGH fuh*

Atroth   *AT rahth*

Atroth-beth-joab   *AT rahth–beth–JOH ab*

Atrothbethjoab   *AT rahth–beth–JOH ab*

Atroth beth Joab   *AT rahth–beth–JOH ab*

Atrothshophan   *AT rahth–SHOH fan*

Atroth-shophan   *AT rahth–SHOH fan*

Atroth Shophan   *AT rahth–SHOH fan*

Attai   *AT igh, AT ay igh (eye)*

Attalia   *at uh LIGH uh*

Attalus   *AT uh luhs*

Attharates   *ath uh RAY teez*

Attharias   *ath uh RIGH uhs*

Attica   *AT tih kuh*

Augia   *AW jee uh*

Augusta   *aw GUHS tuh*

Augustan   *aw GUHS tuhn*

Augustine   *AW guh steen, aw GUHS tuhn*

Augustinian   *aw guh STIN ee uhn*

Augustus   *aw GUHS tuhs*

Auranus   *aw RAY nuhs*

Auteas   *aw TEE uhs*

Ava   *AY vuh*

Avaran   *AV uh ran*

Avaris   *uh VAHR iss, ah VAHR iss*

Aven   *AY vehn*

Avesta   *uh VESS tuh*

Avim   *AY vim*

Avite   *AY vight*

Avith   *AY vith*

Avva   *AY vuh*

Avvim   *AY vim*

Avvite   *AY vight*

ayin (Hebrew letter)   *A (a) yin*

Ayyah   *A (a) yuh*

Azael   *AY zay el*

Azaelus   *az uh EE luhs*

Azal   *AY zal*

Azaliah   *az uh LIGH uh*

Azaniah   *az uh NIGH uh*

Azaphion   *uh ZAY fee uhn*

Azara   *AZ uh ruh*

Azarael   *az uh RAY el*

Azareel   *az uh REE el*

Azarel   *AZ uh rehl*

Azariah   *az uh RIGH uh*

Azariahu   *az uh RIGH uh hyoo*

Azarias   *az uh RIGH uhs*

---

a-HAT; ah-far FAHR; aw-call KAWL; ay-name NAYM; B-BAD; ch-CHEW; d-DAD; e,eh-met MET; ee-sea SEE; ew-truth TREWTH; f-FOOT, enough ee NUHF; g-GET; h-HIM; hw-whether HWEH thuhr; i, ih-city SI ti, or SIH tih; igh sign SIGHN, eye IGH; igh LIGHT; j-jack JAK, germ JUHRM; k-KISS, chorus KOH ruhss, ks-(for x) ox AHKS; kw-quail KWAYL; l-live LIHV, LIGHV; m-more MOHR; ng-ring RING; oh-go GOH, row ROH (a boat); oo-LOOK; oo-boot BOOT

Azaru   *AZ uh r<u>oo</u>*

Azaryahu   *A (a) zuhr YAH h<u>oo</u>*

Azaz   *AY zaz*

Azazel   *uh ZAY zel*

Azaziah   *az uh ZIGH uh*

Azbazareth   *az BAZ uh reth*

Azbuk   *AZ buhk*

Azekah   *uh ZEE kuh, AH zih kah*

Azel   *AY zel*

Azem   *AY zuhm*

Azephurith   *uh ZEF uh rith*

Azetas   *uh ZEE tuhs*

Azgad   *AZ gad*

Azia   *AZ ih uh*

Aziei   *az uh EE igh (eye)*

Aziel   *AY zih el*

Aziza   *uh ZIGH zuh*

Azmaveth   *AZ may veth*

Azmon   *AZ mahn*

Aznothtabor   *AZ nahth-TAY bawr*

Aznoth-tabor   *AZ nahth-TAY bawr*

Aznoth Tabor   *AZ nahth-TAY bawr*

Azor   *AY zawr*

Azotus   *uh ZOH tuhs*

Azriel   *AZ rih el*

B

Azrikam   *AZ rih kam, az RIGH kam*

Azubah   *uh ZY<u>OO</u> buh*

Azur   *AY zuhr*

Azuran   *uh Z<u>OO</u> ruhn*

Azzah   *AZ uh*

Azzan   *AZ uhn*

Azzur   *AZ uhr*

B

Baal   *BAY uhl*

Baala   *BAY uh luh*

Baalah   *BAY uh luh*

Baalath   *BAY uh lath*

Baalath-beer   *BAY uh lath-BEE uhr*

Baalathbeer   *BAY uh lath-BEE uhr*

Baalath Beer   *BAY uh lath-BEE uhr*

Baalbek   *BAY uhl bek, BAHL bek*

Baal-berith   *BAY uhl-BEE rith*

Baalberith   *BAY uhl-BEE rith*

Baale   *BAY uh lee*

ow-cow KOW, out OWT; oy-boil BOYL; p-PAT; r-RAN; s-star STAHR, tsetse SET see; sh-show SHOH, action AK shuhn, mission MIH shuhn, vicious VIH shuhss; t-tie TIGH, Thomas TAH muhss; th-thin THIN or THIHN; <u>th</u>-there <u>TH</u>EHR; tw-TWIN; u, uh-tub TUB or TUHB, Joshua JAHSH yew uh, term TUHRM; v-veil VAYL, of AHV; w-WAY; wh (whether) see hw; y-year YEER; z-xerox ZIHR ahks, ZEE rahks, his HIZ or HIHZ, zebra ZEE bruh; zh-version VUHR zhuhn

33

B

Baale-judah *BAY uh lee-JOO duh*

Baalejudah *BAY uh lee-JOO duh*

Baale Judah *BAY uh lee-JOO duh*

Baal-gad *BAY uhl-gad*

Baalgad *BAY uhl-gad*

Baal Gad *BAY uhl-gad*

Baal-hamon *BAY uhl-HAY muhn*

Baalhamon *BAY uhl-HAY muhn*

Baal Hamon *BAY uhl-HAY muhn*

Baalhanan *BAY uhl-HAY nan*

Baal-hanan *BAY uhl-HAY nan*

Baal Hanan *BAY uhl-HAY nan*

Baal-hazor *BAY uhl-HAY zawr*

Baalhazor *BAY uhl-HAY zawr*

Baal Hazor *BAY uhl-HAY zawr*

Baal-hermon *BAY uhl-HUHR muhn*

Baalhermon *BAY uhl-HUHR muhn*

Baal Hermon *BAY uhl-HUHR muhn*

Baali *BAY uh ligh*

Baalim *BAY uh lim*

Baalis *BAY uh liss*

Baalmeon *BAY uhl-MEE uhn*

Baal-meon *BAY uhl-MEE uhn*

Baal Meon *BAY uhl-MEE uhn*

Baal-peor *BAY uhl-PEE awr*

Baalpeor *BAY uhl-PEE awr*

Baal Peor *BAY uhl-PEE awr*

Baalperazim *BAY uhl-PEHR uh zim*

Baal-perazim *BAY uhl-PEHR uh zim*

Baal Perazim *BAY uhl-PEHR uh zim*

Baalsamus *BAY uhl-SAY muhs*

Baal-shalisha *BAY uhl-SHAL ih shuh*

Baal Shalisha *BAY uhl-SHAL ih shuh*

Baalshalishah *BAY uhl-SHAL ih shuh*

Baal-shalishah *BAY uhl-SHAL ih shuh*

Baal Shalishah *BAY uhl-SHAL ih shuh*

Baal-tamar *BAY uhl-TAY mahr*

Baaltamar *BAY uhl-TAY mahr*

---

a-HAT; ah-far FAHR; aw-call KAWL; ay-name NAYM; B-BAD; ch-CHEW; d-DAD; e,eh-met MET; ee-sea SEE; ew-truth TREWTH; f-FOOT, enough ee NUHF; g-GET; h-HIM; hw-whether HWEH thuhr; i, ih-city SI ti, or SIH tih; igh sign SIGHN, eye IGH; igh LIGHT; j-jack JAK, germ JUHRM; k-KISS, chorus KOH ruhss, ks-(for x) ox AHKS; kw-quail KWAYL; l-live LIHV, LIGHV; m-more MOHR; ng-ring RING; oh-go GOH, row ROH (a boat); oo-LOOK; oo-boot BOOT

Baal Tamar *BAY uhl–TAY mahr*

Baalzebub *BAY uhl–ZEE buhb*

Baal-zebub *BAY uhl–ZEE buhb*

Baal Zebub *BAY uhl–ZEE buhb*

Baalzephon *BAY uhl–ZEE fahn*

Baal-zephon *BAY uhl–ZEE fahn*

Baal Zephon *BAY uhl–ZEE fahn*

Baana *BAY uh nuh*

Baanah *BAY uh nuh*

Baanias *BAY uh NIGH uhs*

Baara *BAY uh ruh*

Baaseiah *BAY uh SEE yuh*

Baasha *BAY uh shuh*

Ba beh Dhra *BAH beh–DRAH*

Babel *BAY buhl*

Babi *BAY bigh*

Babylon *BAB ih lahn*

Babylonia *BAB ih LOH nih uh*

Babylonian *BAB ih LOH nih uhn*

Babylonish *BAB ih LOH nish*

Baca *BAY kuh*

Bacchides *BAK uh deez*

Bacchurus *ba KYOOR uhs*

Bacchus *BAK uhs*

Bacenor *buh SEE nawr*

Bachrite *BAK right*

Bachuth *BAY kuhth*

Bactria *BAK tree ah*

Bacuth *BAY kuhth*

Baddan *BAD duhn*

Baean *BEE uhn*

Bagathan *BAG uh than (th as in thin)*

Baghdad *BAG dad*

Bago *BAY goh*

Bagoas *buh GOH uhs*

Bagoi *BAY goy*

Bah *BAH*

Baharum *buh HAY ruhm*

Baharumite *buh HAY ruh might*

Bahurim *buh HYOO rim*

Baiterus *BIGH tuh ruhs*

Baither *BIGH thuhr*

Bajith *BAY jith*

Bakbakkar *bak BAK ahr*

Bakbuk *BAK buhk*

Bakbukiah *BAK byoo KIGH uh*

Bakuth *BAY kuhth*

B

Balaam *BAY luhm*

Balac *BAY lak*

Baladan *BAL uh dan*

Balah *BAY luh*

Balak *BAY lak*

Balamo *BAY luh moh*

Balamon *BAL uh mahn*

Balas *BAH lahs, BAY luhs*

Balasamus *buh LASS uh muhs*

Balata *buh LAH tuh*

Balbaim *bal BAY im*

Baldad *BAL dad*

Baliada *BAY LIGH uh duh*

Balikh *bah LEEK*

balk *BAWLK*

Balnuus *BAL noo uhs*

Balthasar *bal THAZ uhr*

Balu'a Stele *bah LOO ah-STEE luh*

bama *BAH mah*

Bamah *BAY muh*

Bamoth *BAY mahth*

bamoth (pl.) *bah MOOT*

Bamoth-baal *BAY mahth-BAY uhl*

Bamothbaal *BAY mahth-BAY uhl*

Bamoth Baal *BAY mahth-BAY uhl*

Ban *BAN*

Bani *BAY nigh*

Banias *buh NAY yuhs, BAN yuhss*

Bannaia *buh NAY yuh*

Bannus *BAN uhs*

Banuas *BAN yoo uhs*

Banyans *BAN yuhns*

Baptist *BAP tist*

Baptizer *bap TIGH zuhr*

Barabbas *buh RAB uhs*

Barachel *BAHR uh kel*

Barachiah *BAHR uh KIGH uh*

Barachias *BAHR uh KIGH uhs*

Barah *BAY ruh*

Barak *BAY rak*

Barakel *BAHR uh kehl*

barbarian *bahr BEHR rih uhn*

Bar Cochba *bahr-KOHK buh*

Bar Cochbah *bahr-KOHK buh*

Bar Cocheba *bahr-KOHK uh buh*

Bar Cochebah *bahr-KOHK uh buh*

Bar Cosiba *bahr-KOH sih buh*

---

a-HAT; ah-far FAHR; aw-call KAWL; ay-name NAYM; B-BAD; ch-CHEW; d-DAD; e,eh-met MET; ee-sea SEE; ew-truth TREWTH; f-FOOT, enough ee NUHF; g-GET; h-HIM; hw-whether HWEH thuhr; i, ih-city SI ti, or SIH tih; igh sign SIGHN, eye IGH; igh LIGHT; j-jack JAK, germ JUHRM; k-KISS, chorus KOH ruhss, ks-(for x) ox AHKS; kw-quail KWAYL; l-live LIHV, LIGHV; m-more MOHR; ng-ring RING; oh-go GOH, row ROH (a boat); oo-LOOK; oo-boot BOOT

Bar Cosibah *bahr-KOH sih buh*

Bar Coziba *bahr-KOH zih buh*

Bar Cozibah *bahr-KOH zih buh*

Barhumite *bahr HYOO might*

Bariah *buh RIGH uh*

Bar-jesus *bahr-JEE zuhs*

Bar-jona *bahr-JOH nuh*

Barjona *bahr-JOH nuh*

Bar-jonah *bahr-JOH nuh*

Bar Kochba *bahr-KOHK buh*

Bar Kochbah *bahr-KOHK buh*

Bar Kocheba *bahr-KOHK uh buh*

Bar Kochebah *bahr-KOHK-uh-buh*

Bar Kokhba *bahr-KOHK buh*

Bar Kokhbah *bahr-KOHK buh*

Barkos *BAHR kahs*

Bar Kosiba *bahr-KOH sih buh*

Bar Kosibah *bahr-KOH sih buh*

Bar Koziba *bahr-KOH zih buh*

Bar Kozibah *bahr-KOH zih buh*

Barnabas *BAHR nuh buhs*

Barnea *bahr NEE uh*

Barodis *buh ROH diss*

Barsabas *BAHR suh buhs*

Barsabbas *bahr SAB uhs*

Bartacus *BAHR tuh kuhs*

Bartholomew *bahr THAHL uh myoo*

Bartimaeus *BAHR tih MEE uhs*

Bartimeus *BAHR tih MEE uhs*

Baruch *BAY rook, BEHR uhk*

Barzillai *bahr ZIL igh (eye), bar ZIL ay igh (eye)*

Basaloth *BASS uh lahth*

basalt *buh SAWLT, BA sawlt*

Bascama *BASS kuh mah*

Bascama *bass KA muh*

Basemath *BASS eh math*

Bashan *BAY shan, BAY shuhn*

Bashan-havoth-jair *BAY shan-HAY vahth-JAY ihr*

Bashan-Havvoth-Jair *BAY shan-HAY vahth-JAY ihr*

Bashemath *BASH uh math*

Baskama *BASS kuh mah*

Basmath *BASS math*

Bastai *BASS tigh*

Bat-gader *bat-GAY duhr*

bath *BATH*

Bath *BATH*

---

ow-cow KOW, out OWT; oy-boil BOYL; p-PAT; r-RAN; s-star STAHR, tsetse SET see; sh-show SHOH, action AK shuhn, mission MIH shuhn, vicious VIH shuhss; t-tie TIGH, Thomas TAH muhss; th-thin THIN or THIHN; th-there THEHR; tw-TWIN; u, uh-tub TUB or TUHB, Joshua JAHSH yew uh, term TUHRM; v-veil VAYL, of AHV; w-WAY; wh (whether) see hw; y-year YEER; z-xerox ZIHR ahks, ZEE rahks, his HIZ or HIHZ, zebra ZEE bruh; zh-version VUHR zhuhn

B

Bathrabbim *bath–RAB im*

Bath-rabbim *bath–RAB im*

Bath Rabbim *bath–RAB im*

Bath-sheba *bath–SHEE buh*

Bathsheba *bath–SHEE buh*

Bath-shua *bath–SHOO uh*

Bathshua *bath SHOO uh*

Bathzacharias *BATH zak uh RIGH uhs*

baulk *BAWLK*

Bavai *BAY vigh, BAY vay igh (eye)*

Bavvai *BAY vigh, BAY vay igh (eye)*

Baz *BAZ*

Bazlith *BAZ lith*

Bazluth *BAZ luhth*

Bealiah *BEE uh LIGH uh*

Bealoth *BEE uh lahth*

Beatitude *bee A (a) tih tyood*

Beatty *BEE tee, BAY tih*

Bebai *BEE bigh, BEE bay igh (eye)*

Becher *BEE kuhr*

Becherite *BEE kuhr ight*

Bechorath *bee KOH rath*

Bechrite *BEK right*

Becorath *bee KOH rath*

Bectileth *BEK tuh leth*

Bedad *BEE dad*

Bedan *BEE dan*

Bedeiah *bee DEE yah*

Beeliada *bee LIGH uh duh*

Beelsarus *bee EL suh ruhs*

Beeltethmus *BEE el TETH muhs*

Beelzebub *bee EL zee buhb*

Beelzebul *bee EL zee buhl*

Beer *BEE ehr*

Beera *bee EE ruh*

Beerah *bee EE ruh*

Beerelim *BEE uhr–EE lim*

Beer-elim *BEE uhr–EE lim*

Beer Elim *BEE uhr EE lim*

Beeri *bee EE righ*

Beer-lahai-roi *BEE ehr–luh HIGH–roy*

Beerlahairoi *BEE ehr–luh HIGH–roy*

Beer Lahai Roi *BEE ehr–luh HIGH–roy*

Beeroth *bee EE rahth*

Beeroth Bene-Jaakan *BEE ee rahth–BEE nee–JAY uh kuhn*

Beerothite *bee EE rahth ight*

Beersheba *bee ehr–SHEE buh*

Beer-sheba *bee ehr–SHEE buh*

Beersheva *BEHR sheh vuh*

---

a-HAT; ah-far FAHR; aw-call KAWL; ay-name NAYM; B-BAD; ch-CHEW; d-DAD; e,eh-met MET; ee-sea SEE; ew-truth TREWTH; f-FOOT, enough ee NUHF; g-GET; h-HIM; hw-whether HWEH thuhr; i, ih-city SI ti, or SIH tih; igh sign SIGHN; eye IGH; igh LIGHT; j-jack JAK, germ JUHRM; k-KISS, chorus KOH ruhss, ks-(for x) ox AHKS; kw-quail KWAYL; l-live LIHV, LIGHV; m-more MOHR; ng-ring RING; oh-go GOH; row ROH (a boat); oo-LOOK; oo-boot BOOT

Be Eshterah *bee ESH teh ruh,*
  BEE ESH tuh ruh

Be-eshterah *bee-ESH teh ruh*

Beesh-terah *bee ESH-teh ruh*

Beeshterah *bee-ESH teh ruh*

Be Eshterah *bee-ESH teh ruh*

Behemoth *BEE hih mahth,*
  bih HEE muhth

Behistun *bee HISS tuhn*

Beirut *bay ROOT*

Beisan *bay SAHN*

Beit Alpha *bayt-AL fuh*

Beitin *bay TEEN*

Beit Jibrin *BAYT-jih BREEN*

beka *BEE kuh*

bekah *BEE kuh*

Beker *BEHK uhr*

Bekerite *BEE kuh right*

Bel *BEL*

Bela *BEE luh*

Belah *BEE luh*

Belaite *BEE luh ight*

Belemus *BEL uh muhs*

Belial *BEE lih uhl*

Belmaim *bel MAY im*

Belmain *BEL mayn*

Belmen *BEL muhn*

Belnuus *BEL noo uhs*

Belshazzar *bel SHAZ uhr*

Belteshazzar *bel tih SHAZ uhr*

Beltethmus *bel TETH muhs*

Belzedek *behl ZEH dek*

bema *BEE muh*

Bemidbar *buh MID bahr*

Ben *BEN*

Ben-abinadab *BEN-uh BIN uh dab*

Benabinadab *BEN-uh BIN uh dab*

Benaiah *bee NIGH uh*

Benammi *ben-AM igh (eye)*

Ben-ammi *ben-AM igh (eye)*

Bendeker *ben-DEE kuhr*

Ben-deker *ben-DEE kuhr*

Bene *BEN ee*

Beneberak *BEN ee-BEE rak*

Bene-berak *BEN ee-BEE rak*

Bene Berak *BEN ee-BEE rak*

benediction *BEN ih DIK shuhn*

Benedictus *BEN ih DIK toohs*

Bene-jaakan *BEN ee-JAY uh kuhn*

Benejaakan *BEN ee-JAY uh kuhn*

ow-cow KOW, out OWT; oy-boil BOYL; p-PAT; r-RAN; s-star STAHR, tsetse SET see; sh-show
SHOH, action AK shuhn, mission MIH shuhn, vicious VIH shuhss; t-tie TIGH, Thomas TAH muhss;
th-thin THIN or THIHN; th-there THEHR; tw-TWIN; u, uh-tub TUB or TUHB, Joshua JAHSH yew
uh, term TUHRM; v-veil VAYL, of AHV; w-WAY; wh (whether) see hw; y-year YEER; z-xerox ZIHR
ahks, ZEE rahks, his HIZ or HIHZ, zebra ZEE bruh; zh-version VUHR zhuhn

39

B

Bene Jaakan *BEN ee-JAY uh kuhn*

Ben-geber *ben-GHEE buhr*

Bengeber *ben-GHEE buhr*

Bengui *BEN gyoo igh (eye)*

Ben-hadad *ben-HAY dad*

Benhadad *ben-HAY dad*

Benhail *ben-HAY ihl*

Ben-hail *ben-HAY ihl*

Benhanan *ben-HAY nan*

Ben-hanan *ben-HAY nan*

Ben-hesed *ben-HEE sed*

Benhesed *ben-HEE sed*

Ben-hinnom *ben-HIN uhm*

Ben Hinnom *ben-HIN uhm*

Ben-hur *ben-HUHR*

Benhur *ben-HUHR*

Beni Hasan *BIH nih-hah SAHN*

Beninu *bee NIGH nyoo*

Ben-jahaziel *BEN-juh HAY zee uhl*

Benjamin *BEN juh min*

Benjaminite *BEN juh MIHN ight*

Benjamite *BEN juh might*

Ben-josiphiah *BEN-jahs uh FIGH uh*

Beno *BEE noh*

Benob *BEE nahb*

Ben-oni *ben-OH nigh*

Benoni *ben OH nigh*

Benoth *BEE nahth*

Ben-zoheth *ben ZOH heth*

Benzoheth *ben ZOH heth*

Beon *BEE ahn*

Beor *BEE awr*

Beqa' Valley *bee KAH-VA lih*

Bera *BEE ruh*

Beracah *BEHR uh kah*

Berachah *BEHR uh kah*

Berachiah *BEHR uh KIGH uh*

Beraiah *buh RIGH uh*

Berea *buh REE uh*

Berean *buh REE uhn*

Berechiah *BEHR uh KIGH uh*

Bered *BEE red*

Berekiah *BEHR uh KIGH uh*

Berenice *buhr uh NEES*

Bereshith *BEHR uh shith*

Beri *BEE righ*

Beriah *buh RIGH uh*

Beriite *buh RIGH ight*

Berite *BEE right*

Berith *BEE rith*

Bernice *buhr NEES*

---

a-HAT; ah-far FAHR; aw-call KAWL; ay-name NAYM; B-BAD; ch-CHEW; d-DAD; e,eh-met MET; ee-sea SEE; ew-truth TREWTH; f-FOOT, enough ee NUHF; g-GET; h-HIM; hw-whether HWEH thuhr; i, ih-city SI ti, or SIH tih; igh sign SIGHN, eye IGH; igh LIGHT; j-jack JAK, germ JUHRM; k-KISS, chorus KOH ruhss, ks-(for x) ox AHKS; kw-quail KWAYL; l-live LIHV, LIGHV; m-more MOHR; ng-ring RING; oh-go GOH, row ROH (a boat); oo-LOOK; oo-boot BOOT

Berodach-baladan   *bih ROH dak-BAL uh dan*

Beroea   *bih REE uh*

Beroean   *bih REE uhn*

Beroth   *BIHR ahth*

Berothah   *bih ROH thuh*

Berothai   *buh ROH thigh*

Berothite   *BEE rahth ight*

Beruit   *bay ROOT*

Berytus   *bay ROOT uhs*

Berzelus   *buhr ZEE luhs*

Besai   *BEE sigh*

Bescaspasmys   *BESS kuhs PAZ muhs*

Beseth   *BEE seth*

Besodeiah   *BESS uh DIGH yah*

besom   *BEE suhm*

Besor   *BEE sawr*

beta (Greek letter)   *BAY tuh*

Betah   *BEE tuh*

Betane   *BET uh nee*

Beten   *BEE tuhn*

beth (Hebrew letter)   *BAYTH*

Bethabara   *beth AB uh ruh*

Beth Acacia   *BETH-uh KAY shuh*

Beth-achzib   *beth-AK zib*

Beth Alpha   *beth-AL fuh*

Bethanath   *beth AY nath*

Beth-anath   *beth-AY nath*

Beth Anath   *beth-AY nath*

Beth-anoth   *beth-AY nahth*

Bethanoth   *beth-AY nahth*

Beth Anoth   *beth-AY nahth*

Bethany   *BETH uh nih*

Beth Aphrah   *beth-AF ruh*

Beth-arabah   *beth-AR uh buh*

Betharabah   *beth-AR uh buh*

Beth Arabah   *beth-AR uh buh*

Beth-aram   *beth-AY ram*

Betharbel   *beth-AHR bel*

Beth-arbel   *beth-AHR bel*

Beth Arbel   *beth-AHR bel*

Bethashbea   *beth-ASH bih uh*

Beth-ashbea   *beth-ASH bih uh*

Beth Ashbea   *beth-ASH bih uh*

Beth-asmoth   *beth-ASS mahth*

Bethasmoth   *beth-ASS mahth*

Beth-astharoth   *beth-ASS thuh rahth*

Beth-aven   *beth-AY vuhn*

Bethaven   *beth-AY vuhn*

Beth Aven   *beth-AY vuhn*

Bethazmaveth   *beth-az MAY veth*

Beth-azmaveth   *beth-az MAY veth*

ow-cow KOW, out OWT; oy-boil BOYL; p-PAT; r-RAN; s-star STAHR, tsetse SET see; sh-show SHOH, action AK shuhn, mission MIH shuhn, vicious VIH shuhss; t-tie TIGH, Thomas TAH muhss; th-thin THIN or THIHN; th-there THEHR; tw-TWIN; u, uh-tub TUB or TUHB, Joshua JAHSH yew uh, term TUHRM; v-veil VAYL, of AHV; w-WAY; wh (whether) see hw; y-year YEER; z-xerox ZIHR ahks, ZEE rahks, his HIZ or HIHZ, zebra ZEE bruh; zh-version VUHR zhuhn

41

B

Beth Azmaveth   *beth-az MAY veth*

Beth-baal-meon   *beth-BAY uhl-MEE ahn*

Bethbaalmeon   *beth-BAY uhl-MEE ahn*

Beth Baal Meon   *beth-BAY uhl-MEE ahn*

Beth-barah   *beth-BEHR uh*

Bethbarah   *beth-BEHR uh*

Beth Barah   *beth-BEHR uh*

Bethbasi   *beth-BAY sigh*

Beth-basi   *beth-BAY sigh*

Beth-birei   *beth-BIHR ih igh (eye)*

Beth-biri   *beth-BIHR igh (eye)*

Bethbiri   *beth-BIHR igh (eye)*

Beth Biri   *beth-BIHR igh (eye)*

Bethcar   *BETH-kahr*

Beth-car   *BETH-kahr*

Beth Car   *BETH-kahr*

Beth-dagon   *beth-DAY gahn*

Bethdagon   *beth-DAY gahn*

Beth Dagon   *beth-DAY gahn*

Bethdiblathaim   *BETH dib-luh THAY im*

Beth-diblathaim   *BETH dib-luh THAY im*

Beth Diblathaim   *BETH dib-luh THAY im*

Beth-eden   *beth-EE den*

Betheden   *beth-EE den*

Beth Eden   *beth-EE den*

Betheglaim   *beth-EG lay im*

Beth-eglaim   *beth-EG lay im*

Beth Eglaim   *beth-EG lay im*

Beth-eked   *beth-EE kid*

Betheked   *beth-EE kid*

Beth Eked   *beth-EE kid*

Beth-eked-haroim   *beth-EE kid-hah ROH im*

Bethel   *BETH-uhl*

Beth-el   *BETH-uhl*

Beth-elite   *BETH-uhl ight*

Bethelite   *BETH uhl ight*

Bethelsarezer   *BETH uhl-suh REE zuhr*

Beth-emek   *beth-EE mek*

Bethemek   *beth-EE mek*

Beth Emek   *beth-EE mek*

Bether   *BEE thuhr*

Bethesda   *buh THEZ duh*

Bethezel   *beth-EE zuhl*

Beth-ezel   *beth-EE zuhl*

Beth Ezel   *beth-EE zuhl*

Bethgader   *beth-GAY duhr*

Beth-gader   *beth-GAY duhr*

Beth Gader   *beth-GAY duhr*

a-HAT; ah-far FAHR; aw-call KAWL; ay-name NAYM; B-BAD; ch-CHEW; d-DAD; e,eh-met MET; ee-sea SEE; ew-truth TREWTH; f-FOOT, enough ee NUHF; g-GET; h-HIM; hw-whether HWEH thuhr; i, ih-city SI ti, or SIH tih; igh sign SIGHN, eye IGH; igh LIGHT; j-jack JAK, germ JUHRM; k-KISS, chorus KOH ruhss, ks-(for x) ox AHKS; kw-quail KWAYL; l-live LIHV, LIGHV; m-more MOHR; ng-ring RING; oh-go GOH, row ROH (a boat); oo-LOOK; oo-boot BOOT

42

Bethgamul *beth-GAY muhl*

Beth-gamul *beth-GAY muhl*

Beth Gamul *beth-GAY muhl*

Beth-gilgal *beth-GIHL gal*

Bethgilgal *beth-GIHL gal*

Beth Gilgal *beth-GIHL gal*

Beth Gubrin *beth-goo BREEN*

Beth Guvrin *beth-goo VREEN*

Beth-haccerem *beth-HAK uh rem*

Beth Haccerem *beth-HAK uh rem*

Beth-haccherem *beth-HAK uh rem*

Bethhaccherem *beth-HAK uh rem*

Beth Haccherem *beth-HAK uh rem*

Beth-haggan *beth-HAG uhn*

Bethhaggan *beth-HAG uhn*

Beth Haggan *beth-HAG uhn*

Beth Hakkerem *BETH-HAK uh rem*

Beth-hanan *beth-HAY nan*

Beth-haram *beth-HAY ram*

Bethharam *beth-HAY ram*

Beth Haram *beth-HAY ram*

Beth-haran *beth-HAY ruhn*

Bethharan *beth-HAY ruhn*

Beth Haran *beth-HAY ruhn*

Beth-hogla *beth-HAHG luh*

Bethhoglah *beth-HAHG luh*

Beth-hoglah *beth-HAHG luh*

Beth Hoglah *beth-HAHG luh*

Bethhoron *beth-HOH rahn*

Beth-horon *beth-HOH rahn*

Beth Horon *beth-HOH rahn*

Bethjeshimoth *beth-JESH ih mahth*

Beth-jeshimoth *beth-JESH ih mahth*

Beth Jeshimoth *beth-JESH ih mahth*

Beth-jesimoth *beth-JESS ih mahth*

Beth Jesimoth *beth-JESS ih mahth*

Beth-leaphrah *BETH-lih-AF ruh*

Bethleaphrah *BETH-lih-AF ruh*

Beth-le-aphrah *BETH-lih-AF ruh*

Beth-lebaoth *BETH-LEB ay ahth*

Bethlebaoth *BETH-LEB ay ahth*

ow-cow KOW, out OWT; oy-boil BOYL; p-PAT; r-RAN; s-star STAHR, tsetse SET see; sh-show SHOH, action AK shuhn, mission MIH shuhn, vicious VIH shuhss; t-tie TIGH, Thomas TAH muhss; th-thin THIN or THIHN; th-there THEHR; tw-TWIN; u, uh-tub TUB or TUHB, Joshua JAHSH yew uh, term TUHRM; v-veil VAYL, of AHV; w-WAY; wh (whether) see hw; y-year YEER; z-xerox ZIHR ahks, ZEE rahks, his HIZ or HIHZ, zebra ZEE bruh; zh-version VUHR zhuhn

43

B

Beth Lebaoth *BETH-LEB ay ahth*

Bethlehem *BETH lih hem*

Beth-lehem *BETH lih hem*

Bethlehem-ephratah *BETH lih hem-EF ruh tah*

Bethlehem Ephratah *BETH lih hem-EF ruh tah*

Bethlehemite *BETH lih hem ight*

Beth-lehemite *BETH lih hem ight*

Beth-lehem-judah *BETH lih hem-JOO duh*

Beth-lomon *beth-LOH mahn*

Beth-maacah *beth-MAY uh kuh*

Bethmaacah *beth-MAY uh kuh*

Beth Maacah *beth-MAY uh kuh*

Beth-marcaboth *beth-MAHR kuh bahth*

Bethmarcaboth *beth-MAHR kuh bahth*

Beth Marcaboth *beth-MAHR kuh bahth*

Beth-meon *beth-MEE ahn*

Bethmeon *beth-MEE ahn*

Beth Meon *beth-MEE ahn*

Beth-millo *beth-MEEL oh, MIHL oh*

Bethmillo *beth-MEEL oh, MIHL oh*

Beth Millo *beth-MEEL oh, MIHL oh*

Beth-nimrah *beth-NIM ruh*

Bethnimrah *beth-NIM ruh*

Beth Nimrah *beth-NIM ruh*

Beth-ophrah *beth-OHF ruh*

Beth Ophrah *beth-OHF ruh*

Beth-oron *beth-AHR uhn*

Beth-palet *beth-PAY luht*

Bethpazzez *beth-PAZ ez*

Beth-pazzez *beth-PAZ ez*

Beth Pazzez *beth-PAZ ez*

Beth-pelet *beth-PEE luht*

Bethpelet *beth-PEE luht*

Beth Pelet *beth-PEE luht*

Bethpeor *beth-PEE awr*

Beth-peor *beth-PEE awr*

Beth Peor *beth-PEE awr*

Bethphage *BETH fuh jee, BETH fayj*

Beth-phelet *beth-FEE luht*

Bethrapha *beth-RAY fuh*

Beth-rapha *beth-RAY fuh*

Beth Rapha *beth-RAY fuh*

Bethrehob *beth-REE hahb*

---

a-HAT; ah-far FAHR; aw-call KAWL; ay-name NAYM; B-BAD; ch-CHEW; d-DAD; e,eh-met MET; ee-sea SEE; ew-truth TREWTH; f-FOOT, enough ee NUHF; g-GET; h-HIM; hw-whether HWEH thuhr; i, ih-city SI ti, or SIH tih; igh sign SIGHN, eye IGH; igh LIGHT; j-jack JAK, germ JUHRM; k-KISS, chorus KOH ruhss, ks-(for x) ox AHKS; kw-quail KWAYL; l-live LIHV, LIGHV; m-more MOHR; ng-ring RING; oh-go GOH, row ROH (a boat); oo-LOOK; oo-boot BOOT

Beth-rehob   *beth-REE hahb*

Beth Rehob   *beth-REE hahb*

Beth-saida   *beth-SAY ih duh*

Bethsaida   *beth-SAY ih duh*

Bethsamos   *beth SAM ahs*

Bethshan   *beth-SHAHN*

Beth-shan   *beth-SHAHN*

Beth-Shan   *beth-SHAHN*

Beth Shan   *beth-SHAHN*

Beth-shean   *beth-SHEE uhn*

Bethshean   *beth-SHEE uhn*

Beth Shean   *beth-SHEE uhn*

Beth Shearim   *BETH-sheh uh REEM*

Beth-shemesh   *beth-SHEM mesh*

Bethshemesh   *beth-SHEM mesh*

Beth Shemesh   *beth-SHEM mesh*

Beth-shemite   *beth-SHEM might*

Bethshemite   *beth-SHEM might*

Beth-shitta   *beth-SHIT uh*

Bethshitta   *beth-SHIT uh*

Beth Shitta   *beth-SHIT uh*

Bethsura   *beth SOOR uh*

Beth-tappuah   *beth-TAP yoo uh*

Bethtappuah   *beth-TAP yoo uh*

Beth Tappuah   *beth-TAP yoo uh*

Beth-togarmah   *BETH-toh GAHR muh*

Bethtogarmah   *BETH-toh GAHR muh*

Beth Togarmah   *BETH-toh GAHR muh*

Bethuel   *beh THYOO uhl*

Bethul   *BETH uhl, BEE thuhl*

Bethulia   *bih THOO lee uh*

Beth-Yerah   *BETH-yuh RAY uh*

Beth-zacharias   *BETH-zak uh RIGH uhs*

Beth-zaith   *beth-ZAY ith*

Beth-Zaith   *beth-ZAY ith*

Bethzatha   *beth-ZAY thuh*

Beth-zatha   *beth-ZAY thuh*

Beth-zechariah   *beth-ZEK uh RIGH uh*

Beth Zeita   *beth-ZIGH tuh*

Bethzur   *beth-ZUHR*

Beth-zur   *beth-ZUHR*

Beth Zur   *beth-ZUHR*

Betolius   *bih TOH lih uhs*

B

Betomasthaim   *BET uh mass THAY im*

Betomastham   *BET uh MASS thuhm*

Betomesthaim   *BET uh miss THAY im*

Betomestham   *BET uh MESS thuhm*

Betonim   *BET oh nim*

Beulah   *BY<u>OO</u> luh*

Bezaanannim   *bih ZAY uh NAN im*

Bezai   *BEE zay igh (eye), BEE zigh*

Bezaleel   *beh ZAL eh el, BEZ uh leel*

Bezalel   *BEHZ uh lehl*

Bezek   *BEE zek*

Bezer   *BEE zuhr*

Bezeth   *BEE zith, beh ZETH*

Bezetha   *BEE zuh thuh*

Bhogazkoy   *BOHG haz koy*

Biatas   *BIGH uh tuhs*

Bichri   *BIK righ*

Bichrite   *BIK ri<u>ght</u>*

bichrom   *BAK ruhm*

Bicri   *BIK righ*

Bidkar   *BID kahr*

Bigtha   *BIG thuh*

Bigthan   *BIG than*

Bigthana   *big THAY nuh*

Bigvai   *BIG vay igh, BIG vigh*

Bikri   *BIK righ*

Bildad   *BIL dad*

Bileam   *BIL ee uhm*

Bilgah   *BIL guh*

Bilgai   *BIL gay igh, BIL gigh*

Bilhah   *BIL hah*

Bilhan   *BIL han*

Bilshan   *BIL shan*

Bimhal   *BIM hal*

Binea   *BIN ih uh*

Binnui   *BIN y<u>oo</u> igh (eye)*

Birei   *BIHR ee igh   (eye)*

Biri   *BIHR igh (eye)*

Birsha   *BIHR shuh*

Birzaith   *bihr ZAY ith*

Birzavith   *bihr ZAY vith*

Bishlam   *BISH lam*

bishop   *BISH uhp*

Bithia   *BITH ih uh, BIH thih uh*

Bithiah   *BITH ih uh*

Bithron   *BITH rahn*

Bithynia   *bih THIN ih uh*

Biziothiah   *BIZ ee oh THIGH uh*

Bizjothjah   *biz JAHTH juh*

Biztha   *BIZ thuh*

---

a-HAT; ah-far FAHR; aw-call KAWL; ay-name NAYM; B-BAD; ch-CHEW; d-DAD; e,eh-met MET; ee-sea SEE; ew-truth TREWTH; f-FOOT, enough ee NUHF; g-GET; h-HIM; hw-whether HWEH thuhr; i, ih-city SI ti, or SIH tih; igh sign SIGHN, eye IGH; <u>igh</u> LIGHT; j-jack JAK, germ JUHRM; k-KISS, chorus KOH ruhss, ks-(for x) ox AHKS; kw-quail KWAYL; l-live LIHV, LIGHV; m-more MOHR; ng-ring RING; oh-go GOH, row ROH (a boat); oo-LOOK; <u>oo</u>-boot B<u>OO</u>T

Blastus *BLASS tuhs*

Boanerges *BOH uh NUHR jeez*

Boaz *BOH az*

Boccas *BAHK uhs*

Bocheru *BAHK ih roo*

Bochim *BOH kim*

Boghazkoi *bohg haz KOY, buh GHAHZ koy*

Bohan *BOH han*

Bokeru *BOH ker roo*

Bokim *BOH kim*

booths *BOOTHS*

Booz *BOH ahz*

Bor-ashan *bohr-AY shahn*

Borashan *bohr-AY shahn*

Bor Ashan *bohr-AY shahn*

Borith *BAHR ith*

Borsippa *bohr SIP puh*

Boscath *BAHS kath*

Bosketh *BAHS keth*

Bosor *BOH sawr*

Bosora *BAHS uh ruh*

Bosphorus *BAHS fuh ruhs*

Bosporus *BAHS puh ruhs*

Bosra *BAHZ ruh*

Bougaean *boo JEE uhn*

Bozez *BOH zehz*

Bozkath *BAHZ kath*

Boznai *BAHZ nigh*

Bozrah *BAHZ ruh*

Bubastis *byoo BAS tiss*

Bugean *boo GHEE uhn*

Bukki *BUHK igh (eye)*

Bukkiah *buh KIGH uh*

Bul *BULL*

bulla *BOO luh (OO as in look)*

bullae (pl.) *BOO lih (OO as in look)*

Bunah *BYOO nuh*

Bunni *BUHN igh (eye)*

Buqei'ah Valley *boo KEE uh-VA lih (oo as in look)*

burnish *BUHR nish*

Busiris *buh SIGH ruhs*

Buz *BUHZ*

Buzi *BYOO zigh*

Buzite *BYOO zight*

Byblos *BIB lohss, BIB lahss*

Byzantine *BIH zuhn teen*

C

Caanan *KAY uh nuhn, KAY nuhn*

cab *KAB*

---

ow-cow KOW, out OWT; oy-boil BOYL; p-PAT; r-RAN; s-star STAHR, tsetse SET see; sh-show SHOH, action AK shuhn, mission MIH shuhn, vicious VIH shuhss; t-tie TIGH, Thomas TAH muhss; th-thin THIN or THIHN; th-there THEHR; tw-TWIN; u, uh-tub TUB or TUHB, Joshua JAHSH yew uh, term TUHRM; v-veil VAYL, of AHV; w-WAY; wh (whether) see hw; y-year YEER; z-xerox ZIHR ahks, ZEE rahks, his HIZ or HIHZ, zebra ZEE bruh; zh-version VUHR zhuhn

Cabbon   *KAB uhn*

Cabul   *KAY buhl*

Caddis   *KAD iss*

Cades   *KAY deez*

Cades-barne   *KAY deez-BAHR nee*

Cadmiel   *KAD mih uhl*

Caesar   *SEE zuhr*

Caesar Augustus   *SEE zuhr aw GUHS tuhs*

Caesaraea   *SESS uh REE uh*

Caesaraea-Philippi   *SESS uh REE uh-FIL ih pigh*

Caesarea   *SESS uh REE uh*

Caesarean   *SESS uh REE uhn*

Caesarea-Philippi   *SESS uh REE uh-FIL ih pigh*

Caiaphas   *KAY uh fuhs, KIGH uh fuhs*

Cain   *KAYN*

Cainan   *KAY nuhn*

Calah   *KAY luh, kah LAY*

Calamolalus   *KAL uh MAHL uh luhs*

calamus   *KAL uh muhs*

Calcedon   *KAL see dahn, kal SEE duhn*

Calcol   *KAL kahl*

Caleb   *KAY luhb*

Caleb-ephratah   *KAY luhb-EF ruh tuh*

Caleb-Ephrath   *KAY luhb-EF rahth*

Caleb-ephrathah   *KAY luhb-EF ruh thuh*

Caleb Ephrathah   *KAY luhb-EF ruh thuh*

Calebite   *KAY luh bight*

Caligula   *kuh LIHG yuh luh*

Calitas   *kuh LIGHT uhs*

Callisthenes   *kuh LISS thuh neez*

Calneh   *KAL neh*

Calno   *KAL noh*

Calvary   *KAL vuh rih*

Cambyses   *kam BIGH seez*

Camon   *KAY mahn*

camphire   *KAM fighr*

Cana   *KAY nuh*

Canaan   *KAY nuhn*

Canaanite   *KAY nuhn ight*

Canaanitess   *KAY nuhn ight ess*

Canaanitish   *KAY nuhn ight ish*

Cananaean   *KAY nuh NEE uhn*

Candace   *KAN duh see*

Canneh   *KAN eh*

canon   *KA nuhn*

a-HAT; ah-far FAHR; aw-call KAWL; ay-name NAYM; B-BAD; ch-CHEW; d-DAD; e,eh-met MET; ee-sea SEE; ew-truth TREWTH; f-FOOT, enough ee NUHF; g-GET; h-HIM; hw-whether HWEH thuhr; i, ih-city SI ti, or SIH tih; igh sign SIGHN, eye IGH; igh LIGHT; j-jack JAK, germ JUHRM; k-KISS, chorus KOH ruhss, ks-(for x) ox AHKS; kw-quail KWAYL; l-live LIHV, LIGHV; m-more MOHR; ng-ring RING; oh-go GOH, row ROH (a boat); oo-LOOK; oo-boot BOOT

canonical   *kuh NAHN ih kuhl*

canonicity   *KAN uh NISS uh tih*

canonization   *KAN uh nigh ZAY shuhn*

canonize   *KAN uh nighz*

Canticle (Song of Solomon)   *KAN tih kuhl*

Capernaum   *kuh PUHR nay uhm*

Cape-salmone   *KAYP-sal MOH nih*

caph   *KAHF*

Capharnaum   *kuh FAHR nay uhm*

Capharsalama   *KAF uhr-SAL uh muh*

Caphar-salama   *KAF uhr-SAL uh muh*

Caphenatha   *kuh FEN uh thuh*

Caphira   *kuh FIGH ruh*

Caphirim   *kuh FIGH rim*

Caphthorim   *KAF thath rim*

Caphtor (Cyprus)   *KAP thawr*

Caphtorim   *KAF toh rim*

Caphtorite   *KAF toh right*

Cappadocia   *KAP uh DOH shih uh*

Capthor   *KAF tawr*

Car   *KAHR*

Carabasion   *KEHR uh BAY zhee uhn*

caravanseri   *KA ruh van SAY righ*

Carcas   *KAHR kuhs*

Carchemish   *KAHR kem ish*

cardo   *KAHR doh*

Careah   *kuh REE uh*

Carem   *KEHR uhm*

Caria   *KEHR ee uh*

Carian   *KEHR ee uhn*

carinated   *KA rih NAY tehd*

Carite   *KEHR ight*

Carkas   *KAHR kuhs*

Carmanian   *kahr MAY nih uhn*

Carme   *KAHR mee*

Carmel   *KAHR m'l*

Carmelite   *KAHR muhl ight*

Carmelitess   *KAHR muhl ight ess*

Carmi   *KAHR migh*

Carmite   *KAHR might*

Carmonian   *kahr MOH nih uhn*

Carnaim   *kahr NAY im*

Carnion   *KAHR nih uhn*

ow-cow KOW, out OWT; oy-boil BOYL; p-PAT; r-RAN; s-star STAHR, tsetse SET see; sh-show SHOH, action AK shuhn, mission MIH shuhn, vicious VIH shuhss; t-tie TIGH, Thomas TAH muhss; th-thin THIN or THIHN; th-there THEHR; tw-TWIN; u, uh-tub TUB or TUHB, Joshua JAHSH yew uh, term TUHRM; v-veil VAYL, of AHV; w-WAY; wh (whether) see hw; y-year YEER; z-xerox ZIHR ahks, ZEE rahks, his HIZ or HIHZ, zebra ZEE bruh; zh-version VUHR zhuhn

49

Carpus *KAHR puhs*

Carshena *kahr SHEE nuh*

Carthage *KAHR thehg (th as in thin)*

cartouche *kahr TOOSH*

casemate *KAYSS mayt*

Casiphia *kuh SIF ih uh*

Casleu *KASS loo*

Casluh *KASS luh*

Casluhim *KASS lyoo him*

Casluhite *KASS lyoo hight*

Casphor *KASS fawr*

Caspian *KASS pih uhn*

Caspin *KASS pin*

cassia *KASH uh*

Castor *KASS tawr*

casuistic *KASS yoo ISS tik*

catacomb *KAT uh kohmb*

Catal Huyuk *KAT uhl-HOO yook*

catechetical *KAT uh KET ih kuhl*

catechism *KA tuh KIZ uhm*

catholic *KATH uh lik*

Cathua *kuh THOO uh*

Cauda *KAW duh*

Cedemite *KED uh might*

Cedron *SEE druhn*

Ceilan *SEE luhn*

cella *SELL uh*

Celosyria *SEE loh SIHR ih uh*

Celsus *SEL suhs*

Cenchrea *SEN kree uh*

Cenchreae *SEN kree uh, kihn KREE uh*

Cendebaeus *SEN duh BEE uhs*

Cendebeus *SEN duh BEE uhs*

centurion *sen TYOOR ee uhn*

Cephar Haammonai *KEE fahr-ha AM uh nigh*

Cephas *SEE fuhs*

Cesar *SEE zuhr*

Cesarea *SEHS uh REE uh*

Cetab *SEE tab*

Chabod *kah BAHD*

Chabris *KAB riss*

Chadias *KAY dih uhs*

Chadiasa *KAY dih ASS suh*

Chaereas *KIHR ee uhs*

Chalcedon *KAHL sih dahn, kahl SEE duhn*

chalcedony *kal SEE duh nee*

Chalcol *KAL kahl*

Chalcolithic *KAL kuh LITH ik*

Chaldaea *kal DEE uh*

Chaldaean *kal DEE uhn*

Chaldea *kal DEE uh*

Chaldean *kal DEE uhn*

Chaldee *kal DEE*

chalice *CHA liss*

Chalphi *KAL figh*

Chalsis *KAL siss*

Cham *KAM*

Chanaan *KAY nuhn*

Channuneus *KAN uh NEE uhs*

Chanukkah *HAH nuh kuh*

Chaphenatha *kuh FEN uh thuh*

Charaathalar *KEHR ay ATH uh lahr*

Characa *KEHR uh kuh*

Charashim *KEHR uh shim*

Charax *KEHR aks*

Charchamis *KEHR kuh miss*

Charchemish *KAHR kem ish*

Charcus *KAHR kuhs*

Charea *KEHR ee uh*

charisma *kuh RIZ muh*

charismatic *KAR iz MAT ik*

Charmis *KAHR miss*

Charran *KEHR uhn*

Chaseba *KASS uh buh*

Chaspho *KASS foh*

Chebar *KEE bahr*

Chedorlaomer *KED awr lay OH muhr*

Chelal *KEE lal*

Chelcias *KEHL shee uhs*

Cheleoud *KEHL ee ood*

Chellean *KEHL ee uhn*

Chellian *KEHL ih uhn*

Chelluh *KEHL uh*

Chellus *KEHL uhs*

Chelod *KEE lahd*

Chelous *KEHL uhs*

Chelub *KEE luhb*

Chelubai *kih LOO bigh*

Cheluh *KEHL uh*

Cheluhi *KEL yoo high*

Chemarim *KEM uh rim*

Chemosh *KEE mahsh*

Chenaanah *kih NAY uh nuh*

Chenani *kih NAY nigh*

Chenaniah *KEN uh NIGH uh*

Chephar-ammoni *KEE fahr-AM uh nigh*

Chepharammoni *KEE fahr-AM uh nigh*

Chephar-haammonai *KEE fahr-ha AM uh nigh*

Chephirah *kih FIGH ruh*

Chephirim *KEF ih rim*

Cheran *KEE ruhn*

Chereas *KIHR ee uhs*

cherem *KEHR im*

C

ow-cow KOW, out OWT; oy-boil BOYL; p-PAT; r-RAN; s-star STAHR, tsetse SET see; sh-show SHOH, action AK shuhn, mission MIH shuhn, vicious VIH shuhss; t-tie TIGH, Thomas TAH muhss; th-thin THIN or THIHN; th-there THEHR; tw-TWIN; u, uh-tub TUB or TUHB, Joshua JAHSH yew uh, term TUHRM; v-veil VAYL, of AHV; w-WAY; wh (whether) see hw; y-year YEER; z-xerox ZIHR ahks, ZEE rahks, his HIZ or HIHZ, zebra ZEE bruh; zh-version VUHR zhuhn

C

Cherethim *KEHR uh thim*

Cherethite *KER ih thight*

Cherith *KEE rith*

cherub (angel) *CHEHR uhb*

Cherub (city) *KEHR uhb*

cherubim *CHEHR uh bim*

Chesalon *KESS uh lahn*

chesed *KEE sid*

Chesed *KEE sed*

Chesil *KEE suhl*

Chesulloth *kih SUHL ahth*

Cheth *KETH*

Chettiim *KET uh im*

Chezib *KEE zib*

chiasm *KIGH a zuhm*

chiastic *kigh ASS tik*

Chidon *KIGH d'n*

Chileab *KIL ih ab*

Chilion *KIL ih ahn*

Chilmad *KIL mad*

Chimham *KIM ham*

Chinnereth *KIN ih reth*

Chinneroth *KIN ih rahth*

Chios *KIGH ahs*

Chisleu *KISS loo*

Chislev *KISS lehv*

Chislon *KISS lahn*

Chislothtabor KISS *lahth–TAY bawr*

Chisloth-tabor KISS *lahth–TAY bawr*

Chisloth Tabor KISS *lahth–TAY bawr*

Chitlish *KIT lish*

Chittim *KIT im*

Chiun *KIGH uhn*

Chloe *KLOH ee*

Choba *KOH buh*

Chola *KOH luh*

Chonae *KOH nay*

Choraizin *koh RAY zin*

Chor-ashan *kawr–ASH uhn*

Chorashan *kawr–ASH uhn*

Chorazin *koh RAY zin*

Chorbe *KAWR bee*

Chosamaeus KOHS *uh MEE uhs*

Chosameus KOH *suh MEE uhs*

Chosiba *KOH sih buh*

Chosibah *KOH sih buh*

Chozeba *koh ZEE buh*

Choziba *KOH zih buh*

Chozibah *KOH zih buh*

Christ *KRIGHST*

Christian *KRISS chuhn*

---

a-HAT; ah-far FAHR; aw-call KAWL; ay-name NAYM; B-BAD; ch-CHEW; d-DAD; e,eh-met MET; ee-sea SEE; ew-truth TREWTH; f-FOOT, enough ee NUHF; g-GET; h-HIM; hw-whether HWEH thuhr; i, ih-city SI ti, or SIH tih; igh sign SIGHN, eye IGH; igh LIGHT; j-jack JAK, germ JUHRM; k-KISS, chorus KOH ruhss, ks-(for x) ox AHKS; kw-quail KWAYL; l-live LIHV, LIGHV; m-more MOHR; ng-ring RING; oh-go GOH; row ROH (a boat); oo-LOOK; oo-boot BOOT

christological *KRIST uh LAHJ ih kuhl*

Christology *kris TAHL uh jee*

Chronicle *KRAHN ih kuhl*

Chronicler *KRAHN ih kluhr*

Chronicles *KRAHN ih kuhls*

chronos *KROH nahs*

chrysoprase *KRISS uh prayz*

chrysoprasus *KRISS uh PRAY zuhs*

Chub *KUHB*

Chun *KUHN*

Chushan-rishathaim *KOO shan-RISH uh THAY im*

Chusi *KYOO sigh*

Chuzu *KYOO zuh*

Cicero *SISS uh roh*

Cilicia *sih LISH ih uh*

Cilician Gates *sih LISH ih uhn-GAYTS*

cincture *SINK chuhr*

Cinneroth *SIN uh rahth*

Cirama *suh RAY muh*

Cis *SISS*

Cisai *SIGH sigh*

cithara *SITH uh ruh*

cithern *SITH uhrn*

Citim *SIT im*

Clauda *KLAW duh*

Claudia *KLAW dih uh*

Claudius *KLAW dih uhs*

Claudius Lysias *KLAW dih uhs LISS ih uhs*

Clement *KLEM uhnt*

Clementine *KLEM uhn tighn*

Cleopas *KLEE oh puhs*

Cleopatra *KLEE uh PAT ruh*

Cleophas *KLEE oh fuhs*

Clopas *KLOH puhs*

Cnidus *NIGH duhs*

Cochba *KOHK buh*

Cochbah *KOHK buh*

codex *KOH deks*

codices *KOH duh seez, KAH duh seez*

Codomanus *KOH duh MAH nuhs*

Coele-syria *SEE lee-SIHR ih uh*

Coelesyria *SEE lee SIHR ih uh*

Col *KAHL*

Cola *KOH luh*

Colhozeh *kahl-HOH zeh*

Col-hozeh *kahl-HOH zeh*

Colius *koh LIGH uhs*

collate *KOH layt*

collation *koh LAY shuhn*

colon *KOH luhn*

colophon *KAH luh fahn*

C

ow-cow KOW, out OWT; oy-boil BOYL; p-PAT; r-RAN; s-star STAHR, tsetse SET see; sh-show SHOH, action AK shuhn, mission MIH shuhn, vicious VIH shuhss; t-tie TIGH, Thomas TAH muhss; th-thin THIN or THIHN; th-there THEHR; tw-TWIN; u, uh-tub TUB or TUHB, Joshua JAHSH yew uh, term TUHRM; v-veil VAYL, of AHV; w-WAY; wh (whether) see hw; y-year YEER; z-xerox ZIHR ahks, ZEE rahks, his HIZ or HIHZ, zebra ZEE bruh; zh-version VUHR zhuhn

53

C

Colossae   *koh LAHS sih*

Colosse   *koh LAHS sih*

Colossian   *kuh LAHSH uhn*

Comforter   *KUHM fuhr tuhr*

Commentary   *KAHM uhn tehr ih*

Conaniah   *KAHN uh NIGH uh*

concordance   *kahn KAWRD uhnss*

Coniah   *koh NIGH uh*

Cononiah   *KAHN uh NIGH uh*

consul   *KAHN suhl*

Coos   *KOH ahs*

Copt   *KAHPT*

Coptic   *KAHP tik*

cor   *KAWR*

Corashan   *kawr ASH uhn*

corban   *KAWR ban*

Corbe   *KAWR bee*

Core   *KOH ree, KOH rih*

Corinth   *KAWR inth*

Corinthian   *koh RIN thih uhn*

Corinthians   *koh RIN thih uhns*

Corinthus   *koh RIN thuhs*

Cornelius   *kawr NEE lih uhs*

Corsica   *KAWR sih kuh*

Cos   *KAHS*

Cosam   *KOH sam*

Cosbi   *KAHZ bigh*

Cosiba   *KOH sih buh*

Cosibah   *KOH sih buh*

cosmological   *KAHZ muh LAHJ ih kuhl*

cosmology   *kahz MAHL uh jee*

coulter   *KOHL tuhr*

Council   *KOWN suhl*

Counseller   *KOWN suh luhr*

Counsellor   *KOWN suh luhr*

Counselor   *KOWN suh luhr*

Coutha   *KOO thuh (OO as in look)*

Covenant   *KUHV uh nuhnt*

Covenant-box   *KUHV uh nuhnt–BAKS*

Covenant-tent   *KUHV uh nuhnt–TENT*

Coverdale   *KUHV uhr dayl*

Coz   *KAHZ*

Cozeba   *koh ZEE buh*

Coziba   *KOH zih buh*

Cozibah   *KOH zih buh*

Crates   *KRAY teez*

Creator   *kree AY tuhr*

credo   *KREE doh*

Crescens   *KRESS uhnz*

Cretan   *KREE tuhn*

Crete   *KREET*

Cretian   *KREE shuhn*

---

a-HAT; ah-far FAHR; aw-call KAWL; ay-name NAYM; B-BAD; ch-CHEW; d-DAD; e,eh-met MET; ee-sea SEE; ew-truth TREWTH; f-FOOT, enough ee NUHF; g-GET; h-HIM; hw-whether HWEH thuhr; i, ih-city SI ti, or SIH tih; igh sign SIGHN, eye IGH; igh LIGHT; j-jack JAK, germ JUHRM; k-KISS, chorus KOH ruhss, ks-(for x) ox AHKS; kw-quail KWAYL; l-live LIHV, LIGHV; m-more MOHR; ng-ring RING; oh-go GOH, row ROH (a boat); oo-LOOK; oo-boot BOOT

Crispus   *KRISS puhs*

Crocodilopolis   *KRAH kuh digh LAH poh liss*

Crucifixion   *kroo suh FIK shuhn*

crucify   *KROO suh figh*

cryptogram   *KRIP tuh gram*

cryptography   *krip TAHG ruh fih*

Cub   *KUHB*

cubit   *KYOO bit*

Culom   *KOO lahm*

Culon   *KOO luhn*

cumi   *KYOO mih*

cumin   *KUH min*

cummin   *KUH min*

Cun   *KYOON*

Cuneiform   *kyoo NEE uh fohrm*

cursive   *KUHR sihv*

Cush   *KUHSH*

Cushan   *KYOO shan*

Cushan-rishathaim   *KYOO shan-RISH uh THAY im*

Cushanrishathaim   *KYOO shan-RISH uh THAY im*

Cushi   *KYOO shigh*

Cushite   *KYOO shight*

Cuth   *KUHTH*

Cutha   *KYOO thuh*

Cuthah   *KYOO thuh*

Cuza   *KOO zuh*

Cyamon   *SIGH uh muhn*

Cyaxares   *sigh AKS uh reez*

Cybele   *SIB uh lee*

Cyclades   *sigh KLA deez*

cyclopean   *sigh kloh PEE uhn*

Cydnus   *SID nuhs*

cynic   *SIN ik*

cynicism   *SIN uh SIZ uhm*

Cyprian   *SIH prih uhn*

Cypriot   *SIP rih aht*

Cypros   *SIGH prahs*

Cyprus   *SIGH pruhs*

Cyrenaica   *SIGH ruh NAY ih kuh*

Cyrene   *sigh REE nee*

Cyrenean   *sigh REE nih uhn*

Cyreni   *sigh REE nih*

Cyrenian   *sigh REE nih uhn*

Cyrenius   *sigh REE nih uhs*

Cyrus   *SIGH ruhs*

Cyzicus   *SIGHZ ih kuhs*

---

ow-cow KOW, out OWT; oy-boil BOYL; p-PAT; r-RAN; s-star STAHR, tsetse SET see; sh-show SHOH, action AK shuhn, mission MIH shuhn, vicious VIH shuhss; t-tie TIGH, Thomas TAH muhss; th-thin THIN or THIHN; th-there THEHR; tw-TWIN; u, uh-tub TUB or TUHB, Joshua JAHSH yew uh, term TUHRM; v-veil VAYL, of AHV; w-WAY; wh (whether) see hw; y-year YEER; z-xerox ZIHR ahks, ZEE rahks, his HIZ or HIHZ, zebra ZEE bruh; zh-version VUHR zhuhn

D

Dabareh   *DAB uh reh*

Dabbasheth   *DAB uh sheth*

Dabbesheth   *DAB uh sheth*

Daberath   *DAB uh rath*

Dabria   *DAB rih uh*

Dacobi   *DAY kuh bigh*

Daddeus   *DAD ih uhs*

Dadu   *DAY doo*

Dagon   *DAY gahn*

Daisan   *DAY suhn*

Dalaiah   *duh LIGH uh, duh LAY uh*

daleth (Hebrew letter)   *DAH leth*

Dalila   *duh LIGH luh*

Dalmanutha   *DAL muh NOO thuh*

Dalmatia   *dal MAY shih uh*

Dalphon   *DAL fahn*

Damaris   *DAM uh riss*

Damascene   *DAM uh seen*

Damascus   *duh MASS kuhs*

Dammin   *DAM in*

Dan   *DAN*

Daniel   *DAN yuhl*

Danite   *DAN ight*

Dan-jaan   *dan-JAY uhn*

Dan Jaan   *dan-JAY uhn*

Dannah   *DAN uh*

Daphne   *DAF nee*

Dara   *DAHR uh*

Darda   *DAHR duh*

daric   *DEHR ik*

Darius   *duh RIGH uhs*

Darkon   *DAHR kahn*

Dathan   *DAY thuhn*

Dathema   *DATH uh muh*

David   *DAY vid*

Davidic   *duh VID ik*

daysman   *DAYZ muhn*

Day-star   *DAY-stahr*

Daystar   *DAY-stahr*

Day Star   *DAY-stahr*

deacon   *DEE kuhn*

deaconess   *DEE kuh niss*

Dead Sea   *DED-SEE*

Debar   *DEE buhr*

Debarim   *DEE buh rim*

Debir   *DEE buhr*

Debora   *DEB uh ruh*

Deborah   *DEB uh ruh*

decalogue   *DEK uh lahg*

Decapolis   *dih KAP oh liss*

---

a-HAT; ah-far FAHR; aw-call KAWL; ay-name NAYM; B-BAD; ch-CHEW; d-DAD; e,eh-met MET; ee-sea SEE; ew-truth TREWTH; f-FOOT, enough ee NUHF; g-GET; h-HIM; hw-whether HWEH thuhr; i, ih-city SI ti, or SIH tih; igh sign SIGHN, eye IGH; igh LIGHT; j-jack JAK, germ JUHRM; k-KISS, chorus KOH ruhss, ks-(for x) ox AHKS; kw-quail KWAYL; l-live LIHV, LIGHV; m-more MOHR; ng-ring RING; oh-go GOH, row ROH (a boat); oo-LOOK; oo-boot BOOT

D

decision *dee SIHZ uhn*

decumani *deh KOO man ee*

decumanus *deh KOO men uhs*

Dedan *DEE duhn*

Dedanim *DED duh nim*

Dedanite *DED uh night*

Dehavite *dih HAY vight*

Deity *DEE uh tih*

Dekar *DEE kahr*

Deker *DEE kuhr*

Delaiah *dih LAY yuh*

Delilah *dih LIGH luh*

Delos *DEE lahs*

Delphi *DEHL figh*

Delus *DEE luhs*

Demas *DEE muhs*

Demeter *dih MEE tuhr*

Demetrius *dih MEE trih uhs*

Demiurge *DEM ih uhrj*

demoniac *dih MOH nih ak*

demonology *DEE muh NAH luh jih*

Demophon *DEM oh fahn*

demotic *dee MAH tik*

demythologize *DEE mith AHL uh jighz*

denarii (pl.) *dih NEHR ih igh (eye)*

denarius *dih NEHR ih uhs*

dendrochronology *DEN droh kroh NAH luh jih*

Derbe *DUHR bih*

Desolating Sacrilege *DES oh lay ting-SAK ruh lihj*

Dessau *DESS aw*

Deuel *DOO uhl*

Deuterocanon *DYOO tuh roh KAN uhn*

Deutero-Isaiah *DYOO tuh roh-igh ZAY uh*

Deuteronomic *DYOO tuh ruh NAHM ik*

Deuteronomy *DOO tuh RAHN uh mih*

Devil *DEV uhl*

Dhiban *dih BAN*

Diana *digh AN uh*

Diaspora *digh ASS puh ruh*

diatribe *DIGH uh trighb*

Diblah *DIB luh*

Diblaim *DIB lay im*

Diblath *DIB lath*

Diblathaim *DIB luh THAY im*

Dibon *DIGH bahn, dih BAHN*

Dibon-gad *DIGH bahn-GAD*

Dibongad *DIGH bahn-GAD*

Dibon Gad *DIGH bahn-GAD*

D

Dibri   *DIB righ*

Didache   *DID uh kee*

Didymus   *DID ih muhs*

Diklah   *DIK lah*

Dilean   *DIGH lih uhn, DIL ee uhn*

Dilmun   *DIHL muhn*

Dimnah   *DIM nuh*

Dimon   *DIGH mahn*

Dimonah   *digh MOH nuh*

Dinah   *DIGH nuh*

Dinaite   *DIGH nay ight*

Dinhabah   *DIN huh buh*

Dionysia   *DIGH uh NISH ih uh*

Dionysius   *DIGH oh NISH ih uhs*

Dionysus   *DIGH uh NIGH suhs*

Dioscorinthius   *DIGH uhs kuh RIN thih uhs*

Diotrephes   *digh AHT rih feez*

Diphath   *DIGH fath*

disciple   *dih SIGH puhl*

Dishan   *DIGH shan*

Dishon   *DIGH shahn*

dispersion   *diss PUHR zhuhn*

dittography   *dih TAHG ruh fee*

Dizahab   *DIZ uh hab*

Docetism   *DOH suh* TIZ *uhm*

Docus   *DOH kuhs*

Dodai   *DOH digh*

Dodanim   *DOH dah nim*

Dodavah   *DAHD uh vah*

Dodavahu   *doh duh VAY hyoo, doh DAV uh hyoo*

Dodavhu   *doh DAV hyoo*

Dodo   *DOH duh*

Doeg   *DOH ehg*

Dok   *DAHK*

dolmen   *DAHL men*

Domitian   *doh MISH uhn*

Dophkah   *DAHF kah*

Dor   *DAWR*

Dora   *DOHR uh*

Dorcas   *DAWR kuhs*

Dorymenes   *dawr IM uh neez*

Dositheus   *doh SITH ee uhs*

Dotan   *doh TAHN*

Dothaim   *DOH thay im*

Dothan   *DOH thuhn*

Douay   *DOO ay*

doxology   *daks AHL uh jee*

drachma   *DRAK muh*

dram   *DRAM*

Drimylus   *DRIM uh luhs*

Drusilla   *droo SIL uh*

Dumah   *DOO muh*

Dumuzi   *doo MOO zih*

---

a-HAT; ah-far FAHR; aw-call KAWL; ay-name NAYM; B-BAD; ch-CHEW; d-DAD; e,eh-met MET; ee-sea SEE; ew-truth TREWTH; f-FOOT, enough ee NUHF; g-GET; h-HIM; hw-whether HWEH thuhr; i, ih-city SI ti, or SIH tih; igh sign SIGHN, eye IGH; igh LIGHT; j-jack JAK, germ JUHRM; k-KISS, chorus KOH ruhss, ks-(for x) ox AHKS; kw-quail KWAYL; l-live LIHV, LIGHV; m-more MOHR; ng-ring RING; oh-go GOH, row ROH (a boat); oo-LOOK; oo-boot BOOT

dunam *D$\underline{OO}$ nuhm*

Dura *DY$\underline{OO}$ ruh*

Dura-Europus *D$\underline{OO}$R uh y$\underline{oo}$ ROH puhs*

Dur Sharrukin *D$\underline{OO}$R-shuh R$\underline{OO}$ kim*

E

Eanes *EE uh neez*

Easter *EE stuhr*

Ebal *EE buhl*

Ebed *EE bed*

Ebed-melech *EE bed-MEE lek*

Ebedmelech *EE bed-MEE lek*

Eben-bohan-ben-reuben *EE ben-BOH han-ben-RH$\underline{OO}$ ben*

Ebenezer *EB uh NEE zuhr*

Eben-Ezer *EB ehn-EE zuhr*

Eber *EE buhr*

Ebez *EE behz*

Ebiasaph *ih BIGH uh saf*

Ebla *EB luh*

Ebron *EE brahn*

Ebronah *ih BROH nuh*

Ecanus *ih KAY nuhs*

Ecbatana *ehk BAT uh nuh*

Ecce Homo *EK eh-HOH moh*

ecclesia *ih KLEE zhee uh*

ecclesial *ih KLEE zee uhl*

Ecclesiastes *ih KLEE zih ASS teez*

ecclesiastic *ih KLEE zee ASS tik*

ecclesiastical *ih KLEE zee ASS tik kuhl*

Ecclesiasticus (Sirach) *ih KLEE zih ASS tih kuhs*

ecstasy *EK stuh sih*

ecstatic *ek STAT ik*

ecumenical *EK y$\underline{oo}$ MEN ih kuhl*

Ed *ED*

Edar *EE dahr*

Eddias *ih DIGH uhs*

Eddinus *ED uh nuhs*

Eden *EE duhn*

Edenite *EE duh night*

Eder *EE duhr*

Edes *EE deez*

Edessa *eh DESS uh*

Edfu *ED f$\underline{oo}$*

Edna *ED nuh*

Edom *EE duhm*

---

ow-cow KOW, out OWT; oy-boil BOYL; p-PAT; r-RAN; s-star STAHR, tsetse SET see; sh-show SHOH, action AK shuhn, mission MIH shuhn, vicious VIH shuhss; t-tie TIGH, Thomas TAH muhss; th-thin THIN or THIHN; <u>th</u>-there <u>TH</u>EHR; tw-TWIN; u, uh-tub TUB or TUHB, Joshua JAHSH yew uh, term TUHRM; v-veil VAYL, of AHV; w-WAY; wh (whether) see hw; y-year YEER; z-xerox ZIHR ahks, ZEE rahks, his HIZ or HIHZ, zebra ZEE bruh; zh-version VUHR zhuhn

E

Edomite   *EE duhm ight*

Edrei   *ED rih igh (eye)*

Eglah   *EG lah*

Eglaim   *EG lay im*

Eglath-shelishiyah   *EG lath-sheh LISH ih yuh*

Eglathshelishiyah   *EG lath-sheh LISH ih yuh*

Eglath Shelishiyah   *EG lath-sheh LISH ih yuh*

Eglon   *EG lahn*

Egnatian   *EG NAY shuhn*

Egrebel   *ih GREE bel*

Egypt   *EE jipt*

Egyptian   *ee JIPT shuhn*

Ehi   *EE high*

Ehud   *EE huhd*

Eilat   *ee LAHT*

Ekah   *EE kuh*

Eker   *EE kuhr*

ekklesia   *EK klih SEE uh*

Ekrebel   *EK ruh buhl*

Ekron   *EK rahn*

Ekronite   *EK rahn ight*

El   *EHL*

Ela   *EE luh*

Eladah   *EL uh duh*

Elah   *EE luh*

Elam   *EE luhm*

el-Amarna   *el-ah MAHR nuh*

Elamite   *EE luhm ight*

Elasa   *EL uh suh*

Elasah   *EL uh suh, el AY suh*

Elath   *EE lahth, ee LAHT*

Elath   *EE lath*

Elberith   *el-BIHR ith*

El Berith   *el-BIHR ith*

El-beth-el   *el-BETH-uhl*

Elbethel   *el-BETH uhl*

El Bethel   *el-BETH uhl*

Elcia   *el KIGH uh*

Eldaah   *el DAY ah*

Eldad   *EL dad*

Elead   *EL ih uhd*

Eleadah   *EL ih AY duh*

Elealeh   *EE lih AY leh*

Eleasa   *EL ih AY suh*

Eleasah   *EL ih AY suh*

Eleazar   *EL ih AY zuhr*

Eleazurus   *EL ih uh ZOOR uhs*

El-elohe-israel   *el-IH LOH heh-IZ ray el*

El Elohe Israel   *el-IH LOH heh-IZ ray el*

El-elyon   *EL-el YOHN*

El Elyon   *EL-el YOHN*

Eleph   *EE lef*

---

a-HAT; ah-far FAHR; aw-call KAWL; ay-name NAYM; B-BAD; ch-CHEW; d-DAD; e,eh-met MET; ee-sea SEE; ew-truth TREWTH; f-FOOT, enough ee NUHF; g-GET; h-HIM; hw-whether HWEH thuhr; i, ih-city SI ti, or SIH tih; igh sign SIGHN, eye IGH; igh LIGHT; j-jack JAK, germ JUHRM; k-KISS, chorus KOH ruhss, ks-(for x) ox AHKS; kw-quail KWAYL; l-live LIHV, LIGHV; m-more MOHR; ng-ring RING; oh-go GOH, row ROH (a boat); oo-LOOK; oo-boot BOOT

E

Elephantine   *EL uh FAHN tighn*

Eleutherus   *ih LOO thuh ruhs*

Elhanan   *el HAY nuhn*

Eli   *EE ligh*

Eliab   *ih LIGH ab*

Eliaba   *ih LIGH uh buh*

Eliada   *ih LIGH uh duh*

Eliadah   *ih LIGH uh duh*

Eliadas   *ih LIGH uh duhs*

Eliadun   *ih LIGH uh duhn*

Eliah   *ih LIGH uh*

Eliahba   *ih LIGH uh buh*

Eliakim   *ih LIGH uh kim*

Eliali   *ih LIGH uh ligh*

Elialis   *ih LIGH uh liss*

Eliam   *ih LIGH uhm*

Eliaonias   *ih LIGH oh NIGH uhs*

Elias   *ih LIGH uhs*

Eliasaph   *ih LIGH uh saf*

Eliashib   *ih LIGH uh shib*

Eliasib   *ih LIGH uh sib*

Eliasis   *ih LIGH uh siss*

Eliathah   *ih LIGH uh thuh*

Elidad   *ih LIGH dad*

Eliehoenai   *EL ih ee hoh EE nigh*

Eliel   *ih LIGH el*

Eli Eli lama sabach-thani   *EE ligh-EE ligh-LAH mah-sah BAHK thah nigh*

Eli-Eli-lama sabachthani   *EE ligh-EE ligh-LAH mah-sah BAHK thah nigh*

Eli Eli lama sabachthani   *EE ligh-EE ligh-LAH mah-sah BAHK thah nigh*

Elienai   *EL ih EE nigh*

Eliezar   *EL ih EE zuhr*

Eliezer   *EL ih EE zuhr*

Elihoenai   *EL ih hoh EE nigh*

Elihoreph   *EL ih HOH ref*

Elihu   *ih LIGH hyoo*

Elijah   *ih LIGH juh*

Elika   *ih LIGH kuh*

Elim   *EE lim*

Elimelech   *ih LIM uh lek*

Elioenai   *EL ih oh EE nigh*

Elionas   *EL ih OH nuhs*

Eliphal   *ih LIGH fal*

Eliphalat   *ih LIF uh lat*

Eliphalet   *ih LIF uh let*

Eliphaz   *EL ih faz*

Elipheleh   *ih LIF uh leh*

Eliphelehu   *ih LIF uh LEE hyoo*

Eliphelet   *ih LIF eh let*

---

ow-cow KOW, out OWT; oy-boil BOYL; p-PAT; r-RAN; s-star STAHR, tsetse SET see; sh-show SHOH, action AK shuhn, mission MIH shuhn, vicious VIH shuhss; t-tie TIGH, Thomas TAH muhss; th-thin THIN or THIHN; th-there THEHR; tw-TWIN; u, uh-tub TUB or TUHB, Joshua JAHSH yew uh, term TUHRM; v-veil VAYL, of AHV; w-WAY; wh (whether) see hw; y-year YEER; z-xerox ZIHR ahks, ZEE rahks, his HIZ or HIHZ, zebra ZEE bruh; zh-version VUHR zhuhn

E

Elipheleth   *ih LIF uh leth*

Elisabeth   *ih LIZ uh beth*

Elisaeus   *EL uh SEE uhs*

Eliseus   *EL uh SEE uhs*

Elisha   *ih LIGH shuh*

Elishah   *ih LIGH shuh*

Elishama   *ih LISH uh muh*

Elishaphat   *ih LISH uh fat*

Elisheba   *ih LISH ih bah*

Elishua   *EL ih SHOO uh*

Elisimus   *ih LISS ih muhs*

Elite   *EE light*

Eliu   *ih LIGH yoo*

Eliud   *ih LIGH uhd*

Elizabeth   *ih LIZ uh beth*

Elizaphan   *EL ih ZAY fuhn*

Elizur   *ih LIGH zuhr*

Eljehoenai   *EL juh hoh EE nigh*

el-Jib   *el-JIB*

Elkanah   *el KAY nuh*

Elkesh   *EL kesh*

Elkiah   *el KIGH uh*

Elkohshite   *EL koh shight*

Elkosh   *EL kahsh*

Elkoshite   *el KAHSH ight*

Ellasar   *el LAY sahr*

Elmadam   *el MAY duhm*

Elmodam   *el MOH dam*

Elnaam   *el NAY am*

Elnathan   *el NAY thuhn*

Eloah   *ih LOH uh*

Elohe   *el OH heh*

Elohim   *EL oh heem*

Elohist   *EL oh hist*

Eloi   *EE loh igh (eye)*

Eloi Eloi lama sabachthani
   EE loh igh-EE loh igh-LAH muh-suh BAHK thah nee

El Olam   *EL-oh LAHM*

Elon   *EE lahn*

Elonbethhanan   *EE lahn-beth-HAY nan*

Elonbeth-hanan   *EE lahn-beth-HAY nan*

Elon-beth-hanan   *EE lahn-beth-HAY nan*

Elon Bethhanan   *EE lahn-beth-HAY nan*

Elon Beth Hanan   *EE lahn-beth-HAY nan*

Elonite   *EE lahn night*

Elon-meonenim   *EE lahn-mee AHN uh nim*

Eloth   *EE lahth*

Elpaal   *el PAY al*

Elpalet   *el PAY let*

El-paran   *el-PAY ruhn*

---

a-HAT; ah-far FAHR; aw-call KAWL; ay-name NAYM; B-BAD; ch-CHEW; d-DAD; e,eh-met MET; ee-sea SEE; ew-truth TREWTH; f-FOOT, enough ee NUHF; g-GET; h-HIM; hw-whether HWEH thuhr; i, ih-city SI ti, or SIH tih; igh sign SIGHN, eye IGH; igh LIGHT; j-jack JAK, germ JUHRM; k-KISS, chorus KOH ruhss, ks-(for x) ox AHKS; kw-quail KWAYL; l-live LIHV, LIGHV; m-more MOHR; ng-ring RING; oh-go GOH; row ROH (a boat); oo-LOOK; oo-boot BOOT

E

Elparan   *el-PAY ruhn*
El Paran   *el-PAY ruhn*
Elpelet   *el PEL uht*
El Shaddai   *el-SHAD igh (eye)*
El Shadday   *el-SHAD igh (eye)*
Eltecheh   *el TEHK uh*
Elteke   *EL teh keh*
Eltekeh   *EL teh keh*
Eltekoh   *EL teh koh*
Eltekon   *EL teh kahn*
Eltolad   *el TOH lad*
Elul   *IH luhl*
Elusa   *eh LOOZ uh*
Eluzai   *ih LYOO zigh*
Elymaean   *EL uh MEE ahn*
Elymais   *EL uh MAY uhs*
Elymas   *EL ih mass*
Elyon   *el YOHN*
Elzabad   *el ZAY bad*
Elzaphan   *el ZAY fan*
Emadabun   *ih MAD uh buhn*
Emath   *EE math*
Ematheis   *ee MAH thih uhs*
Emathis   *EM uh thuhs*
Emek   *EE mek*
Emekkeziz   *EE mek-KEE ziz*
Emek-keziz   *EE mek-KEE ziz*
Emek Keziz   *EE mek-KEE ziz*

Emeq Rephaim   *EE mek-ref ah EEM*
emerod   *EM uh rahd*
Emim   *EE mim*
Emite   *EE might*
Emmanuel   *ih MAN yoo el*
Emmaus   *eh MAY uhs*
Emmer   *EM uhr*
Emmor   *EM awr*
Enac   *EE nak*
Enaim   *ih NAY im*
Enam   *EE nam*
Enan   *EE nan*
Enasibus   *ih NASS ih buhs*
Endor   *EN-dawr*
En-dor   *EN-dawr*
En Dor   *EN-dawr*
Eneas   *ih NEE uhs*
Eneglaim   *en-EGG lay im*
En-eglaim   *en-EGG lay im*
En Eglaim   *en-EGG lay im*
Enemessar   *EN uh MESS uhr*
Enenius   *ih NEN ih uhs*
Engaddi   *en GAD igh (eye)*
En-gannim   *en-GAN im*
Engannim   *en-GAN im*
En Gannim   *en-GAN im*
En-gedi   *en-GED ih*

ow-cow KOW, out OWT; oy-boil BOYL; p-PAT; r-RAN; s-star STAHR, tsetse SET see; sh-show SHOH, action AK shuhn, mission MIH shuhn, vicious VIH shuhss; t-tie TIGH, Thomas TAH muhss; th-thin THIN or THIHN; th-there THEHR; tw-TWIN; u, uh-tub TUB or TUHB, Joshua JAHSH yew uh, term TUHRM; v-veil VAYL, of AHV; w-WAY; wh (whether) see hw; y-year YEER; z-xerox ZIHR ahks, ZEE rahks, his HIZ or HIHZ, zebra ZEE bruh; zh-version VUHR zhuhn

E

Engedi   *en-GED ih*

En Gedi   *en-GED ih*

En Gev   *en-GEV*

En-haddah   *en-HAD uh*

Enhaddah   *en-HAD uh*

En Haddah   *en-HAD uh*

Enhakkore   *en-HAK oh rih*

En-hakkore   *en-HAK oh rih*

En Hakkore   *en-HAK oh rih*

En-harod   *en-HEHR ahd*

Enhazor   *en-HAY zawr*

En-hazor   *en-HAY zawr*

En Hazor   *en-HAY zawr*

Enkidu   *en KIGH doo*

Enkidu   *AHN kih doo*

Enlil   *EN lil*

Enmishpat   *en-MISH pat*

En-mishpat   *en-MISH pat*

En Mishpat   *en-MISH pat*

Ennom   *EN uhm*

Enoch   *EE nuhk*

Enon   *EE nahn*

Enon-City   *EE nahn-SIT ih*

Enos   *EE nahs*

Enosh   *EE nahsh*

Enrimmon   *en-RIM uhn*

En-rimmon   *en-RIM uhn*

En Rimmon   *en-RIM uhn*

En-rogel   *en-ROH guhl*

Enrogel   *en-ROH guhl*

En Rogel   *en-ROH guhl*

Enshemesh   *en-SHEE mesh, en-SHEM ish*

En-shemesh   *en-SHEE mesh, en-SHEM ish*

En Shemesh   *en-SHEE mesh, en-SHEM ish*

Entappuah   *en-TAP yoo uh*

En-tappuah   *en-TAP yoo uh*

En Tappuah   *en-TAP yoo uh*

Epaenetus   *ih PEE neh tuhs*

Epaphras   *EP uh frass*

Epaphroditus   *ih PAF roh DIGH tuhs*

Epeiph   *EE fif*

Epenetus   *ih PEE nih tuhs*

ephah   *EE fuh*

Ephah   *EE fuh*

Ephai   *EE figh*

Epher   *EE fuhr*

Ephes-dammim   *EE fess-DAM im*

Ephesdammim   *EE fess-DAM im*

Ephes Dammim   *EE fess-DAM im*

Ephes-dammin   *EE fess-DAM in*

a-HAT; ah-far FAHR; aw-call KAWL; ay-name NAYM; B-BAD; ch-CHEW; d-DAD; e,eh-met MET; ee-sea SEE; ew-truth TREWTH; f-FOOT, enough ee NUHF; g-GET; h-HIM; hw-whether HWEH thuhr; i, ih-city SI ti, or SIH tih; igh sign SIGHN, eye IGH; igh LIGHT; j-jack JAK, germ JUHRM; k-KISS, chorus KOH ruhss, ks-(for x) ox AHKS; kw-quail KWAYL; l-live LIHV, LIGHV; m-more MOHR; ng-ring RING; oh-go GOH, row ROH (a boat); oo-LOOK; oo-boot BOOT

64

Ephesian *ih FEE zhuhn*

Ephesians *ih FEE shuhnz*

Ephesus *EF uh suhs*

Ephlal *EF lal*

ephod *EE fahd*

Ephod *EE fahd*

ephphatha *EF uh thuh*

Ephraim *EE fra ihm*

Ephrain *EE fra in*

Ephraimite *EE fra ihm ight*

Ephratah *EF ruh tuh*

Ephrath *EE frath*

Ephrathah *EF ruh thuh*

Ephrathite *EF ruh thight*

Ephron *EE frahn*

Epictetus *EP ih TEE tuhs*

Epicurean *EP ih kyoo REE uhn*

Epicureanism *EP ih kyoo REE uhn iz uhm*

Epicurus *EP ih KYOOR uhs*

epigraphic *ehp uh GRAF ik*

epigraphy *ih PIH gruh fih*

Epimenides *EHP ih MEN ih deez*

Epiphanes *ih PIF uh neez*

Epiphi *EP ih figh*

episcopal *ih PISS kuh puhl*

epistle *ih PISS uhl*

eponym *EP uh nim*

epsilon (Greek letter) *EP sih lahn*

Er *UHR*

Eran *EE ran*

Eranite *EE ran night*

Erastus *ih RASS tuhs*

Erech *EE rek*

Eri *EE righ*

Eridu *EH rih doo*

Erite *EE right*

Esaias *ih ZAY uhs*

Esar-haddon *EE sahr-HAD uhn*

Esarhaddon *EE sahr-HAD uhn*

Esau *EE saw*

eschatological *ES kat uh LAHJ ih kuhl*

eschatology *ES kuh TAHL uh jih*

eschaton *ES kuh tahn*

Esdraelon *ehz DRAY lehn, ehz DREE luhn*

Esdras (Ezra) *EZ druhs*

Esdris *EZ driss*

Esebon *ES ih bahn*

Esebrias *es ih BRIGH uhs*

Esek *EE sek*

Eshan *EE shuhn*

---

ow-cow KOW, out OWT; oy-boil BOYL; p-PAT; r-RAN; s-star STAHR, tsetse SET see; sh-show SHOH, action AK shuhn, mission MIH shuhn, vicious VIH shuhss; t-tie TIGH, Thomas TAH muhss; th-thin THIN or THIHN; th-there THEHR; tw-TWIN; u, uh-tub TUB or TUHB, Joshua JAHSH yew uh, term TUHRM; v-veil VAYL, of AHV; w-WAY; wh (whether) see hw; y-year YEER; z-xerox ZIHR ahks, ZEE rahks, his HIZ or HIHZ, zebra ZEE bruh; zh-version VUHR zhuhn

E

Eshbaal   *esh–BAY uhl*

Esh-baal   *esh–BAY uhl*

Esh Baal   *esh–BAY uhl*

Esh-ban   *ESH–ban*

Eshban   *ESH–ban*

Esh Ban   *ESH–ban*

Eshcol   *ESH kahl*

Eshean   *ESH ih uhn*

Eshek   *EE shek*

Eshkalonite   *ESH kuh lahn ight*

Eshnunna   *esh NOO nuh*

Eshtaol   *ESH tay ahl*

Eshtaolite   *ESH tuh uh light*

Eshtarah   *ESH tuh ruh*

Eshtaulite   *ESH tuh YOO light*

Eshtemoa   *ESH tih MOH uh*

Eshtemoh   *ESH tih moh*

Eshton   *ESH tahn*

Esli   *ESS ligh*

Esora   *ih SAHR uh*

Esril   *ES rihl*

Esrom   *ESS rahm*

Essene   *ESS een*

Ester   *ESS tuhr*

Esther   *ESS tuhr, ESS thuhr*

eta (Greek letter)   *AY tuh*

Etam   *EE tam*

Etham   *EE tham*

Ethan   *EE thuhn*

Ethanim   *ETH uh nim*

Ethanus   *ih THAY nuhs (TH as in thin)*

Ethbaal   *eth BAY uhl*

Ether   *EE thuhr*

Ethiopia   *EE thih OH pih uh*

Ethiopian   *EE thih OH pih uhn*

Ethiopic   *EE thee AHP ik*

Ethkazin   *eth–KAY zin*

Eth-kazin   *eth–KAY zin*

Eth Kazin   *eth–KAY zin*

Ethma   *ETH muh*

Ethnan   *ETH nan*

ethnarch   *ETH nahrk*

Ethni   *ETH nigh*

etiology   *EE tee AHL uh jee*

Etna   *ET nuh*

et-Tell   *et–TELL*

etymological   *ET uh muh LAHJ ih kuhl*

etymology   *ET uh MAH luh jee*

Eubulus   *yoo BYOO luhs*

Eucharist   *YOO kuh rist*

Euergetes   *yoo UHR juh teez*

Euhemerias   *yoo HIM uh RIGH uhs*

---

a-HAT; ah-far FAHR; aw-call KAWL; ay-name NAYM; B-BAD; ch-CHEW; d-DAD; e,eh-met MET; ee-sea SEE; ew-truth TREWTH; f-FOOT, enough ee NUHF; g-GET; h-HIM; hw-whether HWEH thuhr; i, ih-city SI ti, or SIH tih; igh sign SIGHN, eye IGH; igh LIGHT; j-jack JAK, germ JUHRM; k-KISS, chorus KOH ruhss, ks-(for x) ox AHKS; kw-quail KWAYL; l-live LIHV, LIGHV; m-more MOHR; ng-ring RING; oh-go GOH, row ROH (a boat); oo-LOOK; oo-boot BOOT

E

Eumenes *YOO muh neez*

Eunatan *yoo NAY tuhn*

Eunice *YOO niss*

eunuch *YOO nuhk*

Euodia *yoo OH dih uh*

Euodias *yoo OH dih uhs*

Eupator *YOO puh tawr*

Euphrates *yoo FRAY teez*

Eupolemus *yoo PAHL uh muhs*

Eurakylon *yoo RAHK ih lahn*

Euraquila *yoo RAHK wih luh*

Euraquilo *yoo RAK wih loh*

Euripedes *yoo RIP ih deez*

Euroclydon *yoo RAHK lih dahn*

Eusebius *yoo SEE bih uhs*

Eutychus *YOO tih kuhs*

Euxine *yook SEEN*

evangelist *ih VAN juh list*

Eve *EEV*

Evi *EE vigh*

Evil-merodach *EE vihl–mih ROH dak*

Evilmerodach *EE vihl–mih ROH dak*

Evodia *ih VOH dih uh*

execration *EKS ih KRAY shuhn*

exegesis *EK suh JEE suhs*

exegete *EK suh jeet*

exegetical *EK suh JEH tih kuhl*

existential *EG zih STEN shul*

existentialism *EG zih STEN shul IHZ uhm*

exodus *EK suh duhs*

Exodus *EK suh duhs*

exorcise *EK sawr sighz*

exorcism *EK sawr siz uhm*

exorcist *EK sawr sist*

exorcize *EK sawr sighz*

exposition *EK spuh ZIH shuhn*

expository *ek SPAHS uh TOHR ih*

Ezar *EE zuhr*

Ezbai *EZ bigh, EZ bay igh (eye)*

Ezbon *EZ bahn*

Ezechias *EZ uh KIGH uhs*

Ezechiel (Ezekiel) *ih ZEE kih uhl*

Ezecias *EZ uh KIGH uhs*

Ezekias *ez uh KIGH uhs*

Ezekiel (Ezechiel) *ih ZEE kih uhl*

Ezel *EE zel*

Ezem *EE zem*

Ezer *EE zuhr*

ow-cow KOW, out OWT; oy-boil BOYL; p-PAT; r-RAN; s-star STAHR, tsetse SET see; sh-show SHOH, action AK shuhn, mission MIH shuhn, vicious VIH shuhss; t-tie TIGH, Thomas TAH muhss; th-thin THIN or THIHN; th-there THEHR; tw-TWIN; u, uh-tub TUB or TUHB, Joshua JAHSH yew uh, term TUHRM; v-veil VAYL, of AHV; w-WAY; wh (whether) see hw; y-year YEER; z-xerox ZIHR ahks, ZEE rahks, his HIZ or HIHZ, zebra ZEE bruh; zh-version VUHR zhuhn

67

F

Ezerias   *EZ uh RIGH uhs*

Ezias   *ih ZIGH uhs*

Ezion-gaber   *EE zih ahn-GAY buhr*

Eziongeber   *EE zih ahn-GHEE buhr*

Ezion-geber   *EE zih ahn-GHEE buhr*

Ezion Geber   *EE zih ahn-GHEE buhr*

Eznite   *EZ night*

Ezora   *ih ZAWR uh*

Ezra (Esdras)   *EZ ruh*

Ezrah   *EZ ruh*

Ezrahite   *EZ ruh hight*

Ezra-Nehemyah   *EZ ruh-nih HEM yuh*

Ezri   *EZ righ*

Ezrite   *EZ right*

F

faience   *FAY ahnss*

Fair-Havens   *fehr-HAY vuhnz*

Fair Havens   *fehr-HAY vuhnz*

Faiyum   *figh YOOM*

farthing   *FAHR thing (th as in there)*

fauchion   *FAW chuhn*

favissa   *fah VISS uh*

Felix   *FEE liks*

felloe   *FEL oh*

fenestrated   *FEN uh STRAY ted*

Festus   *FESS tuhs*

firkin   *FUHR kin*

Flavius   *FLAY vih uhs*

Florilegium   *FLOHR uh LEEJ ee uhm*

Fortunatus   *FAWR tyoo NAY tuhs*

forum   *FOHR uhm*

fosse   *FAHSS*

G

Gaal   *GAY uhl*

Gaash   *GAY ash*

Gaba   *GAY buh*

Gabael   *GAB ay el*

Gabaon   *GAB ay ahn*

Gabatha   *GAB uh thuh*

Gabbai   *GAB bay igh (eye)*

---

a-HAT; ah-far FAHR; aw-call KAWL; ay-name NAYM; B-BAD; ch-CHEW; d-DAD; e,eh-met MET; ee-sea SEE; ew-truth TREWTH; f-FOOT, enough ee NUHF; g-GET; h-HIM; hw-whether HWEH thuhr; i, ih-city SI ti, or SIH tih; igh sign SIGHN, eye IGH; igh LIGHT; j-jack JAK, germ JUHRM; k-KISS, chorus KOH ruhss, ks-(for x) ox AHKS; kw-quail KWAYL; l-live LIHV, LIGHV; m-more MOHR; ng-ring RING; oh-go GOH, row ROH (a boat); oo-LOOK; oo-boot BOOT

Gabbatha   *GAB uh thuh*

Gabdes   *GAB deez*

Gaber   *GAY buhr*

Gaboes   *GAY bohz*

Gabri   *GAY brigh*

Gabrias   *GAY brih uhs*

Gabriel   *GAY brih el*

Gad   *GAD*

Gadara   *GAD uh ruh*

Gadarene   *GAD uh reen*

Gaddah   *GAD uh*

Gaddi   *GAD igh (eye)*

Gaddiel   *GAD ih uhl*

Gader   *GAY duhr*

Gadi   *GAY digh*

Gadite   *GAD ight*

Gaham   *GAY ham*

Gahar   *GAY hahr*

Gaher   *GAY huhr*

Gai   *GIGH*

Gaius   *GAY yuhs*

Galaad   *GAL ay uhd*

Galal   *GAY lal*

Galatia   *guh LAY shuh*

Galatian   *guh LAY shuhn*

Galatians   *guh LAY shuhnz*

galbanum   *GAL buh nuhm*

Galgal   *GAL gal*

Galgala   *GAL guh luh*

Galilaean   *GAL ih LEE uhn*

Galilean   *GAL ih LEE uhn*

Galilee   *GAL ih lee*

Gallienus   *GAH lih IN uhs*

Gallim   *GAL im*

Gallio   *GAL ih oh*

Gamad   *GAY mad*

Gamadite   *GAY muh dight*

Gamael   *GAM ay el*

Gamaliel   *guh MAY lih uhl*

Gamla   *GAHM luh*

Gammad   *GAM muhd*

Gammadim   *GAM uh dim*

Gamul   *GAY muhl*

Gannim   *GAN im*

Gar   *GAHR*

Gareb   *GAY reb*

Garizim   *GAHR uh zim*

Garmite   *GAHR might*

Gas   *GAS*

Gashmu   *GASH myoo*

Gatam   *GAY tam*

Gath   *GATH*

Gath-hepher   *gath-HEE fuhr*

Gathhepher   *gath-HEE fuhr*

Gathrimmon   *gath-RIM uhn*

Gath-rimmon   *gath-RIM uhn*

G

ow-cow KOW, out OWT; oy-boil BOYL; p-PAT; r-RAN; s-star STAHR, tsetse SET see; sh-show SHOH, action AK shuhn, mission MIH shuhn, vicious VIH shuhss; t-tie TIGH, Thomas TAH muhss; th-thin THIN or THIHN; th-there THEHR; tw-TWIN; u, uh-tub TUB or TUHB, Joshua JAHSH yew uh, term TUHRM; v-veil VAYL, of AHV; w-WAY; wh (whether) see hw; y-year YEER; z-xerox ZIHR ahks, ZEE rahks, his HIZ or HIHZ, zebra ZEE bruh; zh-version VUHR zhuhn

G

Gath Rimmon *gath-RIM uhn*

Gaugamela *gah GAH muh luh*

Gaul *GAWL*

Gaulanitis *GAWL uh NIGH tiss*

Gaza *GAY zuh, GAH zuh*

Gazara *guh ZAY ruh*

Gazathite *GAY zuh thight, GAH zuh thight*

Gazer *GAY zuhr*

Gazera *guh ZEE ruh*

Gazez *GAY zez*

Gazite *GAY zight*

Gazzam *GAZ uhm*

Gazzan *GAZ uhn*

Geba *GHEE buh*

Gebal *GHEE buhl*

Gebalite *GHEE buh light*

Geber *GHEE buhr*

Gebim *GHEE bim*

gecko *GEK oh*

Gedaliah *GED uh LIGH uh*

Geddur *GED uhr*

Gedeon *GED ih uhn*

Geder *GHEE duhr*

Gederah *gih DEE ruh*

Gederathite *geh DEE ruh thight*

Gederite *gih DEER ight*

Gederoth *gih DEE rahth*

Gederothaim *gih DEE ruh THAY im*

Gedi *GED igh (eye)*

Gedor *GHEE dawr*

Geharashim *ghee-HAHR uh shim*

Ge-harashim *ghee-HAHR uh shim*

Ge Harashim *ghee-HAHR uh shim*

Gehazi *gih HAY zigh*

Gehenna *gih HEN uh*

Ge-hinnom *gih-HIN uhm*

Gelboe *gehl BOH uh*

Geliloth *gih LIGH lahth*

Gemalli *gih MAL igh (eye)*

Gemara *guh MAH ruh*

Gemariah *GHEM uh RIGH uh*

genealogical *JEE nee uh LAHJ ih kuhl*

genealogy *JEE nee AL uh jih*

Genesis *JEN ih siss*

genizah *guh NEE zuh*

Gennaeus *gih NEE uhs*

Gennesar *gih NEE sahr*

---

a-HAT; ah-far FAHR; aw-call KAWL; ay-name NAYM; B-BAD; ch-CHEW; d-DAD; e,eh-met MET; ee-sea SEE; ew-truth TREWTH; f-FOOT, enough ee NUHF; g-GET; h-HIM; hw-whether HWEH thuhr; i, ih-city SI ti, or SIH tih; igh sign SIGHN, eye IGH; igh LIGHT; j-jack JAK, germ JUHRM; k-KISS, chorus KOH ruhss; ks-(for x) ox AHKS; kw-quail KWAYL; l-live LIHV, LIGHV; m-more MOHR; ng-ring RING; oh-go GOH, row ROH (a boat); oo-LOOK; oo-boot BOOT

Gennesaret *gih NESS uh ret*

Genneus *gih NEE uhs*

genre *ZHAHN ruh*

Gentile *JEN tighl*

Genubath *gih NYOO bath*

Geon *GHEE ahn*

Gera *GHEE ruh*

gerah *GHEE ruh*

Gerah *GHEE ruh*

Gerar *GHEE rahr, geh RAHR*

Gerasa *GEHR uh suh*

Gerasene *GEHR uh seen*

Gergesa *GUHR guh suh*

Gergesene *GUHR guh seen*

Gergesite *GEHR guh sight*

Gerizim *GEHR uh zim*

Geron *GIHR ahn*

Gerrene *guh REE nee*

Gerrhenian *guh REE nee uhn*

Gershom *GUHR shuhm*

Gershomite *GUHR shuh might*

Gershon *GUHR shahn*

Gershonite *GUHR shahn ight*

Gerson *GUHR sahn*

Geruth Chimham *GHEE rooth-KIM ham*

Geruth Kimham *GHEE rooth-KIM ham*

Gerzite *GUHR zight*

Gesem *GHEE suhm*

Gesham *GESH uhm, GHEE shuhm*

Geshan *GESH uhn, GHEE shuhn*

Geshem *GESH ehm*

Geshur *GHEE shuhr*

Geshuri *gih SHOO righ*

Geshurite *GESH yoo right*

Gessen *GHESS uhn*

Gether *GHEE thuhr*

Gethsemane *geth SEM uh nih*

Geuel *gih YOO uhl*

Gezer *GHEE zuhr*

Gezrite *GEHZ right*

Giah *GIGH uh*

Gibbar *GIB ahr*

Gibbeah *GIB ee uh*

Gibbeath *GIB ee ahth*

Gibbethon *GIB uh thahn*

Gibea *GIB ih uh*

Gibeah *GIB ih uh*

Gibea-Saul *GIB ih uh-SAWL*

Gibeath *GIB ih ath*

Gibeathelohim *GIB ee ath-EH loh heem*

ow-cow KOW, out OWT; oy-boil BOYL; p-PAT; r-RAN; s-star STAHR, tsetse SET see; sh-show SHOH, action AK shuhn, mission MIH shuhn, vicious VIH shuhss; t-tie TIGH, Thomas TAH muhss; th-thin THIN or THIHN; th-there THEHR; tw-TWIN; u, uh-tub TUB or TUHB, Joshua JAHSH yew uh, term TUHRM; v-veil VAYL, of AHV; w-WAY; wh (whether) see hw; y-year YEER; z-xerox ZIHR ahks, ZEE rahks, his HIZ or HIHZ, zebra ZEE bruh; zh-version VUHR zhuhn

71

G

Gibeath-elohim   *GIB ee ath-EH loh heem*

Gibeath-haaraloth   *GIB ee ath-hah-AHR uh lahth*

Gibeath-ha-araloth   *GIB ee ath-hah-AHR uh lahth*

Gibeath Haaraloth   *GIB ee ath-hah-AHR uh lahth*

Gibeath-hammoreh   *GIB ee ath-hah MAHR uh*

Gibeathite   *GIB ih uh thight*

Gibeon   *GIB ih uhn*

Gibeon el-Jib   *GIB ih ahn-el-JIB*

Gibeonite   *GIB ih uh night*

Giblite   *GIB light*

Giddalti   *gih DAL tigh*

Giddel   *GID uhl*

Gideon   *GID ih uhn*

Gideoni   *GID ih OH nigh*

Gidgad   *GID gad*

Gidom   *GIGH dahm*   ·

gier   *JIHR*

Giezi   *gih EE zigh*

Gihon   *GHEE hohn, GIGH hahn*

Gilalai   *GIL uh ligh*

Gilat   *GHEE laht*

Gilboa   *gil BOH uh*

Gilead   *GIL ih uhd*

Gileadite   *GIL ih uh dight*

Gilgal   *GIL gal*

Gilgamesh   *gil GAM esh, GIL guh mesh*

Gilo   *GIGH loh*

Giloh   *GIGH loh*

Gilonite   *GIGH loh night*

gimel (Hebrew letter)   *GHEE mehl*

Gimzo   *GIM zoh*

Gina   *GHEE nuh, JEE nuh*

Ginae   *GHIH nigh, JEE nigh*

Ginea   *GIH nigh, JEE nigh*

Ginath   *GIGH nath*

Ginnetho   *GIHN ih thoh*

Ginnethoi   *GIHN ih thoy (oy as in boy)*

Ginnethon   *GIHN nih thahn*

Ginnosar   *GIHN noh sawr*

Girgashite   *GUHR guh shight*

Girgasite   *GUHR guh sight*

Girgushite   *GUHR guh shight*

Girzite   *GUHR zight*

Gishpa   *GISH puh*

Gispa   *GIS puh*

Gittah-hepher   *GIT tah-HEE fuhr*

Gittaim   *GIT ay im*

Gittite   *GIT ight*

---

a-HAT; ah-far FAHR; aw-call KAWL; ay-name NAYM; B-BAD; ch-CHEW; d-DAD; e,eh-met MET; ee-sea SEE; ew-truth TREWTH; f-FOOT, enough ee NUHF; g-GET; h-HIM; hw-whether HWEH thuhr; i, ih-city SI ti, or SIH tih; igh sign SIGHN, eye IGH; igh LIGHT; j-jack JAK, germ JUHRM; k-KISS, chorus KOH ruhss, ks-(for x) ox AHKS; kw-quail KWAYL; l-live LIHV, LIGHV; m-more MOHR; ng-ring RING; oh-go GOH; row ROH (a boat); oo-LOOK; oo-boot BOOT

Gittith   *GIT ith*

Giza   *GHEE zuh*

Gizonite   *GIGH zoh night*

glacis   *glah SEE*

glede   *GLEED*

glossalalia   *GLAHS uh LAY lih uh*

gnosis   *NOH siss*

Gnostic   *NAHS tik*

Gnosticism   *NAHS tuh SIH zuhm*

Goah   *GOH ah*

Goath   *GOH ath*

Gob   *GAHB*

God   *GAHD*

Godhead   *GAHD hed*

Gog   *GAHG*

Goiim   *GOY im (OY as in boy)*

Golan   *GOH lan*

Golgotha   *GAHL guh thuh, gahl GAHTH uh*

Goliath   *guh LIGH uhth*

Gomer   *GOH muhr*

Gomorrah   *guh MAHR uh*

Gomorrha   *guh MAHR uh*

Gordium   *GAWR dih uhm*

Goren-ha-atad   *GAWR in-hah-AY tad*

Gorgias   *GAWR juhs*

Gortyn   *GAWR tin*

Gortyna   *gawr TIGH nuh*

Goshen   *GOH shuhn*

Gospel   *GAHS puhl*

Gotholiah   *GAHTH uh LIGH uh*

Gotholias   *GAHTH uh LIGH uhs*

Gothoniel   *goh THAHN ih el*

Goyim   *GOY im (OY as in boy)*

Gozan   *GOH zan*

Gozen   *GOH zen*

Graba   *GRAH buh*

Granicus   *GRAN ih kuhs*

Grecia   *GREE shih uh, GREE shuh*

Grecian   *GREE shuhn*

Greece   *GREES*

Greek   *GREEK*

Gudgogah   *guhd GOH duh*

Guni   *GYOO nigh*

Gunite   *GYOO night*

Gur   *GUHR*

Gur-baal   *guhr-BAY uhl*

Gurbaal   *guhr-BAY uhl*

Gur Baal   *guhr-BAY uhl*

Gutium   *ghoo TEE uhm*

G

ow-cow KOW, out OWT; oy-boil BOYL; p-PAT; r-RAN; s-star STAHR, tsetse SET see; sh-show SHOH, action AK shuhn, mission MIH shuhn, vicious VIH shuhss; t-tie TIGH, Thomas TAH muhss; th-thin THIN or THIHN; th-there THEHR; tw-TWIN; u, uh-tub TUB or TUHB; Joshua JAHSH yew uh; term TUHRM; v-veil VAYL, of AHV; w-WAY; wh (whether) see hw; y-year YEER; z-xerox ZIHR ahks, ZEE rahks, his HIZ or HIHZ, zebra ZEE bruh; zh-version VUHR zhuhn

H

Haahashtari   *HAY uh HASH tuh righ*

Haammonai   *hay AM uh nigh*

Habacuc (Habakkuk)   *HAB uh kuhk*

Habaiah   *huh BAY yuh*

Habakkuk (Habacuc)   *huh BAK kuk*

Habaziniah   *HAB uh zih NIGH uh*

Habazziniah   *HAB uh zih NIGH uh*

Habbacuc   *huh BAK uhk*

habergeon   *HAB uhr juhn*

Habiru   *hah BEE roo*

Habor   *HAY bawr, hah BOHR*

Habucuc   *HAB uh kuhk*

Hacaliah   *HAK uh LIGH uh*

Haccerem   *HAK uh rem*

Hachaliah   *HAK uh LIGH uh*

Hachamoni   *HAK uh MOH nigh*

Hachilah   *huh KIGH luh*

Hachmon   *HAK muhn*

Hachmoni   *HAK moh nigh*

Hachmonite   *HAK moh night*

Hacmoni   *HAK moh nigh*

Hacmonite   *HAK moh night*

Hadad   *HAY dad*

Hadadezer   *HAD ad EE zuhr*

Hadadrimmon   *HAY dad-RIM uhn*

Hadad Rimmon   *HAY dad-RIM uhn*

Hadar   *HAY dahr*

Hadarezer   *HAD ad EE zuhr*

Hadashah   *huh DASH uh*

Hadassah   *huh DASS uh*

Hadattah   *huh DAT uh*

Haddah   *HAD uh*

Haddon   *HAD ahn*

Hadera   *ha DEHR uh*

Hades   *HAY deez*

Hadid   *HAY did*

Hadlai   *HAD lay igh, HAD ligh*

Hadoram   *huh DOH ram*

Hadrach   *HAY drak, HAD rak*

Hadrian   *HAY drih uhn*

Haeleph   *ha EE lef, hay EE lif*

Hagab   *HAY gab*

Hagaba   *HAG uh buh*

Hagabah   *HAG uh buh*

Hagar   *HAY gahr*

Hagarene   *HAG uh reen*

Hagarite *HAG ahr ight*

Hagerite *HAY guhr ight*

Haggadah *HAG guh duh, huh GAH duh*

Haggadol *HAG uh dahl*

Haggai (Aggeus) *HAG igh (eye)*

Haggedolim *HAG eh DOH lihm*

Haggeri *huh GHEE righ*

Haggi *HAG igh (eye)*

Haggiah *huh GIGH uh*

Haggite *HAG ight*

Haggith *HAG ith*

Hagia *HAY ghee uh*

Hagiographa *HAG ee AHG ruh fuh*

Hagri *HAG righ*

Hagrite *HAG right*

Hahiroth *huh HIGH rahth*

Hai *HIGH*

Haifa *HIGH fuh*

Hail *HAYL*

Hakeldama *huh KEHL duh muh*

Hakilah *huh KIGH luh*

Hakkatan *HAK uh tan*

Hakkore *HAK oh rih*

Hakkoz *HAK ahz*

Hakupha *huh KYOO fuh*

Halah *HAY luh*

Halak *HAY lak*

Halakah *HAH lah KAH*

Halhul *HAY huhl*

Hali *HAY ligh*

Halicarnassus *HAL uh kahr NASS uhs*

hallel *HAL el*

hallelujah *ha luh LOO yuh*

Hallohesh *huh LOH hesh*

Halohesh *huh LOH hesh*

Halys *HAY liss*

Ham *HAM*

Hamadan *HAH muh dahn*

Haman *HAY muhn*

Hamath *HAY math*

Hamathite *HAY muhth ight*

Hamath-zobah *HAY math-ZOH buh*

Hamathzobah *HAY math-ZOH buh*

Hamath Zobah *HAY math-ZOH buh*

Hamite *HAM ight*

Hammahlekoth *huh MAH lih kahth*

Hammath *HAM uhth*

ow-cow KOW, out OWT; oy-boil BOYL; p-PAT; r-RAN; s-star STAHR, tsetse SET see; sh-show SHOH, action AK shuhn, mission MIH shuhn, vicious VIH shuhss; t-tie TIGH, Thomas TAH muhss; th-thin THIN or THIHN; th-there THEHR; tw-TWIN; u, uh-tub TUB or TUHB, Joshua JAHSH yew uh, term TUHRM; v-veil VAYL, of AHV; w-WAY; wh (whether) see hw; y-year YEER; z-xerox ZIHR ahks, ZEE rahks, his HIZ or HIHZ, zebra ZEE bruh; zh-version VUHR zhuhn

75

Hammedatha *HAM mih DAY thuh*

Hammelech *HAM uh lek*

Hammolecheth *ha MAHL eh keth*

Hammoleketh *hah MOH lih keth*

Hammon *HAM uhn*

Hammothdor *HAM uhth-DAWR*

Hammoth-dor *HAM uhth-DAWR*

Hammoth Dor *HAM uhth-DAWR*

Hammuel *HAM yoo el*

Hammurabi *HAM uh RAH bih*

Hammurapi *HAM uh RAH pih*

Hamon *HAY muhn*

Hamonah *huh MOH nuh*

Hamongog *HAY muhn-GAHG*

Hamon-gog *HAY muhn-GAHG*

Hamon Gog *HAY muhn-GAHG*

Hamor *HAY mawr*

Hamran *HAM ran*

Hamuel *HAM yoo el*

Hamul *HAY muhl*

Hamulite *HAY muhl ight*

Hamutal *huh MYOO tuhl*

Hana *HAY nuh*

Hanameel *huh NAM ih el*

Hanamel *HAN uh mehl*

Hanan *HAY nan*

Hananeal *huh NAN ee uhl*

Hananeel *huh NAN ih el*

Hananel *HAN uh nehl*

Hanani *huh NAY nigh*

Hananiah *HAN uh NIGH uh*

Hananiel *huh NAN ih el*

Hanes *HAY neez*

Haniel *HAN ih el*

Hannah *HAN uh*

Hannathon *HAN uh thahn*

Hanniel *HAN ih el*

Hanoch *HAY nahk*

Hanochite *HAY nahk ight*

Hanukkah *HAH nuh kuh*

Hanun *HAY nuhn*

hapax *HAH pahks*

Hapharaim *HAF uh RAY im*

Haphraim *haf RAY im*

Hapiru *hah PEE roo*

Happizzez *HAP ih zez*

Happuch *HAP uhk*

Hara *HAY ruh*

Haradah *huh RAY duh*

---

a-HAT; ah-far FAHR; aw-call KAWL; ay-name NAYM; B-BAD; ch-CHEW; d-DAD; e,eh-met MET; ee-sea SEE; ew-truth TREWTH; f-FOOT, enough ee NUHF; g-GET; h-HIM; hw-whether HWEH thuhr; i, ih-city SI ti, or SIH tih; igh sign SIGHN; eye IGH; igh LIGHT; j-jack JAK, germ JUHRM; k-KISS, chorus KOH ruhss, ks-(for x) ox AHKS; kw-quail KWAYL; l-live LIHV, LIGHV; m-more MOHR; ng-ring RING; oh-go GOH; row ROH (a boat); oo-LOOK; oo-boot BOOT

Haran   *HAY ran*

Harar   *HAY ruhr*

Hararite   *HAY ruh right*

Harbel   *HAHR bel*

Harbona   *hahr BOH nuh*

Harbonah   *hahr BOH nuh*

Harel   *HEHR uhl*

Hareph   *HAY ref*

Haresha   *huh REE shuh*

Hareth   *HAY reth*

Harhaiah   *hahr HIGH uh*

Harhas   *HAHR hass*

Har-heres   *hahr-HEE reez*

Harheres   *hahr-HEE reez*

Harhur   *HAHR huhr*

Harim   *HAY rim*

Hariph   *HAHR if*

Har-magedon   *HAHR-muh GED uhn*

Harmon   *HAHR muhn*

Harnepher   *HAHR nuh fuhr*

Harod   *HAY rahd*

Harodite   *HAY rahd ight*

Haroeh   *huh ROH eh*

Harorite   *HAY roh right*

Harosheth   *huh ROH sheth*

Harosheth Haggoyim   *huh ROH sheth-huh GOY im*

Harosheth-hagoiim   *huh ROH sheth-huh GOY im*

Harosheth-ha-goiim   *huh ROH sheth-huh-GOY im*

Haroshethhagoiim   *huh ROH sheth-huh GOY im*

Harosheth-hagoyim   *huh ROH sheth-huh GOY im*

Harosheth Hagoyim   *huh ROH sheth-huh GOY im*

Harsa   *HAHR suh*

Harsha   *HAHR shuh*

Harsith   *HAHR sith*

Haruan   *HAWR an*

Harum   *HAY ruhm*

Harumaph   *huh ROO maf*

Haruphite   *huh ROO fight*

Haruz   *HAY ruhz*

Hasadiah   *HASS uh DIGH uh*

Hasenuah   *HASS ih NYOO uh*

Hash   *HASH*

Hashabiah   *HASH uh BIGH uh*

Hashabnah   *huh SHAB nuh*

Hashabneah   *HASH uhb NEE uh*

Hashabneiah   *HASH uhb NEE yah*

Hashabniah   *HASH uhb NIGH uh*

ow-cow KOW, out OWT; oy-boil BOYL; p-PAT; r-RAN; s-star STAHR, tsetse SET see; sh-show SHOH, action AK shuhn, mission MIH shuhn, vicious VIH shuhss; t-tie TIGH, Thomas TAH muhss; th-thin THIN or THIHN; th-there THEHR; tw-TWIN; u, uh-tub TUB or TUHB, Joshua JAHSH yew uh, term TUHRM; v-veil VAYL, of AHV; w-WAY; wh (whether) see hw; y-year YEER; z-xerox ZIHR ahks, ZEE rahks, his HIZ or HIHZ, zebra ZEE bruh; zh-version VUHR zhuhn

H

Hashbadana *HASH buh DAY nuh*

Hashbaddanah *hash BAD uh nuh*

Hashem *HAY shem*

Hashmonah *hash MOH nuh*

Hashub *HAY shuhb*

Hashubah *huh SHOO buh*

Hashum *HAY shuhm*

Hashupha *huh SHOO fuh*

Hasid *HAH sid, ha SEED*

Hasidaeans *hass uh DEE uhnz*

Hasidean *HASS uh DEE uhn*

Hasidic *hah SID ik*

Hasidim *HASS uh deem*

Hasmonaean *HAZ moh NEE uhn*

Hasmonean *HAZ moh NEE uhn*

Hasrah *HAZ ruh*

Hassenaah *HASS ih NAY uh*

Hassenuah *HASS ih NOO uh*

Hasshub *HASS shuhb*

Hassophereth *hass SOH fih reth*

Hasupha *huh SOO fuh*

Hatach *HAY tak*

Hathach *HAY thak*

Hathath *HAY thath*

Hatipha *huh TIGH fuh*

Hatita *huh TIGH tuh*

Hattaavah *huh TAY uh vah*

Hatti *hah TEE*

Hatticon *HAT ih kahn*

Hattil *HAT ihl*

Hattin *ha TEEN*

Hattush *HAT uhsh*

Hattusha *hah TOO shuh*

Hattushah *hah TOOSH uh*

Hauran *HAH ran, HAW ran*

Havilah *HAV ih luh*

Havilah-by-shur *HAV ih luh-bigh-SHUHR*

Havoth-Jair *HAY vahth-JAY ihr*

Havvothjair *HAY vahth-JAY ihr*

Havvoth-jair *HAY vahth-JAY ihr*

Havvoth Jair *HAY vahth-JAY ihr*

Hayamim *hay YAH mim*

Hazael *HAZ ay el*

Hazaiah *huh ZIGH uh, huh ZAY yuh*

Hazar *HAY zahr*

Hazaraddar *HAY zahr-AD ahr*

---

a-HAT; ah-far FAHR; aw-call KAWL; ay-name NAYM; B-BAD; ch-CHEW; d-DAD; e,eh-met MET; ee-sea SEE; ew-truth TREWTH; f-FOOT, enough ee NUHF; g-GET; h-HIM; hw-whether HWEH thuhr; i, ih-city SI ti, or SIH tih; igh sign SIGHN, eye IGH; igh LIGHT; j-jack JAK, germ JUHRM; k-KISS, chorus KOH ruhss, ks-(for x) ox AHKS; kw-quail KWAYL; l-live LIHV, LIGHV; m-more MOHR; ng-ring RING; oh-go GOH, row ROH (a boat); oo-LOOK; oo-boot BOOT

Hazar-addar *HAY zahr-AD ahr*

Hazar Addar *HAY zahr-AD ahr*

Hazar-addar-Hezron *HAY zahr-AD ahr-hez RAHN*

Hazarenan *HAY zahr-EE nuhn*

Hazar-enan *HAY zahr-EE nuhn*

Hazar Enan *HAY zahr-EE nuhn*

Hazar-enon *HAY zahr-EE nuhn*

Hazarenon *HAY zahr-EE nuhn*

Hazar-gaddah *HAY zahr-GAD uh*

Hazargaddah *HAY zahr-GAD uh*

Hazar Gaddah *HAY zahr-GAD uh*

Hazar-hatticon *HAY zahr-HAT ih kahn*

Hazar Hatticon *HAY zahr-HAT ih kahn*

Hazar-maveth *HAY zahr-MAY veth*

Hazarmaveth *HAY zahr-MAY veth*

Hazarshual *HAY zahr-SHOO uhl*

Hazar-shual *HAY zahr-SHOO uhl*

Hazar Shual *HAY zahr-SHOO uhl*

Hazarsusah *HAY zahr-SOO suh*

Hazar-susah *HAY zahr-SOO suh*

Hazar Susah *HAY zahr-SOO suh*

Hazarsusim *HAY zahr-SOO sim*

Hazar-susim *HAY zahr-SOO sim*

Hazar Susim *HAY zahr-SOO sim*

Hazazon *HAZ uh zahn*

Hazazon-tamar *HAZ uh zahn-TAY muhr*

Hazazontamar *HAZ uh zahn-TAY muhr*

Hazazon-Tamar *HAZ uh zahn-TAY mahr*

Hazelelponi *HAZ uh lel POH nigh*

Hazerhatticon *HAY zuhr-HAT ih kahn*

Hazer-hatticon *HAY zuhr-HAT ih kahn*

Hazer Hatticon *HAY zuhr-HAT ih kahn*

Hazerim *huh ZEE rim*

H

ow-cow KOW, out OWT; oy-boil BOYL; p-PAT; r-RAN; s-star STAHR, tsetse SET see; sh-show SHOH, action AK shuhn, mission MIH shuhn, vicious VIH shuhss; t-tie TIGH, Thomas TAH muhss; th-thin THIN or THIHN; th-there THEHR; tw-TWIN; u, uh-tub TUB or TUHB, Joshua JAHSH yew uh, term TUHRM; v-veil VAYL, of AHV; w-WAY; wh (whether) see hw; y-year YEER; z-xerox ZIHR ahks, ZEE rahks, his HIZ or HIHZ, zebra ZEE bruh; zh-version VUHR zhuhn

H

Hazeroth *huh ZEE rahth*

Hazezon-tamar *HAZ uh zahn-TAY muhr*

Hazezon Tamar *HAZ uh zahn-TAY muhr*

Haziel *HAY zih el*

Hazo *HAY zoh*

Hazor *HAY zawr*

Hazorea *HAH zoh REE uh*

Hazorhadattah *HAY zawr-huh DAT uh*

Hazor-hadattah *HAY zawr-huh DAT uh*

Hazor Hadattah *HAY zawr-huh DAT uh*

Hazzebaim *HAZ uh BAY im*

Hazzelelponi *HAZ zih lehl POH nigh*

Hazzobebah *HAZ oh BEE buh*

Hazzurim *HAZ uh rim*

he (Hebrew letter) *HAY*

Heber *HEE buhr*

Heberite *HEB uh right*

Hebraic *hee BRAY ihk*

Hebrew *HEE broo*

Hebrews *HEE brooz*

Hebrewess *HEE broo ess*

Hebron *HEE bruhn*

Hebronite *HEE bruhn ight*

hectare *HEHK tahr*

Hegai *HEE gigh*

Hege *HEE ghee*

Hegemonides *HEJ uh MOH nuh deez*

Heglam *HEG luhm*

Helah *HEE lah*

Helam *HEE luhm*

Helbah *HEL buh*

Helbon *HEL bahn*

Helchiah *hehl KIGH uh*

Heldai *HEL digh, HEL day igh (eye)*

Heleb *HEE leb*

Helech *HEE lek*

Heled *HEE led*

Helek *HEE lek*

Helekite *HEE lek ight*

Helem *HEE lem*

Heleph *HEE lef*

Heler *HEE luhr*

Helez *HEE lez*

Heli *HEE ligh*

Helias *HEE lee uhs*

Heliodorus *HEE lee uh DAWR uhs*

Heliopolis *HEE lih AHP uh liss*

Helkai *HEL kay igh, HEL kigh*

Helkath *HEL kath*

---

a-HAT; ah-far FAHR; aw-call KAWL; ay-name NAYM; B-BAD; ch-CHEW; d-DAD; e,eh-met MET; ee-sea SEE; ew-truth TREWTH; f-FOOT, enough ee NUHF; g-GET; h-HIM; hw-whether HWEH thuhr; i, ih-city SI ti, or SIH tih; igh sign SIGHN, eye IGH; igh LIGHT; j-jack JAK, germ JUHRM; k-KISS, chorus KOH ruhss, ks-(for x) ox AHKS; kw-quail KWAYL; l-live LIHV, LIGHV; m-more MOHR; ng-ring RING; oh-go GOH, row ROH (a boat); oo-LOOK; oo-boot BOOT

Helkath-hazzurim *HEL kath-HAZ yoo rim*

Helkathhazzurim *HEL kath-HAZ yoo rim*

Helkath Hazzurim *HEL kath-HAZ yoo rim*

Helkias *hehl KIGH uhs*

Hellenism *HEH luh NIH zuhm*

Hellenist *HEL uh nist*

Hellenistic *HEL uh NISS tik*

Hellenization *HEH luh nuh ZAY shuhn*

hellenize *HEL uh NIGHZ*

Hellespont *HEHL uh spahnt*

Hellez *HEHL ehz*

Helon *HEE lahn*

helper *HELP uhr*

Hemam *HEE mam*

Heman *HEE muhn*

Hemath *HEE math*

Hemdan *HEM dan*

Hen *HEN*

Hena *HEE nuh*

Heena *HEE nuh*

Henadad *HEN uh dad*

Henna *HEE nuh*

Henoch *HEE nahk*

henotheism *HEN oh thee IZ uhm (th as in thin)*

henotheist *HEN oh thee ist*

henotheistic *HEN oh thee ISS tik (th as in thin)*

Hephaestus *hih FESS tuhs*

Hepher *HEE fuhr*

Hepherite *HEE fuhr ight*

Hephzi-bah *HEF zih-buh*

Hephzibah *HEF zih-buh*

Heptateuch *HEP tuh tyook*

Heradonijah *HUHR ad uh NIGH juh*

Herakleid *huh RAHK lid*

Herculaneum *HUHR koo LAYN ih uhm*

Hercules *HUHR kyuh LEEZ*

herem *HEHR im*

Heres *HEE ress*

Heresh *HEE resh*

Hereth *HEE reth*

Hermas *HUHR muhs*

hermeneutic *HUHR muh NYOO tik*

hermeneutical *HUHR muh NYOO tih kuhl*

Hermes *HUHR meez*

Hermogenes *huhr MAHJ ih neez*

Hermon *HUHR muhn*

Hermonite *HUHR muh night*

H

H

Hermus *HUHR muhs*

Herod *HEHR uhd*

Herodian *hih ROH dih uhn*

Herodias *hih ROH dih uhs*

Herodion *hih ROH dih uhn*

Herodium *hih ROH dih uhm*

Herodotus *hih RAHD uh tuhs*

hesed *HEE sid, HEE sed*

Hesed *HEE sed*

Heshbon *HESH bahn*

Heshbonite *HESH bahn ight*

Heshmon *HESH mahn*

Hesli *HESS ligh*

Heth *HETH*

heth (Hebrew letter) *HAYTH*

Hethlon *HETH lahn*

hexapla *HEK suh pluh*

Hexateuch *HEK suh tyook*

Hezeki *HEZ ih kigh*

Hezekiah *HEZ ih kigh uh*

Hezion *HEE zih ahn*

Hezir *HEE zihr*

Hezrai *HEZ ray igh, HEZ righ*

Hezro *HEZ roh*

Hezron *HEZ rahn*

Hezronite *HEZ rahn ight*

Hiddai *HID ay igh, HID igh (eye)*

Hiddekel *HID ih kehl*

Hiel *HIGH el*

Hierapolis *HIGH uhr AHP oh liss*

hierarchy *highr AHRK kee*

hieratic *highr RA tik*

Hiereel *high IHR ee el*

Hieremoth *high IHR uh mahth*

Hierielus *high IHR ih EE luhs*

Hiermas *high UHR muhs*

hierocracy *highr AHK ruh see*

hieroglyph *HIGHR glif*

hieroglyphic *highr GLIF ik*

Hieronymus *HIGH uh RAHN uh muhs*

Higgaion *hih GAY yahn*

hilani *hee LAHN nih*

Hilen *HIGH len*

Hilkiah *hil KIGH uh*

Hillel *HIL el*

hin *HIN*

Hinnom *HIN ahm*

hippodrome *HIP uh DROHM*

Hippos *HIP puhs, HIP pahs*

Hippus *HIP puhs*

Hirah *HIGH ruh*

Hiram *HIGH ruhm*

Hircanus *hihr KAY nuhs*

Hittite *HIT tight*

Hivite *HIGH vight*

Hizki *HIZ kigh*

Hizkiah *hiz KIGH uh*

Hizkijah *hiz KIGH juh*

Hobab *HOH bab*

Hobah *HOH bah*

Hobaiah *hoh BAY yuh*

Hod *HAHD*

Hodaiah *hoh DAY yuh*

Hodaviah *hoh duh VIGH uh*

Hodesh *HOH desh*

Hodevah *HOH dih vah*

Hodiah *hoh DIGH uh*

Hodijah *hoh DIGH juh*

Hodshi *HAHD shigh*

Hoglah *HAHG luh*

Hoham *HOH ham*

holemouth *HOHL mowth*
   (ow as in cow)

Holofernes *HAHL uh FUHR*
   neez

Holon *HOH lahn*

Holy Ghost *HOH lee-GOHST*

Holy Spirit *HOH lee-SPIHR it*

Homam *HOH mam*

homer *HOH muhr*

homiletic *hahm ih LET ik*

homily *HAHM ih lih*

hoopoe *HOO poo*

Hophni *HAHF nigh*

Hophra *HAHF ruh*

Hor *HAWR*

Horam *HOH ram*

Horeb *HOH reb*

Horem *HOH rem*

Horesh *HOR resh*

Hor-haggidgad *HAWR-huh*
   GID gad

Horhaggidgad *HAWR-huh*
   GID gad

Hor Haggidgad *HAWR-huh*
   GID gad

Hor-hagidgad *HAWR-huh*
   GID gad

Hor Hagidgad *HAWR-huh*
   GID gad

Hori *HOH righ*

Horim *HOH rim*

Horite *HOH right*

Hormah *HAWR muh*

Horon *HAWR ahn*

Horonaim *HAWR oh NAY im*

Horonite *HAWR oh night*

H

---

ow-cow KOW, out OWT; oy-boil BOYL; p-PAT; r-RAN; s-star STAHR, tsetse SET see; sh-show
SHOH, action AK shuhn, mission MIH shuhn, vicious VIH shuhss; t-tie TIGH, Thomas TAH muhss;
th-thin THIN or THIHN; th-there THEHR; tw-TWIN; u, uh-tub TUB or TUHB, Joshua JAHSH yew
uh, term TUHRM; v-veil VAYL, of AHV; w-WAY; wh (whether) see hw; y-year YEER; z-xerox ZIHR
ahks, ZEE rahks, his HIZ or HIHZ, zebra ZEE bruh; zh-version VUHR zhuhn

83

Horvat Teman *HOHR vat-TEE mahn*

Horvat Uza *HOHR vat-OO zah*

Hosah *HOH suh*

hosanna *hoh ZAN nuh*

Hosea (Osee) *hoh ZAY uh*

Hoshaiah *hoh SHIGH uh*

Hoshama *HAHSH uh muh*

Hoshea *hoh SHEE uh*

Hotham *HOH tham (th as in thin)*

Hothan *HOH than (th as in thin)*

Hothir *HOH thuhr (th as in thin)*

Hozai *HOH zay igh, HOH zigh*

Hozeh *HOH zeh*

Hubbah *HUH buh*

Huddai *HUH digh*

Hukkok *HUHK ahk*

Hukok *HYOO kahk*

Hul *HUHL*

Hula *HOO luh*

Huldah *HUHL duh*

Huleh *HOO luh*

Humtah *HUHM tuh*

Hupham *HYOO fam*

Huphamite *HYOO fam ight*

Huppah *HUP uh*

Huppim *HUP im*

Huppite *HUP ight*

Hur *HUHR*

Hurai *HYOO ray igh, HYOO righ*

Huram *HYOO ram*

Huram-abi *HYOO ram-AY bih*

Huramabi *HYOO ram-AY bih*

Huri *HYOO righ*

Hurrian *HOOR ih uhn*

Hus *HUHS*

Husha *HYOO shuh*

Hushah *HYOO shuh*

Hushai *HYOO shigh, HYOO shay igh (eye)*

Husham *HYOO sham*

Hushathite *HYOO shuhth ight*

Hushim *HYOO shim*

Hushite *HYOO shight*

Huz *HUHZ*

Huzoth *HUH zahth*

Huzzab *HUHZ ab*

Hydaspes *high DASS peez*

Hyksos *HIK sohss*

Hymenaeus *HIGH meh NEE uhs*

---

a-HAT; ah-far FAHR; aw-call KAWL; ay-name NAYM; B-BAD; ch-CHEW; d-DAD; e,eh-met MET; ee-sea SEE; ew-truth TREWTH; f-FOOT, enough ee NUHF; g-GET; h-HIM; hw-whether HWEH thuhr; i, ih-city SI ti, or SIH tih; igh sign SIGHN, eye IGH; igh LIGHT; j-jack JAK, germ JUHRM; k-KISS, chorus KOH ruhss, ks-(for x) ox AHKS; kw-quail KWAYL; l-live LIHV, LIGHV; m-more MOHR; ng-ring RING; oh-go GOH, row ROH (a boat); oo-LOOK; oo-boot BOOT

Hymeneus   *HIGH meh NEE uhs*

Hyrcania   *huhr KAY nee uh, hihr KAY nih uh*

Hyrcanus   *huhr KAY nuhs*

hyssop   *HISS uhp*

Hystaspes   *hih STAHS peez*

Hystastes   *hih STAHS teez*

I

Ibhar   *IB hahr*

Ibleam   *IB lih uhm*

Ibneiah   *ib NIGH uh*

Ibnijah   *ib NIGH juh*

Ibri   *IB righ*

Ibsam   *IB sam*

Ibzan   *IB zan*

I-chabod   *IH kuh bahd*

Ichabod   *IK uh bahd*

icon   *IGH kahn*

Iconium   *igh (eye) KOH nih uhm*

iconoclasm   *igh KAHN uh KLAZ uhm*

iconoclastic   *IGH kahn uh KLAS tik*

Idalah   *ID uh luh*

Idbash   *ID bash*

Iddo   *ID oh*

Iduel   *IHD yoo el*

Idumaea   *ID yoo MEE uh*

Idumaean   *IHD yoo MEE uhn*

Idumea   *ID yoo MEE uh*

Iezer   *igh (eye) EE zuhr*

Iezerite   *igh (eye) EE zuh right*

Igal   *IGH (eye) gal*

Igdaliah   *IG duh LIGH uh*

Igeal   *IGH (eye) gih uhl*

Ignatius   *ihg NAY shuhs*

Iim   *IGH (eye) im*

Iishvah   *igh (eye) ISH vuh*

Ije-abarim   *IGH (eye) jih–AB uh rim*

Ije Abarim   *IGH (eye) jih–AB uh rim*

Ijim   *IGH (eye) jim*

Ijon   *IGH (eye) jahn*

Ikhnaton   *IHK nah tahn, ik NAY tuhn*

Ikkesh   *IK esh*

Ilai   *IGH ligh, IGH lay igh (eye)*

Iliadun   *ih LIGH uh duhn*

Ilium   *IH lih uhm*

Illyria   *ih LIHR ih uh*

I

ow-cow KOW, out OWT; oy-boil BOYL; p-PAT; r-RAN; s-star STAHR, tsetse SET see; sh-show SHOH, action AK shuhn, mission MIH shuhn, vicious VIH shuhss; t-tie TIGH, Thomas TAH muhss; th-thin THIN or THIHN; th-there THEHR; tw-TWIN; u, uh-tub TUB or TUHB, Joshua JAHSH yew uh, term TUHRM; v-veil VAYL, of AHV; w-WAY; wh (whether) see hw; y-year YEER; z-xerox ZIHR ahks, ZEE rahks, his HIZ or HIHZ, zebra ZEE bruh; zh-version VUHR zhuhn

85

	I

Illyricum   *ih LIHR ih kuhm*

Imalcue   *ih MAL k<u>oo</u>*

Imalkue   *ih MAL ky<u>oo</u> ee*

Imla   *IM lah*

Imlah   *IM lah*

Immanuel   *ih MAN y<u>oo</u> el*

Immer   *IM uhr*

Immite   *IM <u>ight</u>*

Imna   *IM nuh*

Imnah   *IM nuh*

Imnite   *IM ni<u>ght</u>*

Imrah   *IM ruh*

Imri   *IM righ*

Incarnation   *IN kahr NAY shuhn*

India   *IN dih uh*

Indian   *IN dih uhn*

inerrancy   *in EHR uhn see*

inerrant   *in EHR uhnt*

interpolate   *in TUHR poh layt*

interpolation   *in TUHR poh LAY shuhn*

Iob   *IGH (eye) ohb*

Ionian   *igh (eye) OH nih uhn*

iota (Greek letter)   *ih OH tuh*

Iphdeiah   *if DEE yuh*

Iphedeiah   *IF ih DIGH uh*

Iphtah   *IF tuh*

Iphtah-el   *IF tuh-EL*

Iphtahel   *IF tuh EL*

Iphtah EL   *IF tuh-EL*

Ipsus   *IHP s<u>oo</u>s*

Ir   *UHR*

Ira   *IGH (eye) ruh*

Irad   *IGH (eye) rad*

Iram   *IGH (eye) ram*

Iran   *ih RAHN, ih RAN*

Iraq   *ih RAHK, ih RAK*

Irbid   *IHR bid*

Irenaeus   *IGH ruh NEE uhs*

Ir-hamelah   *ihr-HAM uh luh*

Iri   *IGH (eye) righ*

Irijah   *igh (eye) RIGH juh*

Ir-Moab   *ihr-MOH ab*

Ir-nahash   *uhr-NAY hash*

Irnahash   *uhr-NAY hash*

Ir Nahash   *uhr-NAY hash*

Iron   *IGH rahn*

Irpeel   *UHR peh uhl*

Ir-shemesh   *uhr-SHEE mesh*

Irshemesh   *uhr-SHEE mesh*

Ir Shemesh   *uhr-SHEE mesh*

Iru   *IGH (eye) r<u>oo</u>*

Isaac   *IGH (eye) zik*

Isai   *IGH (eye) zigh*

---

a-HAT; ah-far FAHR; aw-call KAWL; ay-name NAYM; B-BAD; ch-CHEW; d-DAD; e,eh-met MET; ee-sea SEE; ew-truth TREWTH; f-FOOT, enough ee NUHF; g-GET; h-HIM; hw-whether HWEH thuhr; i, ih-city SI ti, or SIH tih; igh sign SIGHN, eye IGH; i<u>gh</u> L<u>IGHT</u>; j-jack JAK, germ JUHRM; k-KISS, chorus KOH ruhss; ks-(for x) ox AHKS; kw-quail KWAYL; l-live LIHV, LIGHV; m-more MOHR; ng-ring RING; oh-go GOH, row ROH (a boat); oo-LOOK; <u>oo</u>-boot B<u>OO</u>T

Isaiah (Isaias)   *igh (eye) ZAY uh*

Iscah   *ISS kuh*

Iscariot   *iss KAR ih aht*

Isdael   *IZ dih uhl*

Ish   *ISH*

Ishbaal   *ISH bay uhl*

Ishbah   *ISH buh*

Ishbak   *ISH bak*

Ishbibenob   *ISH bigh-BEE nahb*

Ishbi-benob   *ISH bigh-BEE nahb*

Ish-bosheth   *ish-BOH sheth*

Ishbosheth   *ISH-BOH sheth*

Ish-hai   *ISH-high*

Ishi   *ISH igh (eye)*

Ishiah   *ish IGH (eye) uh*

Ishijah   *ish IGH (eye) juh*

Ishma   *ISH muh*

Ishmachiah   *ISH muh KIGH uh*

Ishmael   *ISH may el*

Ishmaelite   *ISH may el ight*

Ishmaiah   *ish MIGH uh*

Ishmeelite   *ISH mee uh light*

Ishmerai   *ISH mih righ*

Ishod   *IGH (eye) shahd, ISH ahd*

Ishpah   *ISH puh*

Ishpan   *ISH pan*

Ishtar   *ISH tahr*

Ishtob or Ish-tob   *ISH-tahb*

Ishuah   *ISH yoo uh*

Ishuai   *ISH yoo igh (eye)*

Ishui   *ISH yoo igh (eye)*

Ishvah   *ISH vuh*

Ishvi   *ISH vigh*

Ishvite   *ISH vight*

Isin   *IH sin*

Isis   *IGH siss*

Ismachiah or Ismakiah   *ISS muh KIGH uh*

Ismael   *ISS may el*

Ismaiah   *iss MAY yuh*

Ispa   *ISS puh*

Ispah   *ISS puh*

Israel   *IZ ray el*

Israelite   *IZ ray el ight*

Israelitish   *IZ ray uh LIGHT ish*

Issachar   *ISS uh KAHR*

Issacharite   *ISS uh kuh right*

Isshiah   *iss SHIGH uh*

Isshijah   *iss SHIGH juh*

Issus   *IH suhss*

Istalcurus   *ISS tuhl KYOOR uhs*

Isuah   *ISS yoo uh*

Isui   *ISS yoo igh (eye)*

I

ow-cow KOW, out OWT; oy-boil BOYL; p-PAT; r-RAN; s-star STAHR, tsetse SET see; sh-show SHOH, action AK shuhn, mission MIH shuhn, vicious VIH shuhss; t-tie TIGH, Thomas TAH muhss; th-thin THIN or THIHN; th-there THEHR; tw-TWIN; u, uh-tub TUB or TUHB, Joshua JAHSH yew uh, term TUHRM; v-veil VAYL, of AHV; w-WAY; wh (whether) see hw; y-year YEER; z-xerox ZIHR ahks, ZEE rahks, his HIZ or HIHZ, zebra ZEE bruh; zh-version VUHR zhuhn

I

Italian *igh (eye) TAL ih uhn*

Italica *igh (eye) TAL ih kuh*

Italy *IT uh lih*

Ithai *IGH thay igh (eye), ITH igh*

Ithamar *ITH uh mahr*

Ithiel *ITH ih el*

Ithlah *ITH luh*

Ithmah *ITH muh*

Ithnan *ITH nan*

Ithra *ITH ruh*

Ithran *ITH ran*

Ithream *ITH rih am*

Ithrite *ITH right*

Ittah-kazin *IT uh-KAY zin*

Ittai *IT ay igh, IT igh (eye)*

Ituraea *IT yoo REE uh*

Iturea *IT yoo REE uh*

Ivah *IGH vuh*

Ivvah *IGH vuh*

Iye-abarim *IGH (eye) yuh-AB uh rim*

Iyeabarim *IGH (eye) yuh AB uh rim*

Iye Abarim *IGH (eye) yuh-AB uh rim*

Iyim *IGH (eye) yim*

Iyyob *IGH (eye) yahb*

Izar *IGH (eye) zahr*

Izarahiah *IZ uh ruh HIGH uh*

Izbet Sartah *IHZ bet-SAHR tuh*

Izehar *IGH (eye) zih hahr*

Izeharite *IZ ih hahr ight*

Izhar *IZ hahr*

Izharite *IZ hahr IGHT*

Izliah *iz LIGH uh*

Izrahiah *IZ rah HIGH uh*

Izrahite *IZ ruh hight*

Izri *IZ righ*

Izziah *iz IGH (eye) uh*

J

Jaakan *JAY uh kan*

Jaakanite *JAY uh kuh night*

Jaakobah *jay uh KOH buh*

Jaakobath *jay uh KOH bath*

Jaala *JAY uh luh*

Jaalah *JAY uh luh*

Jaalam *JAY uh lam*

Jaanai *JAY uh nigh*

Jaar *JAY ahr*

Jaareoregim *JAY uh rih-AWR ih gim*

---

a-HAT; ah-far FAHR; aw-call KAWL; ay-name NAYM; B-BAD; ch-CHEW; d-DAD; e,eh-met MET; ee-sea SEE; ew-truth TREWTH; f-FOOT, enough ee NUHF; g-GET; h-HIM; hw-whether HWEH thuhr; i, ih-city SI ti, or SIH tih; igh sign SIGHN, eye IGH; igh LIGHT; j-jack JAK, germ JUHRM; k-KISS, chorus KOH ruhss, ks-(for x) ox AHKS; kw-quail KWAYL; l-live LIHV, LIGHV; m-more MOHR; ng-ring RING; oh-go GOH, row ROH (a boat); oo-LOOK; oo-boot BOOT

Jaare-Oregim *JAY uh rih–AWR ih gim*

Jaareshiah *JAY uh rih SHIGH uh*

Jaasai *JAY uh sigh*

Jaasau *JAY uh saw*

Jaasiel *jay ASS ih el*

Jaasu *JAY uh soo*

Jaazaniah *jay AZ uh NIGH uh*

Jaazer *JAY uh zuhr*

Jaaziah *JAY uh ZIGH uh*

Jaaziel *jay AY zih el*

Jabal *JAY bal*

Jabbok *JAB ahk*

Jabesh *JAY besh*

Jabeshgilead *JAY besh–GIL ih uhd*

Jabesh-gilead *JAY besh–GIL ih uhd*

Jabesh Gilead *JAY besh–GIL ih uhd*

Jabez *JAY bez*

Jabin *JAY bin*

Jabneel *JAB nih el*

Jabneh *JAB neh*

Jacan *JAY kan*

Jachan *JAY kan*

Jachin *JAY kin*

Jachinite *JAY kih night*

jacinth *JAY sinth*

Jacob *JAY kuhb*

Jacubus *juh KYOO buhs*

Jada *JAY duh*

Jadah *JAY duh*

Jadau *JAY daw*

Jaddai *JAD digh*

Jaddua *JAD yoo uh*

Jaddus *JAD uhs*

Jadon *JAY dahn*

Jael *JAY uhl*

Jaffa *JAF fuh*

Jagur *JAY guhr*

Jah *JAH*

Jahaleleel *JAY huh LEL ee uhl*

Jahath *JAY hath*

Jahaz *JAY haz*

Jahaza *juh HAY zuh*

Jahazah *juh HAY zuh*

Jahaziah *JAY huh ZIGH uh*

Jahaziel *juh HAY zih el*

Jahdai *JAH day igh, JAH digh*

Jahdiel *JAH dih el*

Jahdo *JAH doh*

Jahel *JAY hel*

Jahleel *JAH lih el*

Jahleelite *JAH lih el ight*

Jahmai *JA may igh, JAH migh*

J

ow-cow KOW, out OWT; oy-boil BOYL; p-PAT; r-RAN; s-star STAHR, tsetse SET see; sh-show SHOH, action AK shuhn, mission MIH shuhn, vicious VIH shuhss; t-tie TIGH, Thomas TAH muhss; th-thin THIN or THIHN; th-there THEHR; tw-TWIN; u, uh-tub TUB or TUHB, Joshua JAHSH yew uh, term TUHRM; v-veil VAYL, of AHV; w-WAY; wh (whether) see hw; y-year YEER; z-xerox ZIHR ahks, ZEE rahks, his HIZ or HIHZ, zebra ZEE bruh; zh-version VUHR zhuhn

89

J

Jahveh *YAH weh*	Janna *JAN uh*
Jahweh *YAH weh*	Jannaeus *juh NAY uhs*
Jahzah *JA zuh*	Jannai *JAN igh, jah NAY igh (eye)*
Jahzeel *JA zih el*	
Jahzeelite *JA zih el ight*	Jannes *JAN eez*
Jahzeiah *ja ZEE yuh*	Janoah *juh NOH uh*
Jahzerah *JA zeh ruh*	Janohah *juh NOH huh*
Jahziel *JA zih el*	Janum *JAY nuhm*
Jair *JAY uhr*	Japheth *JAY feth*
Jairite *JAY uh right*	Japhia *juh FIGH uh, JAH fih uh*
Jairus *JIGH ruhs, JAY uh ruhs*	
Jakan *JAY kuhn*	Japhlet *JAF let*
Jakeh *JAY keh*	Japhleti *jaf LEE tigh*
Jakim *JAY kim*	Japhletite *JAF lee tight*
Jakin *JAY kin*	Japho *JAY foh*
Jakinite *JAY kih night*	Jarah *JAY ruh*
Jalam *JAY luhm*	Jareb *JAY reb*
Jalon *JAY lahn*	Jared *JAY red*
Jambres *JAM breez*	Jaresiah *JEHR uh SIGH uh*
Jambri *JAM brigh*	Jarha *JAHR huh*
James *JAYMZ*	Jarib *JAY rib*
Jamin *JAY min*	Jarimoth *JEHR ih mahth*
Jaminite *JAY min ight*	Jarkon *JAHR kahn*
Jamlech *JAM lek*	Jarmo *JAHR moh*
Jamnia *JAM nih uh*	Jarmuth *JAHR muhth*
Jamnian *JAM nih uhn*	Jaroah *juh ROH uh*
Janai *JAY nay igh, JAY nigh*	Jasael *JAY say el*
Janim *JAY nim*	Jashar *JASH uhr*

a-HAT; ah-far FAHR; aw-call KAWL; ay-name NAYM; B-BAD; ch-CHEW; d-DAD; e,eh-met MET; ee-sea SEE; ew-truth TREWTH; f-FOOT, enough ee NUHF; g-GET; h-HIM; hw-whether HWEH thuhr; i, ih-city SI ti, or SIH tih; igh sign SIGHN, eye IGH; igh LIGHT; j-jack JAK, germ JUHRM; k-KISS, chorus KOH ruhss, ks-(for x) ox AHKS; kw-quail KWAYL; l-live LIHV, LIGHV; m-more MOHR; ng-ring RING; oh-go GOH, row ROH (a boat); oo-LOOK; oo-boot BOOT

Jashen *JAY shen*

Jasher *JAY shuhr*

Jashobeam *juh SHOH bih am*

Jashub *JAY shuhb*

Jashubi-lehem *juh SHOO bigh-LEE hem*

Jashubi Lehem *juh SHOO bigh-LEE hem*

Jashubite *JAY shub ight*

Jasiel *JAS ih el*

Jason *JAY suhn*

Jasubus *juh SOO buhs*

Jatal *JAY tuhl*

Jathan *JAY thuhn*

Jathniel *JATH nih el*

Jattir *JAT uhr*

Javan *JAY van*

Jazer *JAY zuhr, JAH zuhr*

Jaziz *JAY ziz*

Jearim *JEE uh rim*

Jeaterai *jih AT uh righ*

Jeatherai *jih ATH uh righ*

Jebel et-Tor (Gerezim) *JAY buhl-et-TAWR*

Jebel Musa (Mt. of Moses) *JAY buhl-MOO suh*

Jeberechiah *jih BEHR ih KIGH uh*

Jeberekiah *jeh BEHR ih KIGH uh*

Jebus *JEE buhs*

Jebusi *JEB yoo sigh*

Jebusite *JEB yoo sight*

Jecamiah *JEK uh MIGH uh*

Jechiliah *JEK uh LIGH uh*

Jecholiah *JEK oh LIGH uh*

Jechoniah *JEK uh NIGH uh*

Jechonias *JEK oh NIGH uhs*

Jecoliah *JEK oh LIGH uh*

Jeconiah *JEK oh NIGH uh*

Jeconias *JEK oh NIGH uhs*

Jedaiah *jih DIGH uh*

Jeddu *JED oo*

Jedeus *JED ih uhs*

Jediael *jih DIGH ay el*

Jedidah *jih DIGH duh*

Jedidiah *JED uh DIGH uh*

Jeduthun *jih DYOO thuhn*

Jeeli *JEE uh ligh*

Jeelus *jih EE luhs*

Jeezer *jih EE zuhr*

Jeezerite *jih EE zuhr ight*

Jegarsahadutha *JEE gahr-say huh DYOO thuh*

Jegar-sahadutha *JEE gahr-say huh DYOO thuh*

J

Jegar Sahadutha   *JEE gahr-say huh DYOO thuh*

Jehaleleel   *JIH huh LEE lih el*

Jehalelel   *jih HAL uh luhl*

Jehallel   *juh HAL uhl*

Jehallelel   *jeh HAL lih lehl*

Jehath   *JEE hath*

Jehaziel   *jih HAZ ih el*

Jehdeiah   *jeh DEE yuh*

Jehezekel   *jih HEZ ih kel*

Jehezkel   *jih HEZ kel*

Jehiah   *jih HIGH uh*

Jehiel   *jih HIGH el*

Jehieli   *jih HIGH uh ligh*

Jehielite   *jeh HIGH uh light*

Jehizkiah   *JEE hiz KIGH uh*

Jehoadah   *jih HOH uh duh*

Jehoaddah   *jeh HOH ad duh*

Jehoaddan   *JEE hoh AD uhn*

Jehoaddin   *JEE hoh AD in*

Jehoahaz   *jih HOH uh haz*

Jehoash   *jih HOH ash*

Jehohanan   *JEE huh HAY nan*

Jehoiachin   *jih HOY uh kin*

Jehoiada   *jih HOY uh duh*

Jehoiakim   *jih HOY uh kim*

Jehoiarib   *jih HOY uh rib*

Jehonadab   *jih HAHN uh dab*

Jehonathan   *jih HAHN uh thuhn*

Jehoram   *jih HOH ruhm*

Jehoshabeath   *JEE hoh SHAB ih ath*

Jehoshaphat   *jih HAHSH uh fat*

Jehosheba   *jih HAHSH ih buh*

Jehoshua   *jih HAHSH yoo uh*

Jehoshuah   *jih HAHSH yoo uh*

Jehovah   *jeh HOH vuh*

Jehovah-jireh   *jeh HOH vuh-JIGH reh*

Jehovah-nissi   *jeh HOH vuh-NISS igh*

Jehovah-shalom   *jeh HOH vuh-shah LOHM*

Jehovah-shamma   *jeh HOH vuh-SHAM uh*

Jehovah-tsidkenu   *jeh HOH vuh-tsid KEN oo*

Jehozabad   *jih HAHZ uh bad*

Jehozadak   *jih HAHZ uh dak*

Jehu   *JEE hyoo*

Jehubbah   *jih HUHB uh*

Jehucal   *jih HYOO kuhl*

Jehud   *JEE huhd*

Jehudi   *jih HYOO digh*

Jehudijah   *JEE hyoo DIGH juh*

Jehuel   *jih HYOO el*

---

a-HAT; ah-far FAHR; aw-call KAWL; ay-name NAYM; B-BAD; ch-CHEW; d-DAD; e,eh-met MET; ee-sea SEE; ew-truth TREWTH; f-FOOT, enough ee NUHF; g-GET; h-HIM; hw-whether HWEH thuhr; i, ih-city SI ti, or SIH tih; igh sign SIGHN, eye IGH; igh LIGHT; j-jack JAK, germ JUHRM; k-KISS, chorus KOH ruhss; ks-(for x) ox AHKS; kw-quail KWAYL; l-live LIHV, LIGHV; m-more MOHR; ng-ring RING; oh-go GOH, row ROH (a boat); oo-LOOK; oo-boot BOOT

Jehus   *JEE huhs*

Jehush   *JEE huhsh*

Jeiel   *jih IGII (eye) el*

Jekabzeel   *jih KAB zih el*

Jekameam   *JEK uh MEE am*

Jekamiah   *JEK uh MIGH uh*

Jekuthiel   *jih KYOO thih el*

Jemdet Nasr   *JIM det–NA'sr*

Jemima   *jeh MIGH muh*

Jemimah   *jeh MIGH muh*

Jeminah   *jeh MIGH nuh*

Jemnaan   *JEM nay uhn*

Jemuel   *jih MYOO el*

Jenual   *jih NYOO uhl*

Jephte   *JEF tee*

Jephthae   *JEF thee (th as in thin)*

Jephthah   *JEF thuh (th as in thin)*

Jephunneh   *jih FUHN nee*

Jerah   *JEE ruh*

Jerahmeel   *jih RAH mih el*

Jerahmeelite   *jih RAH mih uhl ight*

Jerash   *JEHR ash*

Jerechus   *JEHR uh kuhs*

Jered   *JEE red*

Jeremai   *JER ih migh*

Jeremiah (Jeremias)   *JER ih MIGH uh*

Jeremias (Jeremiah)   *JER ih MIGH uhs*

Jeremiel   *jih REM ee el*

Jeremoth   *JER ih mahth*

Jeremy   *JER uh mih*

Jeriah   *jih RIGH uh*

Jeribai   *JER ih bay igh, JER ih bigh*

Jericho   *JER ih koh*

Jeriel   *JER ih el*

Jerijah   *jih RIGH jah*

Jerimoth   *JER ih mahth*

Jerioth   *JER ih ahth*

Jeroboam   *JER uh BOH uhm*

Jeroham   *jih ROH ham*

Jerome   *juh ROHM*

Jerub-baal   *JEHR uhb–BAY uhl*

Jerubbaal   *JER uhb–BAY uhl*

Jerub-besheth   *jih RUB-bih sheth*

Jerubbesheth   *jih RUB-bih sheth*

Jeruel   *jih ROO el*

Jerusa   *jih ROO suh*

Jerusah   *jih ROO suh*

Jerusalem   *jih ROO suh lem*

Jerusha   *jih ROO shuh*

J

---

ow-cow KOW, out OWT; oy-boil BOYL; p-PAT; r-RAN; s-star STAHR, tsetse SET see; sh-show SHOH, action AK shuhn, mission MIH shuhn, vicious VIH shuhss; t-tie TIGH, Thomas TAH muhss; th-thin THIN or THIHN; th-there THEHR; tw-TWIN; u, uh-tub TUB or TUHB, Joshua JAHSH yew uh, term TUHRM; v-veil VAYL, of AHV; w-WAY; wh (whether) see hw; y-year YEER; z-xerox ZIHR ahks, ZEE rahks, his HIZ or HIHZ, zebra ZEE bruh; zh-version VUHR zhuhn

J

Jerushah   *jeh R**OO** shuh*

Jesaiah   *jih SIGH uh*

Jesarelah   *JESS uh REE luh*

Jeshaiah   *jih SHIGH uh*

Jeshanah   *JESH uh nuh, jih SHAY nuh*

Jesharelah   *JESH uh REE luh*

Jeshebeab   *jih SHEB ih ab*

Jesher   *JEE shuhr*

Jeshimon   *jih SHIGH mahn*

Jeshimoth   *jih SHIGH mahth*

Jeshishai   *jih SHISH igh (eye)*

Jeshohaiah   *JESH oh HIGH uh*

Jeshoshaphat   *jih SHAHSH uh fat*

Jeshua   *JESH y**oo** uh*

Jeshuah   *JESH y**oo** uh*

Jeshurun   *jih SH**OO** ruhn*

Jeshush   *JESH uhsh*

Jesiah   *jih SIGH uh*

Jesimiel   *jih SIM ih el*

Jesimoth   *jih SIGH mahth*

Jesse   *JESS ih*

Jesshiah   *jih SHIGH uh*

Jessue   *JESH y**oo** ee*

Jesu   *JEH s**oo***

Jesui   *JESS y**oo** igh*

Jesuite   *JESS y**oo** i**gh**t*

Jesurun   *jih S**OO** ruhn*

Jesus   *JEE zuhs*

Jesus ben-sira   *JEE zuhs-ben-SIGH ruh*

Jesus ben-Sirach   *JEE zuhs-ben-SIGH ruhk*

Jether   *JEE thuhr (th as in thin)*

Jetherai   *JETH uh righ*

Jetheth   *JEE theth (th as in thin)*

Jethlah   *JETH luh*

Jethro   *JETH roh*

Jetta   *JET uh*

Jetur   *JEE tuhr*

Jeuel   *J**OO** el, jeh Y**OO** el*

Jeush   *JEE uhsh*

Jeuz   *JEE uhz*

Jew   *J**OO***

Jewess   *J**OO** ess*

Jewish   *J**OO** ish*

Jewry   *J**OO** rih*

Jezaniah   *JEZ uh NIGH uh*

Jezebel   *JEZ uh bel*

Jezelus   *JEZ uh luhs*

Jezer   *JEE zuhr*

Jezerite   *JEE zuhr i**gh**t*

Jeziah   *jeh ZIGH uh*

Jeziel   *JEE zih el*

---

a-HAT; ah-far FAHR; aw-call KAWL; ay-name NAYM; B-BAD; ch-CHEW; d-DAD; e,eh-met MET; ee-sea SEE; ew-truth TREWTH; f-FOOT, enough ee NUHF; g-GET; h-HIM; hw-whether HWEH thuhr; i, ih-city SI ti, or SIH tih; igh sign SIGHN, eye IGH; igh LIGHT; j-jack JAK, germ JUHRM; k-KISS, chorus KOH ruhss, ks-(for x) ox AHKS; kw-quail KWAYL; l-live LIHV, LIGHV; m-more MOHR; ng-ring RING; oh-go GOH, row ROH (a boat); oo-LOOK; oo-boot BOOT

Jezliah   *jez LIGH uh*

Jezoar   *jih ZOH uhr*

Jezrahel   *JEZ ruh hel*

Jezrahiah   *JEZ ruh HIGH uh*

Jezreel   *JEZ reel*

Jezreelite   *JEZ reel ight*

Jezreelitess   *JEZ reel light ess*

Jibsam   *JIB sam*

Jidlaph   *JID laf*

Jimna   *JIM nuh*

Jimnah   *JIM nuh*

Jimnite   *JIM night*

Jiphtah   *JIF tuh*

Jiphthah-el   *JIF thuh-el (th a in thin)*

Jipithah El   *JIF thuh-el*

Jiptah   *JIP tuh*

Jishui   *JISH yoo ih*

Jisshiah   *jih SHIGH uh*

Jithra   *JITH ruh*

Jithran   *JITH ruhn*

Jizliah   *jiz LIGH uh*

Jizri   *JIZ righ*

Joab   *JOH ab*

Joachaz   *JOH uh kaz*

Joachim   *JOH uh kim*

Joacim   *JOH uh kim*

Joadanus   *joh AD uh nuhs*

Joah   *JOH uh*

Joahaz   *JOH uh haz*

Joakim   *JOH uh kim*

Joanan   *joh AY nuhn*

Joanna   *joh AN uh*

Joannan   *joh AN uhn*

Joannas   *joh AN uhs*

Joarib   *JOH uh rib*

Joash   *JOH ash*

Joatham   *JOH uh tham (th as in thin)*

Joazabdus   *JOH uh ZAB duhs*

Job   *JOHB*

Jobab   *JOH bab*

Jochanan   *JOH kuh nan*

Jochebed   *JAHK uh bed*

jod (Hebrew letter)   *YOHD*

Joda   *JOH duh*

Jodan   *JOH dan*

Joed   *JOH ed*

Joel   *JOH el*

Joelah   *joh EE luh*

Joezer   *joh EE zuhr*

Jogbehah   *JAHG bih ha*

Jogli   *JOG ligh*

Joha   *JOH huh*

Johanan   *joh HAY nuhn*

Johannan   *joh HAY nuhn*

---

ow-cow KOW, out OWT; oy-boil BOYL; p-PAT; r-RAN; s-star STAHR, tsetse SET see; sh-show
SHOH, action AK shuhn, mission MIH shuhn, vicious VIH shuhss; t-tie TIGH, Thomas TAH muhss;
th-thin THIN or THIHN; th-there THEHR; tw-TWIN; u, uh-tub TUB or TUHB, Joshua JAHSH yew
uh, term TUHRM; v-veil VAYL, of AHV; w-WAY; wh (whether) see hw; y-year YEER; z-xerox ZIHR
ahks, ZEE rahks, his HIZ or HIHZ, zebra ZEE bruh; zh-version VUHR zhuhn

Johannes   *joh HAN iz*

Johannine   *joh HAN ighn*

John   *JAHN*

John-Mark   *jahn-MAHRK*

Johojanan   *JOH hoh JAY nan*

Joiada   *JOY uh duh*

Joiakim   *JOY uh kim*

Joiarib   *JOY uh rib*

Jokdeam   *JAHK dih am*

Jokim   *JOH kim*

Jokmeam   *JAHK mih am*

Jokneam   *JAHK nih am*

Jokshan   *JAHK shan*

Joktan   *JAHK tan*

Joktheel   *JAHK thih el (th as in thin)*

Jona   *JOH nuh*

Jonadab   *JAHN uh dab*

Jonah   *JOH nuh*

Jonam   *JOH nuhm*

Jonan   *JOH nan*

Jonas   *JOH nuhs*

Jonathan   *JAHN uh thuhn*

Jonathas   *JAHN uh thuhs*

Jonath-elem-rechokim   *JOH nath-EE lem-rih KOH kim*

Jonath Elem Rehoqim   *JOH nath-EE lem-rih HOH kim*

Joppa   *JAHP uh*

Jorah   *JOH ruh*

Jorai   *JOH ray igh (eye)*

Joram   *JOH ruhm*

Jordan   *JAWR duhn*

Joribas   *juh RIGH buhs*

Joribus   *juh RIGH buhs*

Jorim   *JOH rim*

Jorkeam   *JAWR kih am*

Jorkoam   *JAWR koh am*

Josabad   *JAHS uh bad*

Josaphat   *JAHS uh fat*

Josaphias   *JOH sah FIGH uhs*

Jose   *JOH sih*

Josech   *JOH sek*

Josedec   *JAHS uh dek*

Josedech   *JAHS uh dek*

Joseph   *JOH zif*

Josephite   *JOH seh fight*

Josephus   *joh SEE fuhs*

Joses   *JOH seez*

Joshah   *JOH shuh*

Joshaphat   *JAHSH uh fat*

Joshaviah   *JAHSH uh VIGH uh*

Joshbekashah   *JAHSH bih KAY shuh*

Josheb   *JOH sheb*

Joshebbasshebeth   *JOH sheb-bass SHEE beth*

---

a-HAT; ah-far FAHR; aw-call KAWL; ay-name NAYM; B-BAD; ch-CHEW; d-DAD; e,eh-met MET; ee-sea SEE; ew-truth TREWTH; f-FOOT, enough ee NUHF; g-GET; h-HIM; hw-whether HWEH thuhr; i, ih-city SI ti, or SIH tih; igh sign SIGHN, eye IGH; <u>igh</u> LIGHT; j-jack JAK, germ JUHRM; k-KISS, chorus KOH ruhss, ks-(for x) ox AHKS; kw-quail KWAYL; l-live LIHV, LIGHV; m-more MOHR; ng-ring RING; oh-go GOH, row ROH (a boat); oo-LOOK; <u>oo</u>-boot B<u>OO</u>T

Josheb-basshebeth *JOH*
  sheb-bass SHEE beth

Joshibiah *jahsh uh BIGH uh*

Joshua (Josue) *JAHSH yoo*
  uh

Josiah (Josias) *joh SIGH uh*

Josias (Josiah) *joh SIGH uhs*

Josibiah *jahs ih BIGH uh*

Josiphiah *jahs ih FIGH uh*

Josue (Joshua) *jahs OO ee*

jot (dot) *JAHT*

Jotbah *JAHT buh*

Jotbath *JAHT bath*

Jotbathah *JAHT buh thuh*

Jotham *JOH thuhm*

Jozabad *JAHZ uh bad*

Jozacar *JOH zuh kahr*

Jozachar *JAHZ uh kahr*

Jozadak *JAHZ uh dak*

Jubal *JOO buhl*

jubile *JOO buh lee*

jubilee *JOO buh lee*

Jucal *JOO kal*

Juda *JOO duh*

Judaea *joo DEE uh*

Judaean *joo DEE uhn*

Judaeus *joo DEE uhs*

Judah *JOO duh*

Judahite *JOO duh hight*

Judaic *joo DAY ik*

Judaism *JOO day iz uhm*

Judaizer *JOO day ighz uhr*
  (eyes)

Judaizing *joo day IGHZ ing*
  (EYES)

Judas *JOO duhs*

Judas Iscariot *JOO duhs–iss*
  KA(a)R ih aht

Jude *JOOD*

Judea *joo DEE uh*

Judean *joo DEE uhn*

Judges *JUH jihz*

Judith *JOO dith*

Juel *JOO uhl*

Julia *JOO lih uh*

Julius *JOO lih uhs*

Jung *YOONG*

Junia *JOO nih uh*

Junias *JOO nih uhs*

Jupiter *JOO pih tuhr*

Jushab-hesed *joo shab–HEE*
  sed

Jushabhesed *joo shab–HEE*
  sed

Justin Martyr *JUHS*
  tin–MAHR tuhr

Justus *JUHS tuhs*

J

---

ow-cow KOW, out OWT; oy-boil BOYL; p-PAT; r-RAN; s-star STAHR, tsetse SET see; sh-show
SHOH, action AK shuhn, mission MIH shuhn, vicious VIH shuhss; t-tie TIGH, Thomas TAH muhss;
th-thin THIN or THIHN; th-there THEHR; tw-TWIN; u, uh-tub TUB or TUHB, Joshua JAHSH yew
uh, term TUHRM; v-veil VAYL, of AHV; w-WAY; wh (whether) see hw; y-year YEER; z-xerox ZIHR
ahks, ZEE rahks, his HIZ or HIHZ, zebra ZEE bruh; zh-version VUHR zhuhn

Jutah *JUHT uh*

Juttah *JUHT uh*

K

kab *KAB*

Kabul *KAH buhl*

Kabzeel *KAB zih el*

Kaddish *KAH dish*

Kades *KAY deez*

Kadesh *KAY desh*

Kadesh-barnea *KAY desh-bahr NEE uh*

Kadeshbarnea *KAY desh-bahr NEE uh*

Kadesh Barnea *KAY desh-bahr NEE uh*

Kadesh-Meribah *KAY desh-MEHR ih bah*

Kadish *KAY desh*

Kadmiel *KAD mih el*

Kadmonite *KAD muhn ight*

Kain *KAYN*

kairos *KIGH rahs*

Kaiwan *KIGH wahn*

Kallai *KAL ay igh, KAL igh (eye)*

Kamon *KAY mahn*

Kanah *KAY nuh*

Kanish *KAHN ish*

kaph (Hebrew letter) *KAF*

kappa (Greek letter) *KAP puh*

Karatepe *KA ruh TEH peh, kahr uh TEH peh*

Kareah *kuh REE uh*

Karim *KEHR im*

Karka *KAHR kuh*

Karkaa *KAHR kay uh*

Karkar *KAHR kahr*

Karkor *KAHR kawr*

Karnaim *kahr NAY im*

Karnak *KAHR nak*

Karnion *KAHR nih ahn*

Kartah *KAHR tuh*

Kartan *KAHR tan*

Kaserin *KASS uh rin*

Kassite *KA sight*

Kattah *KAT uh*

Kattath *KAT ath*

Kebar *KEE bahr*

Kebara *keh BAH ruh*

Kedar *KEE duhr*

Kedem *KEE dem*

Kedemah *KED ih muh*

Kedemite *KED ih might*

---

a-HAT; ah-far FAHR; aw-call KAWL; ay-name NAYM; B-BAD; ch-CHEW; d-DAD; e,eh-met MET; ee-sea SEE; ew-truth TREWTH; f-FOOT, enough ee NUHF; g-GET; h-HIM; hw-whether HWEH thuhr; i, ih-city SI ti, or SIH tih; igh sign SIGHN, eye IGH; igh LIGHT; j-jack JAK, germ JUHRM; k-KISS, chorus KOH ruhss, ks-(for x) ox AHKS; kw-quail KWAYL; l-live LIHV, LIGHV; m-more MOHR; ng-ring RING; oh-go GOH, row ROH (a boat); oo-LOOK; oo-boot BOOT

Kedemoth   *KED uh mahth*

Kedesh   *KEE desh*

Kedesh-naphtali   *KEE desh-NAF tuh ligh*

Kedorlaomer   *KED awr LAY oh muhr*

Kedron   *KEE druhn*

Kehelathah   *KEE hih LAY thuh*

Keilah   *kih IGH (eye) luh*

Kelaiah   *kih LIGH uh, kih LAY yuh*

Kelal   *KEE lal*

Kelita   *kih LIGH tuh*

Kelub   *KEE luhb*

Keluhi   *KEL yoo high*

Kemuel   *KEM yoo el*

Kenaanah   *keh NAY uh nuh*

Kenan   *KEE nuhn*

Kenani   *kih NAY nigh*

Kenaniah   *KEN uh NIGH uh*

Kenath   *KEE nath*

Kenaz   *KEE naz*

Kenez   *KEE nez*

Kenezite   *KEE nez ight*

Kenezzite   *KEE nez ight*

Kenite   *KEN ight*

Kenizzite   *KEN iz ight*

Kephar-ammoni   *KEE fahr-AM oh nigh*

Kephirah   *kih FIGH ruh*

Kepphar Ammoni   *KEE fahr-AM oh nigh*

Kerak   *KEHR ahk*

Keran   *KEE ruhn*

kere   *kuh RAY*

Keren-happuch   *KEHR uhn-HAP uhk*

Kerenhappuch   *KEHR uhn-HAP uhk*

Kerethite   *KEHR ih thight*

Kerioth   *KEE rih ahth*

Keriothhezron   *KEE rih ahth-HEZ rahn*

Kerioth-hezron   *KEE rih ahth-HEZ rahn*

Kerioth Hezron   *KEE rih ahth-HEZ rahn*

Kerith   *KEE rith*

kernos   *KEHR nahss*

Keros   *KEE rahs*

Kerub   *KEE ruhb*

kerygma   *keh RIG muh*

kerygmatic   *KEHR ig MAT ihk*

Kesalon   *KEHS uh lahn*

Kesed   *KEE sed*

Kesil   *KEE sihl*

K

ow-cow KOW, out OWT; oy-boil BOYL; p-PAT; r-RAN; s-star STAHR, tsetse SET see; sh-show SHOH, action AK shuhn, mission MIH shuhn, vicious VIH shuhss; t-tie TIGH, Thomas TAH muhss; th-thin THIN or THIHN; th-there THEHR; tw-TWIN; u, uh-tub TUB or TUHB, Joshua JAHSH yew uh, term TUHRM; v-veil VAYL, of AHV; w-WAY; wh (whether) see hw; y-year YEER; z-xerox ZIHR ahks, ZEE rahks, his HIZ or HIHZ, zebra ZEE bruh; zh-version VUHR zhuhn

99

Kesulloth *kih SUHL ahth*

Ketab *KEE tab*

Ketef Hinnon *KEH tef-HIN nuhm*

Kethibh *kuh THEEV*

Kethubhim *kih THOO veem*

Kethuvim *kuh THOO vim, KETH uh veem*

Ketubhim *kih TOO veem*

Keturah *keh TYOO ruh*

Keveh *KEE vuh*

Kezia *kih ZIGH uh*

Keziah *kih ZIGH uh*

Kezib *KEE zib*

Keziz *KEE ziz*

Khabur *kah BOOR*

khirbet *KIHR bet, KEHR vay (Hebraic)*

Khirbet el-Qom *KIHR bet-el-KOHM*

Khirbet Iskander *KIHR bet-iss KAN duhr*

Khirbet Kerak *KIHR bet-KEHR ehk*

Khirbet Qumran *KIHR bet-kuhm RAHN*

Khirbet Rabud *KIHR bet-rah BOOD*

Khorsabad *KAHR sah bad, KAWR suh bad, KAWR suh bahd*

Kibroth-hattaarah *kih BRAHTH-hah TAH hah REH*

Kibroth-hattaavah *KIB rahth-hat TAY uh vuh*

Kibrothhattaavah *KIB rahth-hat TAY uh vuh*

Kibroth Hattaavah *KIB rahth-hat TAY uh vuh*

Kibzaim *kib ZAY im*

Kidon *KIGH dahn*

Kidron *KID ruhn*

Kilan *KIGH lan*

Kileab *KIHL ih ab*

Kilion *KIHL ih ahn*

Kilmad *KIHL mad*

Kimham *KIM ham*

Kinah *KIGH nuh*

King, Kings *KING, KINGZ*

Kinnereth *KIN ih reth*

Kios *KIGH ahs*

Kir *KUHR*

Kir-haraseth *kuhr-HAHR uh seth*

Kir Haraseth *kuhr-HAHR uh seth*

Kir-hareseth *KIHR-hah REH seth, kuhr-HEHR uh seth*

K

---

a-HAT; ah-far FAHR; aw-call KAWL; ay-name NAYM; B-BAD; ch-CHEW; d-DAD; e,eh-met MET; ee-sea SEE; ew-truth TREWTH; f-FOOT, enough ee NUHF; g-GET; h-HIM; hw-whether HWEH thuhr; i, ih-city SI ti, or SIH tih; igh sign SIGHN, eye IGH; igh LIGHT; j-jack JAK, germ JUHRM; k-KISS, chorus KOH ruhss, ks-(for x) ox AHKS; kw-quail KWAYL; l-live LIHV, LIGHV; m-more MOHR; ng-ring RING; oh-go GOH, row ROH (a boat); oo-LOOK; oo-boot BOOT

Kirhareseth *kuhr-HEHR uh seth*

Kir Hareseth *kuhr-HEHR uh seth*

Kir-haresh *kuhr HAY resh*

Kirheres *kuhr-HEE ress*

Kir-heres *kuhr-HEE ress*

Kiriath *KIHR ih ath*

Kiriathaim *KIHR ih uh THAY im (TH as in thin)*

Kiriatharba *KIHR ih ath-AHR buh*

Kiriath-arba *KIHR ih ath-AHR buh*

Kiriath Arba *KIHR ih ath-AHR buh*

Kiriath-arim *KIHR ih ath-AY rim*

Kiriatharim *KIHR ih ath-AY rim*

Kiriathbaal *KIHR ih ath-BAY uhl*

Kiriath-baal *KIHR ih ath-BAY uhl*

Kiriath Baal *KIHR ih ath-BAY uhl*

Kiriathhuzoth *KIHR ih ath-HYOO zahth*

Kiriath-huzoth *KIHR ih ath-HYOO zahth*

Kiriath Huzoth *KIHR ih ath-HYOO zahth*

Kiriathiarius *KIHR ih ath ih EHR ih uhs*

Kiriathjearim *KIHR ih ath-JEE uh rim*

Kiriath-jearim *KIHR ih ath-JEE uh rim*

Kiriath Jearim *KIHR ih ath-JEE uh rim*

Kiriathsannah *KIHR ih ath-SAN nuh*

Kiriath-sannah *KIHR ih ath-SAN nuh*

Kiriath Sannah *KIHR ih ath-SAN nuh*

Kiriathsepher *KIHR ih ath-SEE fuhr*

Kiriath-sepher *KIHR ih ath-SEE fuhr*

Kiriath Sepher *KIHR ih ath-SEE fuhr*

Kirioth *KIHR ih ahth*

Kirjath *KIHR jath*

Kirjathaim *KIHR juh-THAY im (TH as in thin)*

Kirjath-arba *KIHR jath-AHR buh*

Kirjath Arba *KIHR jath-AHR buh*

---

ow-cow KOW, out OWT; oy-boil BOYL; p-PAT; r-RAN; s-star STAHR, tsetse SET see; sh-show SHOH, action AK shuhn, mission MIH shuhn, vicious VIH shuhss; t-tie TIGH, Thomas TAH muhss; th-thin THIN or THIHN; th-there THEHR; tw-TWIN; u, uh-tub TUB or TUHB, Joshua JAHSH yew uh, term TUHRM; v-veil VAYL, of AHV; w-WAY; wh (whether) see hw; y-year YEER; z-xerox ZIHR ahks, ZEE rahks, his HIZ or HIHZ, zebra ZEE bruh; zh-version VUHR zhuhn

Kirjath-arim *KIHR jath-AY rim*

Kirjath Arim *KIHR jath-AY rim*

Kirjath-baal *KIHR jath-BAY uhl*

Kirjath Baal *KIHR jath-BAY uhl*

Kirjath-huzoth *KIHR jath-HYOO zahth*

Kirjath Huzoth *KIHR jath-HYOO zahth*

Kirjath-jearim *KIHR jath-JEE uh rim*

Kirjath Jearim *KIHR jath-JEE uh rim*

Kirjath-sannah *KIHR jath-SAN uh*

Kirjath Sannah *KIHR jath-SAN uh*

Kirjath-sepher *KIHR jath-SEE fuhr*

Kirjath Sepher *KIHR jath-SEE fuhr*

Kish *KISH*

Kishi *KISH igh (eye)*

Kishion *KISH ih ahn*

Kishon *KIGH shahn*

Kislev *KISS lehv*

Kislon *KISS lahn*

Kisloth-tabor *KISS lahth-TAY bawr*

Kisloth Tabor *KISS lahth-TAY bawr*

Kison *KIGH sahn*

Kithlish *KITH lish*

Kition *KIH tih ahn*

Kitlish *KIT lish*

Kitron *KIT rahn*

Kittim *KIT im*

Kittim (Cyprus) *kih TEEM*

Kiyyun *KIGH yuhn*

knop *NAHP*

Knossos *NOH suhss*

Koa *KOH uh*

Kochba *KOHK buh*

Kochbah *KOHK buh*

Kocheba *KOH kuh buh*

Kochebah *KOH kuh buh*

Kohath *KOH hath*

Kohathite *KOH hath ight*

Koheleth *koh HEL eth*

kokh *KOHF*

Kokhba *KOHK buh*

kokhim (pl.) *koh KEEM*

Kola *KOH luh*

Kolaiah *koh LIGH yuh, koh LAY yuh*

Kona *KOH nuh*

---

a-HAT; ah-far FAHR; aw-call KAWL; ay-name NAYM; B-BAD; ch-CHEW; d-DAD; e,eh-met MET; ee-sea SEE; ew-truth TREWTH; f-FOOT, enough ee NUHF; g-GET; h-HIM; hw-whether HWEH thuhr; i, ih-city SI ti, or SIH tih; igh sign SIGHN, eye IGH; igh LIGHT; j-jack JAK, germ JUHRM; k-KISS, chorus KOH ruhss; ks-(for x) ox AHKS; kw-quail KWAYL; l-live LIHV, LIGHV; m-more MOHR; ng-ring RING; oh-go GOH, row ROH (a boat); oo-LOOK; oo-boot BOOT

Konae *KOH nigh*

Koph *KAHF*

kor *KAWR*

Korah *KOH ruh*

Korahite *KAWR uh hight*

Korathite *KOH rath ight*

Korazin *KOH ray zihn*

korban *KAWR ban*

Kordan *KAWR dan*

Kore *KOH rih*

Koreite *KAWR ih ight*

Koressos *koh REES sahs*

Korhite *KAWR hight*

kosher *KOH shuhr*

Kosiba *KOH sih buh*

Kosibah *KOH sih buh*

koum *KOOM (OO as in look)*

Koz *KAHZ*

Koziba *KOH zih buh*

Kozibah *KOH zih buh*

krater *KRAY tuhr*

Krenides *KRIN uh deez*

Kub *KUHB*

Kue *KYOO eh*

Kulom *KYOO lahm*

Kultepe *kool TEP peh*

kum *KOOM*

Kun *KOON*

Kuntillat Ajrud *kuhn TOO lit-ahj ROOD*

Kushaiah *koo SHIGII yuh*

kyrios *KIHR ih ahs*

L

Laadah *LAY uh duh*

Laadan *LAY uh dan*

Laban *LAY buhn*

Labana *luh BAY nuh*

Labaoth *la BAY ahth*

Labashi *lah BAHSH ee*

Labashi-Marduk *lah BAH shee-MAHR dook*

Labo *LAY boh*

Laccunus *luh KOO nuhs*

Lacedaemonian *LAS uh dih MOH nih uhn*

Lachish *LAY kish*

Laconia *lah KOHN ih uh*

Lacunus *luh KOO nuhs*

Ladan *LAY duhn*

Lael *LAY uhl*

Lagash *la GAHSH*

Lahad *LAY had*

---

ow-cow KOW, out OWT; oy-boil BOYL; p-PAT; r-RAN; s-star STAHR, tsetse SET see; sh-show SHOH, action AK shuhn, mission MIH shuhn, vicious VIH shuhss; t-tie TIGH, Thomas TAH muhss; th-thin THIN or THIHN; th-there THEHR; tw-TWIN; u, uh-tub TUB or TUHB, Joshua JAHSH yew uh, term TUHRM; v-veil VAYL, of AHV; w-WAY; wh (whether) see hw; y-year YEER; z-xerox ZIHR ahks, ZEE rahks, his HIZ or HIHZ, zebra ZEE bruh; zh-version VUHR zhuhn

Lahai-roi   *luh HIGH-roy (oy as in boy)*

Lahai Roi   *luh HIGH-roy (oy as in boy)*

Lahav   *lah HAHV*

Lahmam   *LA mam*

Lahmas   *LAH muhs*

Lahmi   *LAH migh*

Laish   *LAY ish*

Laishah   *LAY ish uh*

Lakkum   *LAY kuhm, LAK uhm*

Lakum   *LAY kuhm*

lama   *LAH muh*

Lamech   *LAY mek*

lamed   *LAH med*

lamedh (Hebrew letter)   *LAH medth*

lamelekh   *lah MELL ehk*

lamentation   *LA men TAY shuhn*

Lamentations   *LA men TAY shuhnz*

Laodicea   *lay AHD ih SEE uh*

Laodicean   *lay AHD ih SEE uhn*

Lapidoth   *LAP ih dahth*

Lappidoth   *LAP ih dahth*

larnax   *LAHR nax*

Larsa   *LAHR suh*

Larsa   *LAHR suh*

Lasaea   *luh SEE uh*

Lasea   *luh SEE uh*

Lasha   *LAY shuh*

Lasharon   *luh SHEHR uhn*

Lasthenes   *LASS thuh neez*

Latin   *LA tin*

Latinism   *LAT uh NIZ uhm*

Lazarus   *LAZ uh ruhs*

Leah   *LEE uh*

Leannoth   *lee AN ahth*

Lebana   *lih BAY nuh*

Lebanah   *lih BAY nuh*

Lebanon   *LEB uh nuhn*

Lebaoth   *lih BAY ahth*

Lebbaeus   *luh BEE uhs*

Lebbeus   *luh BEE uhs*

Leb-kamai   *leb-KAY migh*

Leb Kamai   *leb-KAY migh*

Lebo-hamath   *LEE boh-HAY math*

Lebo Hamath   *LEE boh-HAY math*

Lebonah   *lih BOH nuh*

Lecah   *LEE kuh*

Lechaeum   *leh KAY uhm*

lectionary   *LEK shuh NEHR ee*

Legion   *LEE juhn*

Lehab   *LEE hab*

---

a-HAT; ah-far FAHR; aw-call KAWL; ay-name NAYM; B-BAD; ch-CHEW; d-DAD; e,eh-met MET; ee-sea SEE; ew-truth TREWTH; f-FOOT, enough ee NUHF; g-GET; h-HIM; hw-whether HWEH thuhr; i, ih-city SI ti, or SIH tih; igh sign SIGHN, eye IGH; igh LIGHT; j-jack JAK, germ JUHRM; k-KISS, chorus KOH ruhss, ks-(for x) ox AHKS; kw-quail KWAYL; l-live LIHV, LIGHV; m-more MOHR; ng-ring RING; oh-go GOH, row ROH (a boat); oo-LOOK; oo-boot BOOT

Lehabim   *lih HAY bim, LEE hay bim*

Lehabite   *LEE huh bight*

Lehem   *LEE hem*

Lehi   *LEE high*

lema   *luh MAH*

Lemuel   *LEM yoo uhl*

Leontes   *lay AHN teez*

Leptis Magna   *LEP tiss-MAHG nuh*

Leshem   *LEE shem*

Lessau   *LEHS sow (ow as in cow)*

lethech   *LEE thek*

lethek   *LEE thek*

Lettus   *LET uhs*

Letushim   *lih TYOO shim*

Letushite   *lih TYOO shight*

Leummim   *lih UHM mim*

Leummite   *lih UHM might*

Leumonite   *lih UHM ah night*

Levant   *luh VANT*

Levantine   *LEV uhn teen*

Levi   *LEE vigh*

Leviathan   *lih VIGH uh thuhn*

Levis   *LEE viss*

Levite   *LEE vight*

Levitical   *lih VIT ih kuhl*

Leviticus   *lih VIT ih kuhs*

lexical   *LEK sih kuhl*

lexicography   *LEK sih KAHG ruh fee*

lexicon   *LEK sih kahn*

lex talionis   *LEKS-tal ih OH niss*

Libertine   *LIB uhr teen*

Libnah   *LIB nuh*

Libnath   *LIB nath*

Libni   *LIB nigh*

Libnite   *LIB night*

Libre Hayamim   *LIB rih-HAY yuh mim*

Libya   *LIB ih uh*

Libyan   *LIB ih uhn*

Lidebir   *LID uh bihr*

Likhi   *LIK high*

Lilith   *LIL ith*

Linus   *LIGH nuhs*

Lisan   *lih SAHN, LIGH san*

Litani   *lih TAH nih*

lithic   *LITH ik*

liturgical   *lih TUHR jih kuhl*

liturgy   *LIH tuhr jih*

Lo-ammi   *lo-AM igh (eye)*

loculi (pl.)   *LAH koo lee*

L

---

ow-cow KOW, out OWT; oy-boil BOYL; p-PAT; r-RAN; s-star STAHR, tsetse SET see; sh-show SHOH, action AK shuhn, mission MIH shuhn, vicious VIH shuhss; t-tie TIGH, Thomas TAH muhss; th-thin THIN or THIHN; th-there THEHR; tw-TWIN; u, uh-tub TUB or TUHB, Joshua JAHSH yew uh, term TUHRM; v-veil VAYL, of AHV; w-WAY; wh (whether) see hw; y-year YEER; z-xerox ZIHR ahks, ZEE rahks, his HIZ or HIHZ, zebra ZEE bruh; zh-version VUHR zhuhn

loculus *LAH koo luhss*

Lod *LOHD*

Lo-debar *loh-DEE bahr*

Lodebar *loh-DEE bahr*

Lo Debar *loh-DEE bahr*

Lo Debar Karnaim *loh-DEE
  bahr-kahr NAY im*

loess *LESS, LUHS, LOH uhs*

log *LAHG*

logia *LOH jee ah*

Logos *LAH gahs, LOH gohs*

Lois *LOH iss*

Longimanus *LAHN jih
  MAHN uhs*

Lord *LAWRD*

Lo-ruhama *LOH-roo HA muh*

Lo-ruhamah *LOH-roo HA
  muh*

Lot *LAHT*

Lotan *LOH tan*

Lothasubus *loh THAH suh
  buhs (TH as in thin)*

Lozon *LOH zahn*

Lubim *LYOO bim*

Lucas *LYOO kuhs*

Lucifer *LYOO sih fuhr*

Lucius *LYOO shuhs*

Lud *LUHD*

Ludim *LYOO dim*

Ludite *LYOO dight*

Luhith *LYOO hith*

Luke *LOOK, (LEWK)*

Luristan *LOOR iss STAN*

Luxor *LUX awr*

Luz *LUHZ*

Lycaonia *LIK ay OH nih uh*

Lycaonian *LIK ay OH nih
  uhn*

Lycia *LISS ih uh, LISH uh*

Lydda *LID uh*

Lydia *LID ih uh*

Lydian *LID ih uhn*

Lysanias *ligh SAY nih uhs*

Lysias *LISS ih uhs*

Lysimachus *lih SIM uh kuhs*

Lystra *LISS truh*

Maacah *MAY uh kuh*

Maacath *MAY uh kath*

Maacathite *may AK uh thight*

Maachah *MAY uh kuh*

Maachathi *may AK uh thigh*

a-HAT; ah-far FAHR; aw-call KAWL; ay-name NAYM; B-BAD; ch-CHEW; d-DAD; e,eh-met MET; ee-sea SEE; ew-truth TREWTH; f-FOOT, enough ee NUHF; g-GET; h-HIM; hw-whether HWEH thuhr; i, ih-city SI ti, or SIH tih; igh sign SIGHN, eye IGH; igh LIGHT; j-jack JAK, germ JUHRM; k-KISS, chorus KOH ruhss, ks-(for x) ox AHKS; kw-quail KWAYL; l-live LIHV, LIGHV; m-more MOHR; ng-ring RING; oh-go GOH; row ROH (a boat); oo-LOOK; oo-boot BOOT

Maachathite *may AK uh thight*

Maadai *MAY uh digh*

Maadiah *MAY uh DIGH uh*

Maai *MAY igh (eye)*

Maaleh-acrabbim *MAY uh leh-ah KRAB bim*

Maani *MAY uh nigh*

Maarath *MAY uh rath*

Maareh-geba *MAY uh reh-GHEE buh*

Maasai *MAY uh sigh*

Maaseiah *MAY uh SEE uh*

Maasiai *MAY uh SIGH igh (eye)*

Maasias *may uh SIGH uhs*

Maasmas *may ASS muhs*

Maath *MAY ath*

Maaz *MAY az*

Maaziah *MAY uh ZIGH uh*

Mabdai *MAB digh*

Macalon *muh KAL ahn*

Macbannai *MAK buh nigh*

Macbenah *mak BEE nuh*

Maccabean *mak uh BEE uhn*

Maccabee *MAK uh bee*

Maccabeus *MAK uh BEE uhs*

Macedon *MASS uh dahn*

Macedonia *MASS uh DOH nih uh*

Macedonian *MASS uh DOH nih uhn*

Machabee *MAK uh bee*

Machabeus *MAK uh BEE uhs*

Machaerus *muh KIHR uhs*

Machbanai *MAK buh nigh*

Machbannai *MAK buh nigh*

Machbena *mak BEE nuh*

Machbenah *mak BEE nuh*

Machi *MAY kigh*

Machir *MAY kihr*

Machirite *MAY kuh right*

Machmas *MAK muhs*

Machnadebai *mak NAD ih bigh*

Machpelah *mak PEE luh*

Macnadebai *mak NAD ih bigh*

Macron *MAY krahn*

Madaba *MAH dah bah*

Madai *MAY digh*

Madiabun *muh DIGH uh buhn*

Madian *MAY dih uhn*

Madmannah *mad MAN nuh*

Madmen *MAD men*

Madmenah *mad MEE nuh*

M

---

ow-cow KOW, out OWT; oy-boil BOYL; p-PAT; r-RAN; s-star STAHR, tsetse SET see; sh-show SHOH, action AK shuhn, mission MIH shuhn, vicious VIH shuhss; t-tie TIGH, Thomas TAH muhss; th-thin THIN or THIHN; th-there THEHR; tw-TWIN; u, uh-tub TUB or TUHB, Joshua JAHSH yew uh, term TUHRM; v-veil VAYL, of AHV; w-WAY; wh (whether) see hw; y-year YEER; z-xerox ZIHR ahks, ZEE rahks, his HIZ or HIHZ, zebra ZEE bruh; zh-version VUHR zhuhn

Madon   *MAY dahn*

Maelus   *MAY uh luhs*

Mag   *MAG*

Magadan   *MAG uh dan*

Magbish   *MAG bish*

Magdala   *MAG duh luh*

Magdal-eder   *MAG duhl-EE duhr*

Magdalen   *MAG duh len*

Magdalene   *MAG duh leen, mag duh LEE nih*

Magdiel   *MAG dih el*

Maged   *MAY ged*

Magi   *MAY jigh*

Magnificate   *mag NIF ih kat*

Magog   *MAY gahg*

Magor-missabib   *MAY gahr-mih SAY bib*

Magpiash   *MAG pih ash*

Magus   *MAY guhs*

Mahalab   *muh HAY luhb*

Mahalah   *muh HAY luh*

Mahalaleel   *muh HAY luh LEE el*

Mahalalel   *muh HAL uh lihl*

Mahalath   *MAY huh lath*

Mahalath-leannoth   *MAY huh lath-lih AN ahth*

Mahalath Leannoth   *MAY huh lath-lih AN ahth*

Mahaleb   *MAY huh leb*

Mahali   *MAY huh ligh*

Mahanaim   *MAY huh NAY im*

Mahanath   *MAY huh nath*

Mahaneh-dan   *MAY hun neh-DAN*

Mahanehdan   *MAY huh neh-DAN*

Maharai   *muh HEHR ay igh (eye)*

Mahath   *MAY hath*

Mahavite   *MAY huh vight*

Mahazioth   *muh HAY zih ahth*

Maheneh Dan   *MAY hun neh-DAN*

Mahershalalhashbaz   *MAY hehr-SHAL al-HASH baz*

Maher-shaslal-hash-baz   *MAY hehr-SHAL al-HASH baz*

Mahlah   *MA luh (A as in cat)*

Mahli   *MA ligh (A as in cat)*

Mahlite   *MA light (A as in cat)*

Mahlon   *MA lahn (A as in cat)*

Mahol   *MAY hahl*

Mahseiah   *MAH see uh*

Maianeas   *may AN ih uhs*

Makaz   *MAY kaz*

---

a-HAT; ah-far FAHR; aw-call KAWL; ay-name NAYM; B-BAD; ch-CHEW; d-DAD; e,eh-met MET; ee-sea SEE; ew-truth TREWTH; f-FOOT, enough ee NUHF; g-GET; h-HIM; hw-whether HWEH thuhr; i, ih-city SI ti, or SIH tih; igh sign SIGHN, eye IGH; igh LIGHT; j-jack JAK, germ JUHRM; k-KISS, chorus KOH ruhss, ks-(for x) ox AHKS; kw-quail KWAYL; l-live LIHV, LIGHV; m-more MOHR; ng-ring RING; oh-go GOH; row ROH (a boat); oo-LOOK; oo-boot BOOT

Maked   *MAY ked*

Makheloth   *mak HEE lahth*

Maki   *MAY kigh*

Makir   *MAY kuhr*

Makirite   *MAY kih right*

Makkedah   *ma KEE duh (a as in cat)*

Maktesh   *MAK tesh*

Malachi (Malachias)   *MAL uh kigh*

Malachias (Malachi)   *MAL uh KIGH uhs*

Malachy   *MAL uh kee*

Malcam   *MAL kam*

Malcham   *MAL kam*

Malchiah   *mal KIGH uh*

Malchiel   *MAL kih el*

Malchielite   *MAL kih el ight*

Malchijah   *mal KIGH juh*

Malchiram   *mal KIGH ram*

Malchishua   *MAL kigh-SHOO uh*

Malchi-shua   *MAL kigh-SHOO uh*

Malchus   *MAL kuhs*

Maleleel   *muh LEE lih el*

Malkiel   *MAL kih el*

Malkielite   *MAL kih ih light*

Malkijah   *mal KIGH juh*

Malkiram   *mal KIH rahm*

Malki-shua   *MAL kigh-SHOO uh*

Malkishua   *MAL kigh SHOO uh*

Mallos   *MAL ahs*

Mallothi   *MAL oh thigh*

Malluch   *MAL uhk*

Malluchi   *MAL yoo kigh*

Mallus   *MAL uhs*

Malta   *MAWL tuh*

Mamaias   *muh MAY yuhs*

Mamdai   *MAM digh, MAM day igh (eye)*

mammon   *MAM uhn*

Mampsis   *MAM siss*

Mamre   *MAM rih*

Mamuchus   *muh MYOO kuhs*

Manach   *MAN ak*

Manaen   *MAN uh en*

Manahath   *MAN uh hath*

Manahathite   *MAN uh HATH ight*

Manahethite   *MUH NAY heth ight*

Manasseas   *muh NASS ih uhs*

Manasseh   *muh NASS uh*

Manassehite   *muh NASS uh hight*

M

ow-cow KOW, out OWT; oy-boil BOYL; p-PAT; r-RAN; s-star STAHR, tsetse SET see; sh-show SHOH, action AK shuhn, mission MIH shuhn, vicious VIH shuhss; t-tie TIGH, Thomas TAH muhss; th-thin THIN or THIHN; th-there THEHR; tw-TWIN; u, uh-tub TUB or TUHB, Joshua JAHSH yew uh, term TUHRM; v-veil VAYL, of AHV; w-WAY; wh (whether) see hw; y-year YEER; z-xerox ZIHR ahks, ZEE rahks, his HIZ or HIHZ, zebra ZEE bruh; zh-version VUHR zhuhn

Manasses *muh NASS eez*

Manassite *muh NASS ight*

maneh *MAY neh*

Mani *MAY nigh*

Manicheism *MAN ih kee IZ uhm*

Manius *MAY nih uhs*

Manlius *MAN lih uhs*

manna *MAN uh*

Manna *MAN uh*

Manoah *muh NOH uh*

Manoko *MAN uh koh*

Manuhoth *muh NYOO hahth*

Maoch *MAY ahk*

Maon *MAY ahn*

Maonite *MAY ahn ight*

Mara *MAH ruh*

Marah *MAH ruh*

Maralah *MAHR uh luh*

mara-natha *MAHR uh–NATH uh, MA ruh NATH uh*

mara natha *MAHR uh–NATH uh, MA ruh NATH uh*

maranatha *MAHR uh–NATH uh, MA ruh NATH uh*

Marcaboth *MAHR kuh bahth*

Marchesran *mahr chess RAHN*

Marcion *MAHR shuhn*

Marcus *MAHR kuhs*

Mardochai *MAHR duh kigh*

Mardocheus *MAHR duh KEE uhs*

Marduk *MAHR dyook*

Mareal *MAR ih uhl (A as in cat)*

Mareshah *muh REE shuh*

Mari *MAH ree*

Mariamne *MEHR ih AM nih*

Marimoth *MAHR ih mahth*

Marisa *MAHR ih suh*

Maritima *mar uh TEE muh*

Mark *MAHRK*

Marmoth *MAHR mahth*

Maroth *MAY rahth*

Mars *MAHRZ*

Marsena *mahr SEE nuh*

Martha *MAHR thuh*

Martyr *MAHR tuhr*

martyrdom *MAHR tuhr duhm*

Mary *MAY rih*

Masada *muh SAH duh*

Masaloth *MASS uh lahth*

Maschil *MAHS keel*

Mash *MASH*

Mashal *MAY shal*

Masiah *muh SIGH uh*

Masias   *muh SIGH uhs*

Maskil   *MAHS keel*

Masman   *MASS man*

Masora   *muh SAWR uh*

Masorah   *muh SAWR uh*

Masorete   *MASS oh reet*

Masoretic   *MASS oh RET ik*

Maspha   *MASS fuh*

Masrekah   *MASS rih kuh*

Massa   *MASS uh*

Massah   *MASS uh*

Massaite   *MASS ay ight*

Masseiah   *muh SEE yah*

Massias   *muh SIGH uhs*

Mathanias   *MATH uh NIGH uhs*

Mathusala   *muh THOO suh luh*

Matred   *MAY tred*

Matri   *MAY trigh*

Matrite   *MAY tright*

Mattan   *MAT uhn*

Mattanah   *MAT uh nuh*

Mattaniah   *MAT uh NIGH uh*

Mattatha   *MAT uh thuh*

Mattathah   *MAT uh thuh*

Mattathiah   *MAT uh THIGH uh*

Mattathias   *MAT uh THIGH uhs*

Mattattah   *MAT uh tuh*

Mattenai   *MAT uh nigh*

Matthan   *MAT than (th as in thin)*

Matthanias   *MATH uh NIGH uhs*

Matthat   *MAT that (th as in thin)*

Matthelas   *MATH uh luhs*

Matthew   *MATH yoo*

Matthias   *muh THIGH uhs*

Mattithiah   *MAT uh THIGH uh*

Mauritania   *MAWR uh TAYN ih uh*

Mazitias   *MAZ uh TIGH uhs*

Mazzaroth   *MAZ uh rahth*

Meah   *MEE uh*

Meani   *mih AY nigh*

Mearah   *mih AY ruh*

Mebunnai   *mih BUHN igh (eye)*

Mecherathite   *mih KEHR uh thight*

Meconah   *mih KOH nuh*

Medaba   *MED uh buh*

Medad   *MEE dad*

Medan   *MEE dan*

---

ow-cow KOW, out OWT; oy-boil BOYL; p-PAT; r-RAN; s-star STAHR, tsetse SET see; sh-show SHOH, action AK shuhn, mission MIH shuhn, vicious VIH shuhss; t-tie TIGH, Thomas TAH muhss; th-thin THIN or THIHN; th-there THEHR; tw-TWIN; u, uh-tub TUB or TUHB, Joshua JAHSH yew uh, term TUHRM; v-veil VAYL, of AHV; w-WAY; wh (whether) see hw; y-year YEER; z-xerox ZIHR ahks, ZEE rahks; his HIZ or HIHZ, zebra ZEE bruh; zh-version VUHR zhuhn

M

Mede *MEED*

Medeba *MED uh buh*

Media *MEE dih uh*

Median *MEE dih uhn*

Medinet Habu *meh DEE net-hah BOO*

Mediterranean *MED ih tuh RAY nih uhn*

Meeda *mih EE duh*

megalithic *MEG uh LITH ik*

megaron *MEH guh rahn*

Megiddo *mih GID oh*

Megiddon *mih GID ahn*

Megillah *mih GIL uh*

Megillot *mih GIL aht*

Megilloth *mih GIL ahth*

Mehallalel *muh HAL uh lel*

Mehetabeel *mih HET uh BEEL*

Mehetabel *mih HET uh bel*

Mehida *mih HIGH duh*

Mehir *MEE huhr*

Meholah *mih HOH luh*

Meholathite *mih HOH luh thight*

Mehujael *mih HYOO jay el*

Mehuman *mih HYOO man*

Mehunim *mih HYOO nim*

Mejarkon *mih-JAHR kahn*

Me-jarkon *mih-JAHR kahn*

Me Jarkon *mih-JAHR kahn*

Mekerathite *meh KEE ruh thight*

Mekonah *mih KOH nuh*

Melah *MEE luh*

Melakim *MEL uh kim*

Melatiah *MEL uh TIGH uh*

Melchi *MEL kigh*

Melchiah *mel KIGH uh*

Melchias *mel KIGH uhs*

Melchiel *MEL kee el*

Melchior *MEL kee awr*

Melchisedec *mel KIZ uh dek*

Melchi-shua *MEL kigh-SHOO uh*

Melchishua *MEL kigh-SHOO uh*

Melchizedek *mel KIZ uh dek*

Melea *MEE lee uh*

Melech *MEE lek*

Melichu *MEL ih kyoo*

Melicu *MEL ih kyoo*

Melita *MEL ih tuh, meh LEET uh*

Melki *MEL kigh*

Melzar *MEL zahr*

mem (Hebrew letter) *MAYM*

Memmius *MEM ih uhs*

a-HAT; ah-far FAHR; aw-call KAWL; ay-name NAYM; B-BAD; ch-CHEW; d-DAD; e,eh-met MET; ee-sea SEE; ew-truth TREWTH; f-FOOT, enough ee NUHF; g-GET; h-HIM; hw-whether HWEH thuhr; i, ih-city SI ti, or SIH tih; igh sign SIGHN, eye IGH; igh LIGHT; j-jack JAK, germ JUHRM; k-KISS, chorus KOH ruhss, ks-(for x) ox AHKS; kw-quail KWAYL; l-live LIHV, LIGHV; m-more MOHR; ng-ring RING; oh-go GOH, row ROH (a boat); oo-LOOK; oo-boot BOOT

Memphis   *MEM fiss*

Memshath   *MEM shahth*

Memucan   *mih MYOO kan*

Menahem   *MEN uh hem*

Menan   *MEE nan*

Menander   *muh NAN duhr*

mene   *MEE nih*

Menelaus   *MEN uh LAY uhs*

Menestheus   *mih NESS thee uhs, (th as in thin)*

menhir   *MEN heer*

Meni   *muh NEE*

Menna   *MEN uh*

menorah   *meh NOH ruh*

Menuhoth   *min YOO hahth*

Menuim   *MEN yoo im*

Meon   *MIH ahn, MEE ahn*

Meonenim   *mih AHN uh nim*

Meonothai   *mih AHN oh thigh*

Mephaath   *mef AY ath*

Mephibosheth   *meh FIB oh sheth*

Merab   *MEE rab*

Meraiah   *mih RIGH uh, mih RAY yuh*

Meraioth   *mih RAY ahth*

Meran   *MEHR uhn*

Merari   *mih RAY righ*

Merarite   *mih RAY right*

Merathaim   *MEHR uh THAY im (TH as in thin)*

Mercurius   *muhr KYOO rih uhs*

Mered   *MEE red*

Meremoth   *MER uh mahth*

Meres   *MEE ress, MEE reez*

Meribah   *MEHR ih buh*

Meribah-kadesh   *MEHR ih buh-KAY desh*

Meribah Kadesh   *MEHR ih buh-KAY desh*

Meribath   *MEHR ih bath*

Meribathkadesh   *MEHR ih bahth-KAY desh*

Meribath Kadesh   *MEHR ih bahth-KAY desh*

Meribbaal   *MEHR ib-BAY uhl*

Merib-baal   *MEHR ib-BAY uhl*

Merib Baal   *MEHR ib-BAY uhl*

Meriboth   *MEHR ih bahth*

Merneptah   *MUHR nep TAH*

Merob   *MEE rahb*

Merodach   *mih ROH dak*

Merodachbaladan   *mih ROH dak-BAL uh dan*

Merodach-baladan   *mih ROH dak-BAL uh dan*

Meroe   *MEH roh ee*

Merom   *MEE rahm*

M

ow-cow KOW, out OWT; oy-boil BOYL; p-PAT; r-RAN; s-star STAHR, tsetse SET see; sh-show SHOH, action AK shuhn, mission MIH shuhn, vicious VIH shuhss; t-tie TIGH, Thomas TAH muhss; th-thin THIN or THIHN; th-there THEHR; tw-TWIN; u, uh-tub TUB or TUHB, Joshua JAHSH yew uh, term TUHRM; v-veil VAYL, of AHV; w-WAY; wh (whether) see hw; y-year YEER; z-xerox ZIHR ahks, ZEE rahks, his HIZ or HIHZ, zebra ZEE bruh; zh-version VUHR zhuhn

113

M

Meron   *MEE rahn*

Meronoth   *mih RAHN ath*

Meronothite   *mih RAHN oh thight*

Meroth   *MEHR ahth*

Meroz   *MEE rahz*

Merran   *MEHR uhn*

Meruth   *MEE ruhth*

Mesad Hashavyahu   *MEH sahd-hahsh uh VAH hoo*

Mesaloth   *MESS uh lahth*

Mesech   *MEE sek*

Mesha   *MEE shuh*

Meshach   *MEE shak*

Meshech   *MEE shek*

Meshek   *MEE shek*

Meshelemiah   *mih SHEL uh MIGH uh*

Meshezabeel   *mih SHEZ uh beel*

Meshezabel   *mih SHEZ uh bel*

Meshillemith   *mih SHIL uh mith*

Meshillemoth   *mih SHIL uh mahth*

Meshobab   *mih SHOH bab*

Meshullam   *mih SHUHL uhm*

Meshullemeth   *mih SHUHL uh meth*

Mesobaite   *mih SOH bay ight*

mesolithic   *meh zoh LITH ik*

Mesopotamia   *MESS uh puh TAY mih uh*

Mesraim   *mess RAY im*

Messiah   *muh SIGH uh*

messiahship   *muh SIGH uh ship*

Messianic   *MESS ih AN ik*

Messias   *muh SIGH uhs*

Messina   *meh SEEN uh*

Meterus   *muh TEE ruhs*

Methegammah   *METH eg-AM uh, MEE theg-AM uh*

Metheg-ammah   *METH eg-AM uh*

Metheg Ammah   *METH eg-AM uh*

Methegh-ammah   *METH eg-AM uh*

Methoar   *mih THOH ahr*

Methusael   *mih THOO say el*

Methuselah   *mih THOOZ uh luh*

Methushael   *mih THOO shih el*

Meunim   *mih YOO nim*

Meunite   *mih YOO night*

Mezahab   *MEZ uh hab, MEE-zuh hab*

---

a-HAT; ah-far FAHR; aw-call KAWL; ay-name NAYM; B-BAD; ch-CHEW; d-DAD; e,eh-met MET; ee-sea SEE; ew-truth TREWTH; f-FOOT, enough ee NUHF; g-GET; h-HIM; hw-whether HWEH thuhr; i, ih-city SI ti, or SIH tih; igh sign SIGHN, eye IGH; igh LIGHT; j-jack JAK, germ JUHRM; k-KISS, chorus KOH ruhss, ks-(for x) ox AHKS; kw-quail KWAYL; l-live LIHV, LIGHV; m-more MOHR; ng-ring RING; oh-go GOH, row ROH (a boat); oo-LOOK; oo-boot BOOT

Me-zahab   *MEZ uh hab,*
  MEE-zuh hab

Mezobaite   *mih ZOH bay ight*

Mezobian   *mih ZOH bih uhn*

mezuzah   *muh ZOO zuh*

Miamin   *MIGH uh min*

Mibhar   *MIB hahr*

Mibsam   *MIB sam*

Mibzar   *MIB zahr*

Mica   *MIGH kuh*

Micah   *MIGH kuh*

Micaiah   *migh KAY yuh*

Micha   *MIGH kuh*

Michael   *MIGH kuhl, MIGH
  kay uhl*

Michah   *MIGH kuh*

Michaiah   *migh KAY yuh*

Michal   *MIGH kuhl*

Micheas (Micah)   *MIK ih uhs*

Michmas   *MIK muhs*

Michmash   *MIK mash*

Michmethah   *MIK mih thuh*

Michmethath   *MIK mih thath*

Michri   *MIK righ*

Michtam   *MIK tam*

Micmash   *MIK mash*

Micmethath   *MIK muh thath*

Micri   *MIK righ*

Middin   *MID in*

Midian   *MID ih uhn*

Midianite   *MID ih uhn ight*

Midianitish   *MID ih uh night
  ish*

midrash   *MID rash*

midrashim   *mid RASH im*

Migdal   *MIG dahl*

Migdal-eder   MIG *dal-EE dihr*

Migdal Eder   MIG *dal-EE dihr*

Migdal-el   *MIG dal-EL*

Migdalel   *MIG dal-EL*

Migdal El   *MIG dal-EL*

Migdalgad   *MIG dal-GAD*

Migdal-gad   *MIG dal-GAD*

Migdal Gad   *MIG dal-GAD*

Migdal-shechem   MIG
  dal-SHEK uhm

Migdol   *MIG dahl*

Migron   *MIG rahn*

Mijamin   *MIHJ uh min*

Mikloth   *MIK lahth*

Mikneiah   *mik NIGH uh, mik
  NEE yah*

Miktam   *MIK tam*

mikva'ot (pl.)   *MIK vah oot*

mikveh   *mik VEH*

Milalai   *MIL uh ligh*

Milcah   *MIL kuh*

ow-cow KOW, out OWT; oy-boil BOYL; p-PAT; r-RAN; s-star STAHR, tsetse SET see; sh-show
SHOH, action AK shuhn, mission MIH shuhn, vicious VIH shuhss; t-tie TIGH, Thomas TAH muhss;
th-thin THIN or THIHN; th-there THEHR; tw-TWIN; u, uh-tub TUB or TUHB, Joshua JAHSH yew
uh, term TUHRM; v-veil VAYL, of AHV; w-WAY; wh (whether) see hw; y-year YEER; z-xerox ZIHR
ahks, ZEE rahks, his HIZ or HIHZ, zebra ZEE bruh; zh-version VUHR zhuhn

Milcham   *MIL kam*

Milcom   *MIL kahm*

Miletum   *migh LEE tuhm*

Miletus   *migh LEE tuhs*

millennial   *muh LEN ih uhl*

millennium   *muh LEN ih uhm*

Millo   *MIL oh*

mina   *MIN uh*

Miniamin   *mih NIGH uh min*

Minjamin   *MIN juh min*

Minni   *MIN igh (eye)*

Minnith   *MIHN ith*

Minoan   *muh NOH uhn, migh NOH uhn*

minuscule   *MIH nuhs kyool*

Miphkad   *MIF kad*

Miriam   *MIHR ih uhm*

Mirma   *MUHR muh*

Mirmah   *MUHR muh*

Misach   *MISS ak*

Misael   *MISS ay el*

Misgab   *MISS gab*

Mishael   *MISH eh uhl*

Mishal   *MIGH shal*

Misham   *MIGH sham*

Misheal   *MIGH shih uhl*

Mishle   *MISH lee*

Mishma   *MISH muh*

Mishmannah   *mish MAN uh*

Mishna   *MISH nah*

Mishnah   *MISH nah*

Mishpat   *MISH pat*

Mishraite   *MISH ray ight*

Mispar   *MISS pahr*

Mispereth   *miss PEH reth*

Misrephoth   *MISS rih fahth*

Misrephoth-maim   *MISS rih fahth-MAY im*

Misrephothmaim   *MISS rih fahth-MAY im*

Mitanni   *mih TAN ee*

mite   *MIGHT*

Mithan   *MITH uhn*

Mithcah   *MITH kuh*

Mithkah   *MITH kuh*

Mithnite   *MITH night*

Mithra   *MITH rah*

Mithradates   *MITH rah DAH teez*

Mithraeum   *mith RAY uhm*

Mithraism   *MITH ruh IHZ uhm*

Mithras   *MITH rahss*

Mithredath   *MITH rih dath*

Mithridates   *MITH rih DAY teez*

Mitylene   *MIT uh LEE nih*

---

a-HAT; ah-far FAHR; aw-call KAWL; ay-name NAYM; B-BAD; ch-CHEW; d-DAD; e,eh-met MET; ee-sea SEE; ew-truth TREWTH; f-FOOT, enough ee NUHF; g-GET; h-HIM; hw-whether HWEH thuhr; i, ih-city SI ti, or SIH tih; igh sign SIGHN, eye IGH; igh LIGHT; j-jack JAK, germ JUHRM; k-KISS, chorus KOH ruhss, ks-(for x) ox AHKS; kw-quail KWAYL; l-live LIHV, LIGHV; m-more MOHR; ng-ring RING; oh-go GOH, row ROH (a boat); oo-LOOK; oo-boot BOOT

Mizar   *MIGH zahr*

Mizpah   *MIZ pah*

Mizpah-gilead   *MIZ pah-GIHL ih uhd*

Mizpar   *MIZ pahr*

Mizpeh   *MIZ peh*

Mizraim   *MIZ ray im*

Mizri (Egypt)   *MEEZ ree*

Mizzah   *MIZ uh*

Mnason   *NAY suhn*

Mnemon   *NEE mahn*

Moab   *MOH ab*

Moabite   *MOH uh bight*

Moabitess   *MOH uh bight ess*

Moabitish   *MOH uh bight ish*

Moadiah   *MOH uh DIGH uh*

Mochmur   *MAHK muhr*

Modein   *MOH deen*

Modin   *MOH din*

Moeth   *MOH eth*

Moladah   *moh LAY duh*

Molech   *MOH lek*

Molecheth   *moh LIK ith*

Moli   *MOH ligh*

Molid   *MOH lid*

Moloch   *MOH lahk*

Momdis   *MAHM diss*

Momdius   *MAHM dih uhs*

monolatry   *muh NAHL uh trih*

monotheism   *MAH noh thee IH zuhm (th as in thin)*

monotheism   *MAHN oh thee IHZ uhm (th as in thin)*

monotheist   *MAHN oh thee ist*

monotheistic   *MAHN oh thee ISS tik (th as in thin)*

Mons Casius   *MAHNS-KASS ih uhs*

Montanism   *MAHN tuh NIZ uhm*

Moosias   *MOH uh SIGH uhs*

Moossias   *MOH uh SIGH uhs*

Mopsuestia   *MAHP soo ESS tih uh*

Morasthite   *moh RASS thight*

Morastite   *moh RASS tight*

Mordecai   *MAWR duh kigh*

Moreh   *MOH reh*

Moresheth   *MOH reh sheth*

Moreshethgath   *MOH reh sheth-GATH*

Moresheth-gath   *MOH reh sheth-GATH*

Moresheth Gath   *MOH reh sheth-GATH*

Moriah   *muh RIGH uh*

Mosaic   *moh ZAY ik*

M

ow-cow KOW, out OWT; oy-boil BOYL; p-PAT; r-RAN; s-star STAHR, tsetse SET see; sh-show SHOH, action AK shuhn, mission MIH shuhn, vicious VIH shuhss; t-tie TIGH, Thomas TAH muhss; th-thin THIN or THIHN; th-there THEHR; tw-TWIN; u, uh-tub TUB or TUHB, Joshua JAHSH yew uh, term TUHRM; v-veil VAYL, of AHV; w-WAY; wh (whether) see hw; y-year YEER; z-xerox ZIHR ahks, ZEE rahks, his HIZ or HIHZ, zebra ZEE bruh; zh-version VUHR zhuhn

117

Mosallamon *moh SAHL uh muhn*

Mosera *moh SEE ruh*

Moserah *moh SEE ruh*

Moseroth *moh SEE rahth*

Moses *MOH ziss*

Mosoch *MOH sahk*

Mosollam *moh SAHL uhm*

Moza *MOH zuh*

Mozah *MOH zuh*

Mt. Ebal *MOWNT-EE bahl (ow as in cow)*

Mt. Gerizim *MOWNT-GEHR ih zeem (ow as in cow)*

Mt. Gilboa *MOWNT-gihl BOH uh (ow as in cow)*

Mt. Moriah *MOWNT-moh RIGH uh (ow as in cow)*

Mt. Nebo *MOWNT-NEE boh (ow as in cow)*

mu (Greek letter) *MEW*

Mugharet Abu Shinjeh *muh GAHR ret-ah BOO-SHIN jeh*

Mugharet el-Kebara *muh GAHR ret-el-keh BAHR uh*

Muppim *MUH pim*

Murabbaat *MOOR uh baht*

Murashu *MOO ruh shoo*

Muratorian *MYOOR uh TAWR ih uhn*

Musa, Jebel (Sinai) *MOO suh, JAY buhl*

Mushi *MYOO shigh*

Mushite *MYOO shight*

Musri *MYOOS righ*

Muth-labben *muhth-LAB en*

Muth Labben *muhth-LAB en*

Mycenae *migh SEE neh*

Mycenaean *migh suh NEE uhn*

Myndos *MIN dahs*

Myndus *MIN duhs*

Myra *MIGH ruh*

myriad *MIHR ih uhd*

Mysia *MISS ih uh*

Mysian *MISS ih uhn*

Naam *NAY am*

Naamah *NAY uh muh*

Naaman *NAY uh muhn, NAY muhn*

Naamanite *NAY uh muh night*

---

a-HAT; ah-far FAHR; aw-call KAWL; ay-name NAYM; B-BAD; ch-CHEW; d-DAD; e,eh-met MET; ee-sea SEE; ew-truth TREWTH; f-FOOT, enough ee NUHF; g-GET; h-HIM; hw-whether HWEH thuhr; i, ih-city SI ti, or SIH tih; igh sign SIGHN, eye IGH; igh LIGHT; j-jack JAK, germ JUHRM; k-KISS, chorus KOH ruhss; ks-(for x) ox AHKS; kw-quail KWAYL; l-live LIHV, LIGHV; m-more MOHR; ng-ring RING; oh-go GOH; row ROH (a boat); oo-LOOK; oo-boot BOOT

Naamath   *NAY uh math*

Naamathite   *NAY uh muh thight*

Naamite   *NAY uh might*

Naarah   *NAY uh ruh*

Naarai   *NAY uh righ*

Naaran   *NAY uh ran*

Naarath   *NAY uh rahth*

Naashon   *NAY ash ahn*

Naasson   *nay ASS uhn*

Naathus   *NAY uh thuhs*

Nabajoth   *NAY buh jahth*

Nabal   *NAY bal, NAY buhl*

Nabariah   *NAB uh RIGH uh*

Nabarias   *NAB uh RIGH uhs*

Nabataea   *NAB uh TEE uh*

Nabataean   *NAB uh TEE uhn*

Nabatea   *NAB uh TEE uh*

Nabatean   *NAB uh TEE uhn*

Nabathite   *NAB uh thight*

nabhi   *nah VEE*

nabi   *nah BEE*

Nablus   *NAB luhs*

Nabonidus   *NAB uh NIGH duhs*

Nabopolassar   *NAB uh puh LASS uhr*

Naboth   *NAY bahth*

Nabuchodonosar   *NAB uh kuh DAHN uh sahr*

Nabuchodonosor   *NAB uh kuh DAHN uh sawr*

Nachon   *NAY kahn*

Nachor   *NAY kawr*

Nacon   *NAY kahn*

Nadab   *NAY dab*

Nadabath   *NAD uh bath*

Nadabatha   *nuh DAB uh thuh*

Nadib   *NAY dib*

Naggae   *NAG ee*

Naggai   *NAG igh (eye)*

Nagge   *NAG eh*

Nag Hammadi   *NAHG-huh MAH dee*

Nahalal   *nuh HAL uhl*

Nahale-gaash   *NAY huh lee-GAY ash*

Nahal Hever   *NAH hahl-HEH vuhr*

Nahaliel   *nuh HAY lih el*

Nahallal   *nuh HAL lal*

Nahal Mishmar   *NAH hahl-MISH mahr*

Nahalol   *NAY huh lahl*

Nahal Oren   *NAH hahl-OH rehn*

Naham   *NAY ham*

N

ow-cow KOW, out OWT; oy-boil BOYL; p-PAT; r-RAN; s-star STAHR, tsetse SET see; sh-show SHOH, action AK shuhn, mission MIH shuhn, vicious VIH shuhss; t-tie TIGH, Thomas TAH muhss; th-thin THIN or THIHN; th-there THEHR; tw-TWIN; u, uh-tub TUB or TUHB, Joshua JAHSH yew uh, term TUHRM; v-veil VAYL, of AHV; w-WAY; wh (whether) see hw; y-year YEER; z-xerox ZIHR ahks, ZEE rahks, his HIZ or HIHZ, zebra ZEE bruh; zh-version VUHR zhuhn

Nahamani   *NAY huh MAY nigh*

Naharai   *NAY huh righ*

Naharaim   *NAY huh RAY im*

Nahari   *NAY huh righ*

Nahariya   *NAH hah RIGH yuh*

Nahash   *NAY hash*

Nahath   *NAY hath*

Nahbi   *NAH bigh*

Nahor   *NAY hawr*

Nahshon   *NAH shahn*

Nahum   *NAY huhm*

Naidus   *NIGH duhs*

Naim   *NAYM*

Nain   *NAYN*

Naioth   *NAY ahth*

Nanaea   *nuh NEE uh*

Nanaeon   *nuh NEE ahn*

Nanea   *nuh NEE uh*

Nangae   *NAN ghee*

Naomi   *nay OH mih*

Naphath   *NAY fath*

Naphath-dor   *NAY fath-DAWR*

Naphathdor   *NAY fath-DAWR*

Napheth   *NAY feth*

Naphhtuhim   *NAF tyoo him (tew)*

Naphish   *NAY fish*

Naphisi   *NAF ih sigh*

Naphoth   *NAY fahth*

Naphoth-dor   *NAY fahth-DAWR*

Naphothdor   *NAY fahth-DAWR*

Naphoth Dor   *NAY fahth-DAWR*

Naphtali   *NAF tuh ligh*

Naphtalite   *NAF tuh light*

naphtha   *NAF thah*

naphthar   *NAF thahr*

Naphtuh   *NAF tuh*

Naphtuhim   *NAF tyoo him*

Naphtuhite   *NAF tuh hight*

Naples   *NAY puhls*

Narcissus   *nahr SISS uhs*

Nasbas   *NAS buhs*

Nash   *NASH*

Nashim   *NAY shim*

Nasith   *NAY sith*

Nasor   *NAY sawr*

Nathan   *NAY thuhn*

Nathanael   *nuh THAN ay uhl (TH as in thin)*

Nathaniah   *NATH uh NIGH uh*

Nathanias   *NATH uh NIGH uhs*

---

a-HAT; ah-far FAHR; aw-call KAWL; ay-name NAYM; B-BAD; ch-CHEW; d-DAD; e,eh-met MET; ee-sea SEE; ew-truth TREWTH; f-FOOT, enough ee NUHF; g-GET; h-HIM; hw-whether HWEH thuhr; i, ih-city SI ti, or SIH tih; igh sign SIGHN, eye IGH; igh LIGHT; j-jack JAK, germ JUHRM; k-KISS, chorus KOH ruhss, ks-(for x) ox AHKS; kw-quail KWAYL; l-live LIHV, LIGHV; m-more MOHR; ng-ring RING; oh-go GOH; row ROH (a boat); oo-LOOK; oo-boot BOOT

Nathan-melech *NAY thuhn-MEE lek*

Nathanmelech *NAY thuhn-MEE lek*

Natufian *nah TOO fih uhn*

Naum *NAY uhm*

Nave *NAYV*

navi *nah VEE*

Nazarene *NAZ uh reen*

Nazareth *NAZ uh reth*

Nazarite *NAZ uh right*

Nazirite *NAZ uh right*

Nazorean *NAZ uh REE uhn*

Neah *NEE uh*

Neapolis *nee AP uh liss*

Neariah *NEE uh RIGH uh*

Nebai *NEE bigh*

Nebaioth *nih BAY ahth*

Nebajoth *nih BAY jahth*

Neballat *nee BAL uht*

Nebat *NEE bat*

nebhiim *nuh VEE eem*

nebiim *nuh BEE eem*

Nebi Samwil *NEH bih-SAHM wuhl*

Nebo *NEE boh*

Nebo-sarsekim *NEE boh-SAHR seh kim*

Nebuchadnezzar *NEB yoo kad NEZ uhr*

Nebuchadrezzar *NEB yoo kad DREZ uhr*

Nebushasban *NEB yoo SHAZ ban*

Nebushazban *NEB yoo SHAZ ban*

Nebuzar-adan *NEB uh zahr-AY dan*

Nebuzaradan *NEB uh zahr-AY dan*

Necho *NEE koh*

Nechoh *NEE koh*

Neco *NEE koh*

Necodan *nih KOH dan*

necromancy *NEK ruh MAN sih*

necropolis *neh KRAHP uh liss*

Nedabiah *NED uh BIGH uh*

Neemias *NEE uh MIGH uhs*

Negeb *NEG eb, NEH gehv*

Negev *NEH gehv*

Neginah *neh GHEE nah*

Neginoth *NEG ih nahth*

Nego *NEE goh*

Nehelam *neh HEL uhm*

Nehelamite *nih HEL uh might*

Nehemiah *NEE huh MIGH uh*

---

ow-cow KOW, out OWT; oy-boil BOYL; p-PAT; r-RAN; s-star STAHR, tsetse SET see; sh-show SHOH, action AK shuhn, mission MIH shuhn, vicious VIH shuhss; t-tie TIGH, Thomas TAH muhss; th-thin THIN or THIHN; th-there THEHR; tw-TWIN; u, uh-tub TUB or TUHB, Joshua JAHSH yew uh, term TUHRM; v-veil VAYL, of AHV; w-WAY; wh (whether) see hw; y-year YEER; z-xerox ZIHR ahks, ZEE rahks, his HIZ or HIHZ, zebra ZEE bruh; zh-version VUHR zhuhn

Nehemias *NEE huh MIGH uhs*

Nehemyah *nih HEM yuh*

Nehiloth *NEE hih lahth*

Nehum *NEE huhm*

Nehushta *nih HUHSH tuh*

Nehushtan *nih HUHSH tan*

Neiel *nih IGH (eye) el*

Nekeb *NEE keb*

Nekoda *nih KOH duh*

Nemuel *NEM yoo el*

Nemuelite *NEM yoo el ight*

Neolithic *NEE uh LITH ik*

Nepheg *NEE feg*

nephi *NEF igh (eye)*

Nephilim *NEF uh lim*

Nephish *NEE fish, NEF ish*

Nephishesim *nih FISH uh sim*

Nephisim *neh FIGH sim*

Nephtali *NEF tuh ligh*

Nephthali *NEF thuh ligh*

Nephthalim *NEF thuh lim*

nephthar *NEF thahr*

Nephtoah *nef TOH uh*

Nephushesim *neh FOOSH ih sim*

Nephusim *nih FYOO sim*

Nephusite *nih FYOO sight*

Nephussim *nih FYOO sim*

Nepthalim *NEP thuh lim*

Ner *NUHR*

Neraiah *neh RAY uh, nih RIGH uh*

Nereus *NEE roos*

Nergal *NUHR gal*

Nergal-sarezer *NUHR gal-sahr-EE zuhr*

Nergal-sar-ezer *NUHR gal-sahr-EE zuhr*

Nergal-sharezer *NUHR gal-shuh REE zuhr*

Nergalsharezer *NUHR gal-shuh REE zuhr*

Neri *NEE righ*

Neriah *nih RIGH uh*

Nerias *nih RIGH uhs*

Neriglissar *NUHR ihg LISS uhr*

Nero *NEE roh, NIHR oh*

Netaim *nih TAY im*

Nethaneal *nih THAN ih al*

Nethaneel *nih THAN ih el (TH as in thin)*

Nethanel *nih THAN el (TH as in thin)*

Nethaniah *NETH uh NIGH uh*

Nethinim *NETH ih nim*

Netopha *nih TOH fuh*

---

a-HAT; ah-far FAHR; aw-call KAWL; ay-name NAYM; B-BAD; ch-CHEW; d-DAD; e,eh-met MET; ee-sea SEE; ew-truth TREWTH; f-FOOT, enough ee NUHF; g-GET; h-HIM; hw-whether HWEH thuhr; i, ih-city SI ti, or SIH tih; igh sign SIGHN, eye IGH; igh LIGHT; j-jack JAK, germ JUHRM; k-KISS, chorus KOH ruhss, ks-(for x) ox AHKS; kw-quail KWAYL; l-live LIHV, LIGHV; m-more MOHR; ng-ring RING; oh-go GOH, row ROH (a boat); oo-LOOK; oo-boot BOOT

Netophah *nih TOH fuh*

Netophathi *nih TAHF uh thigh*

Netophathite *nih TAHF uh thight*

Nevi'im *neh vih EEM, nuh VEE im, NEH vih eem*

neviim *neh vih EEM, nuh VEE im, NEH vih eem*

Neviim *neh vih EEM, nuh VEE im, NEH vih eem*

Neziah *nih ZIGH uh*

Nezib *NEE zib*

Nibhaz *NIB haz*

Nibshan *NIB shan*

Nicaea *nigh SEE uh*

Nicanor *nigh KAY nawr*

Nicodemus *NIK uh DEE muhs*

Nicolaitan *NIK oh LAY uh tuhn*

Nicolaitane *NIH oh LAY uh tayn*

Nicolas *NIK oh luhs*

Nicolaus *NIK uh LAY uhs*

Nicopolis *nih KAHP oh liss*

Nidia *NID ih uh*

Niger *NIGH guhr*

Nile *NIGHL*

Nilometer *nighl AH meh tuhr*

Nimrah *NIM ruh*

Nimrim *NIM rim*

Nimrod *NIM rahd*

Nimrud *NIM rood*

Nimshi *NIM shigh*

Nineve *NIN eh veh*

Nineveh *NIN uh vuh*

Ninevite *NIN uh vight*

Ningirsu *nin GIHR soo*

Niphis *NIF iss*

Nippur *NIH puhr*

Nisan *NIGH san*

Nisibis *nih SIGH biss*

Nison *NEE sahn*

Nisroch *NISS rahk*

Nissi *NISS ih*

nitre *NIGH tuhr*

No *NOH*

Noadiah *NOH uh DIGH uh*

Noah *NOH uh*

No-amon *noh-AY muhn*

Nob *NAHB*

Nobah *NOH buh*

Nobai *NOH bigh*

Nod *NAHD*

Nodab *NOH dab*

Nodan *NOH dan*

Noe *NOH eh*

Noeba *noh EE buh*

Noemi *NOH uh migh*

N

ow-cow KOW, out OWT; oy-boil BOYL; p-PAT; r-RAN; s-star STAHR, tsetse SET see; sh-show SHOH, action AK shuhn, mission MIH shuhn, vicious VIH shuhss; t-tie TIGH, Thomas TAH muhss; th-thin THIN or THIHN; th-there THEHR; tw-TWIN; u, uh-tub TUB or TUHB, Joshua JAHSH yew uh, term TUHRM; v-veil VAYL, of AHV; w-WAY; wh (whether) see hw; y-year YEER; z-xerox ZIHR ahks, ZEE rahks, his HIZ or HIHZ, zebra ZEE bruh; zh-version VUHR zhuhn

Nogah   *NOH guh*

Nohah   *NOH hah*

nomadization   *NOH mad ih ZAY shuhn*

Non   *NAHN*

Noph   *NAHF*

Nophah   *NOH fuh*

Nora   *NOH ruh*

Nothus   *NOH thuhss*

nu (Greek letter)   *NEW*

Nubian   *NYOO bih uhn*

numbers   *NUHM buhrz*

Numbers   *NUHM buhrz*

Numenius   *noo MEE nee uhs*

Nun   *NUHN*

nun (Hebrew letter)   *NOON*

Nunc Dimittis   *NUNK-duh MIT iss*

Nuzi   *NOO zee*

Nympha   *NIM fuh*

Nymphas   *NIM fuhs*

O

Obadiah   *OH buh DIGH uh*

Obal   *OH buhl*

Obdia   *ahb DIGH uh*

Obed   *OH bed*

Obed-edom   *OH bed-EE duhm*

Obededom   *OH bed-EE duhm*

obelisk   *AHB uh lisk*

Obeth   *OH beth*

Obil   *OH bil*

Oboth   *OH bahth*

Ochiel   *oh KIGH el*

Ochielus   *oh CHEE luhs*

Ochran   *AK ran*

Ochus   *OH chuhss*

Ocidelus   *oh sigh DIH luhs*

Ocina   *oh SIGH nuh*

Ocran   *AHK ran*

Octavion   *ahk TAY vih uhn*

Ode   *OHD*

Oded   *OH ded*

Odollam   *oh DAHL uhm*

Odomera   *AHD uh MEHR uh*

Odonarkes   *AHD uh NAHR keez*

Og   *AHG*

Ohad   *OH had*

Ohel   *OH hel*

Oholah   *oh HOH luh*

Oholiab   *oh HOH lih ab*

Oholibah   *oh HAHL uh buh*

---

a-HAT; ah-far FAHR; aw-call KAWL; ay-name NAYM; B-BAD; ch-CHEW; d-DAD; e,eh-met MET; ee-sea SEE; ew-truth TREWTH; f-FOOT, enough ee NUHF; g-GET; h-HIM; hw-whether HWEH thuhr; i, ih-city SI ti, or SIH tih; igh sign SIGHN, eye IGH; igh LIGHT; j-jack JAK, germ JUHRM; k-KISS, chorus KOH ruhss, ks-(for x) ox AHKS; kw-quail KWAYL; l-live LIHV, LIGHV; m-more MOHR; ng-ring RING; oh-go GOH, row ROH (a boat); oo-LOOK; oo-boot BOOT

Oholibamah *oh* HAHL *ih BAY muh*

Olamus *OH luh muhs*

Olive *AHL ihv*

Olivet *AHL ih vet*

Olympas *oh LIM puhs*

Olympian *oh LIM pih uhn*

Olympus *oh LIM puhs*

Omaerus *oh MEE ruhs*

Omar *OH mahr, OH muhr*

omega (Greek letter) *oh MAY guh, oh MEG uh*

omer *OH muhr*

omerful *OH muhr fool (full)*

omicron (Greek letter) *AH mih krahn*

Omri *AHM righ*

On *AHN*

Onam *OH nam*

Onan *OH nan*

Onesimus *oh NESS ih muhs*

Onesiphorus *AHN ih SIF oh ruhs*

Oni *OH nigh*

Oniads *oh NIGH ads*

Onias *oh NIGH uhs*

Ono *OH noh*

Onus *OH nuhs*

onycha *AHN ih kuh*

Ophel *OH fel*

Ophir *OH fuhr*

Ophni *AHF nigh*

Ophrah *AHF ruh*

Opis *OH piss*

oracle *AWR uh kuhl*

Oreb *OH reb*

Oregim *OH ruh gim*

Oren *OH ren*

Origen *AWR uh juhn*

Orion *oh RIGH uhn*

Ornan *AWR nan*

Orontes *oh RAHN teez, awr AHN teez*

Orpah *AWR puh*

Orpheus *AWR fee uhs*

orthodox *AWR thuh dahks*

orthodoxy *AWR thuh* DAHK *sih*

orthographic *awr THUH gra fik*

Orthosia *awr THOH see uh*

Orthosias *awr THOH see uhs*

orthostat *AWR thuh stat*

Osaias *oh SAY yuhs*

Osea *oh SEE uh*

Oseas *oh SEE uhs*

Osee (Hosea) *OH zee*

Oshea *oh SHEE uh*

O

---

ow-cow KOW, out OWT; oy-boil BOYL; p-PAT; r-RAN; s-star STAHR, tsetse SET see; sh-show SHOH, action AK shuhn, mission MIH shuhn, vicious VIH shuhss; t-tie TIGH, Thomas TAH muhss; th-thin THIN or THIHN; th-there THEHR; tw-TWIN; u, uh-tub TUB or TUHB, Joshua JAHSH yew uh, term TUHRM; v-veil VAYL, of AHV; w-WAY; wh (whether) see hw; y-year YEER; z-xerox ZIHR ahks, ZEE rahks; his HIZ or HIHZ, zebra ZEE bruh; zh-version VUHR zhuhn

125

Osiris   *oh SIGH ruhs*

Osnappar   *ahs NAP uhr*

Osnapper   *ahs NAP uhr*

ossuary   *AH shuh WEHR ee*

Ostia   *AHS tee uh*

ostraca   *AHS truh kah*

ostracon   *AHS truh kahn*

Othni   *AHTH nigh*

Othniel   *AHTH nih el*

othography   *awr THAH gruh fih*

Othoniah   *AHTH uh NIGH uh*

Othonias   *AHTH uh NIGH uhs*

ox   *AHKS*

Oxyrhyncus   *AHK sih RING kuhs*

Ozem   *OH zem*

Ozias   *oh ZIGH uhs*

Oziel   *OH zih el*

Ozni   *AHZ nigh*

Oznite   *AHZ night*

Ozora   *oh ZAWR uh*

P

Paaneah   *pay uh NEE uh*

Paarai   *PAY uh righ*

Pacatania   *pak uh TAN ih uh*

Pachon   *PAY kahn*

Padan   *PAY duhn*

Padan-aram   *PAY duhn-AY ram*

Padan Aram   *PAY duhn-AY ram*

Paddan   *PAY duhn*

Paddan-aram   *PAY duhn-AY ram*

Paddan Aram   *PAY duhn-AY ram*

Padon   *PAY dahn*

Pagae   *PAY jigh*

Pagiel   *PAY gih el*

Pahath-moab   *PAY hath-MOH ab*

Pahathmoab   *PAY hath-MOH ab*

Pai   *PAY igh (eye), PIGH*

Palal   *PAY lal*

paleography   *PAY lee AHG ruh fih*

Paleolithic   *PAY lee oh LITH ik*

Palestina   *PAL uhs TIGH nuh*

Palestine   *PAL uhs tighn*

Palet   *PAY let*

palimpsest   *PA limp sest*

---

a-HAT; ah-far FAHR; aw-call KAWL; ay-name NAYM; B-BAD; ch-CHEW; d-DAD; e,eh-met MET; ee-sea SEE; ew-truth TREWTH; f-FOOT, enough ee NUHF; g-GET; h-HIM; hw-whether HWEH thuhr; i, ih-city SI ti, or SIH tih; igh sign SIGHN, eye IGH; igh LIGHT; j-jack JAK, germ JUHRM; k-KISS, chorus KOH ruhss, ks-(for x) ox AHKS; kw-quail KWAYL; l-live LIHV, LIGHV; m-more MOHR; ng-ring RING; oh-go GOH, row ROH (a boat); oo-LOOK; oo-boot BOOT

126

Pallu   *PAL yoo*

Palluite   *PAL yoo ight*

Palmyra   *pal MIGH ruh*

Palti   *PAL tigh*

Paltiel   *PAL tih el*

Paltite   *PAL tight*

palynology   *PAY luhn NAH luh jih*

Pamphylia   *pam FIL ih uh*

Panias   *PAN yuhss*

Pannag   *PAN ag*

Paphos   *PAY fahs, PA fahss*

Papias   *PAY pih uhs*

papyri (pl.)   *puh PIGH ree, puh PIGH righ*

papyrus   *puh PIGH ruhs*

parable   *PAR uh buhl (A as in cat)*

Paraclete   *PAR uh kleet (A as in cat)*

paradigm   *PAR uh dighm (A as in cat)*

Paradise   *PAR uh dighss (A as in cat)*

Parah   *PAY ruh*

Paralipomenon   *PAR uh lih PAHM uh nahn*

parallelism   *PAR uh lel IZ uhm (A as in cat)*

Paran   *PAY ruhn*

parataxis   *PAR uh TAK siss (a as in cat)*

Parath   *PAY rath*

Parbar   *PAHR bahr*

parchment   *PAHRCH muhnt*

parenesis   *PAR uh NEE siss (a as in cat)*

parenetic   *PAR uh NET ik (a as in cat)*

Parmashta   *pahr MASH tuh*

Parmenas   *PAHR mih nuhs*

Parnach   *PAHR nak*

paronomasia   *PAR uh noh MAY zhee uh (A as in cat)*

Parosh   *PAY rahsh*

Parousia   *puh ROO zhee uh*

Parshandatha   *PAHR shan DAY thuh*

parsin   *PAHR sin*

Parthia   *PAHR thih uh*

Parthian   *PAHR thih uhn*

Paruah   *puh ROO uh*

Parvaim   *pahr VAY im*

Parzite   *PAHR zight*

Pas   *PASS*

Pasach   *PAY sak*

Pasargadae   *puh SAHR guh dee*

Paschal   *PASS kuhl*

P

---

ow-cow KOW, out OWT; oy-boil BOYL; p-PAT; r-RAN; s-star STAHR, tsetse SET see; sh-show SHOH, action AK shuhn, mission MIH shuhn, vicious VIH shuhss; t-tie TIGH, Thomas TAH muhss; th-thin THIN or THIHN; th-there THEHR; tw-TWIN; u, uh-tub TUB or TUHB, Joshua JAHSH yew uh, term TUHRM; v-veil VAYL, of AHV; w-WAY; wh (whether) see hw; y-year YEER; z-xerox ZIHR ahks, ZEE rahks, his HIZ or HIHZ, zebra ZEE bruh; zh-version VUHR zhuhn

P

Pasdammim   *pas-DAM im*

Pas-dammim   *pas-DAM im*

Pas Dammim   *pas-DAM im*

Paseah   *puh SEE uh*

Pashhur   *PASH huhr*

Pashur   *PASH uhr*

Passion   *PASH uhn*

Passover   *PASS oh vuhr*

Pastoral   *PAS tuh ruhl*

Patara   *PAT uh ruh*

Patheus   *puh THEE uhs (TH as in thin)*

Pathros   *PATH rahss*

Pathrus   *PATH ruhs*

Pathrusim   *path ROO sim*

Pathrusite   *path ROO sight*

Patmos   *PAT muhs*

patriarch   *PAY trih ahrk*

patriarchal   *PAY trih AHRK uhl*

patristic   *puh TRISS tik*

Patrobas   *PAT roh buhs*

Patroclus   *puh TROH kluhs*

Pau   *PAY oo*

Paul   *PAWL, PAHL*

Pauline   *PAW leen*

Paulus   *PAW luhs*

Pazzez   *PAZ iz*

pe (Hebrew letter)   *PAY*

Pedahel   *PED uh hel*

Pedahzur   *pih DA zuhr*

Pedaiah   *pih DIGH uh*

Pegai   *PEH gigh*

peh   *PAY*

Pekah   *PEE kuh*

Pekahiah   *PEK uh HIGH uh*

Pekod   *PEE kahd*

Pelaiah   *pih LAY yuh*

Pelaliah   *PEL uh LIGH uh*

Pelatiah   *PEL uh TIGH uh*

Peleg   *PEE leg*

Pelet   *PEE let*

Peleth   *PEE leth*

Pelethite   *PEE leth ight*

Pelias   *PEE lih uhs*

Pella   *PEL luh*

Pelon   *PEE lahn*

Pelonite   *PEE loh night, PEHL oh night*

Peloponnesian   *peh luh poh NEE zih uhn*

Peloponnesus   *PEH luh poh NEE suhs*

Pelusium   *peh LOOZ ih uhm*

Peniel   *pih NIGH el, PEN ih el*

Peninnah   *pih NIN uh*

Pentapolis   *pen TAP oh liss*

a-HAT; ah-far FAHR; aw-call KAWL; ay-name NAYM; B-BAD; ch-CHEW; d-DAD; e,eh-met MET; ee-sea SEE; ew-truth TREWTH; f-FOOT, enough ee NUHF; g-GET; h-HIM; hw-whether HWEH thuhr; i, ih-city SI ti, or SIH tih; igh sign SIGHN, eye IGH; igh LIGHT; j-jack JAK, germ JUHRM; k-KISS, chorus KOH ruhss, ks-(for x) ox AHKS; kw-quail KWAYL; l-live LIHV, LIGHV; m-more MOHR; ng-ring RING; oh-go GOH, row ROH (a boat); oo-LOOK; oo-boot BOOT

Pentateuch *PEN tuh tyook*

Pentecost *PEN tih kawst*

Penuel *pih NYOO el*

Peor *PEE awr*

Peraea *puh REE uh*

Perath *PEE rath*

Perazim *pih RAY zim*

perdition *puhr DIH shuhn*

peres *PEE rez*

Peresh *PEE resh*

Perez *PEE rez*

Perezite *PEE rez ight*

Perezuzza *PEE rez-UHZ uh*

Perez-uzza *PEE rez-UHZ uh*

Perezuzzah *PEE rez-UHZ uh*

Perez-uzzah *PEE rez-UHZ uh*

Perez Uzzah *PEE rez-UHZ uh*

Perga *PUHR guh*

Pergamos *PUHR guh muhs*

Pergamum *PUHR guh muhm*

Pericles *PEHR uh kleez*

pericope *puh RIK uh pee*

Perida *pih RIGH duh*

Perizzite *PEHR ih zight*

Persepolis *puhr SEP uh liss*

Perseus *PUHR see uhs*

Persia *PUHR zhuh*

Persian *PUHR zhuhn*

Persis *PUHR sis*

Peruda *pih ROO duh*

pesher *PESH uhr*

pesherim *PESH uh rim*

Peshitta *puh SHEE tuh*

Peter *PEE tuhr*

Pethahiah *PETH uh HIGH uh*

Pethor *PEE thawr*

Pethuel *pih THYOO el*

Petra *PEE truh, PEH truh*

Peullethai *pih UHL uh thigh*

Peulthai *pih UHL thigh*

Phaath Moab *FAY ath-MOH ab*

Phacareth *FAK uh reth*

Phadoura *fuh DOOR uh (OO as in foot)*

Phaisur *FAY zuhr*

Phalaris *FAL uh riss*

Phaldaius *fal DAY uhs*

Phaleas *fuh LEE uhs*

Phalec *FAY lek*

Phallu *FAL oo*

Phalti *FAL tigh*

Phaltiel *FAL tih el*

Phanuel *fuh NYOO uhl*

P

---

ow-cow KOW, out OWT; oy-boil BOYL; p-PAT; r-RAN; s-star STAHR, tsetse SET see; sh-show SHOH, action AK shuhn, mission MIH shuhn, vicious VIH shuhss; t-tie TIGH, Thomas TAH muhss; th-thin THIN or THIHN; th-there THEHR; tw-TWIN; u, uh-tub TUB or TUHB, Joshua JAHSH yew uh, term TUHRM; v-veil VAYL, of AHV; w-WAY; wh (whether) see hw; y-year YEER; z-xerox ZIHR ahks, ZEE rahks, his HIZ or HIHZ, zebra ZEE bruh; zh-version VUHR zhuhn

Pharakim   *FEHR uh kim*

Pharaoh   *FEHR oh*

Pharaoh-hophra   *FEHR oh-HAHF ruh*

Pharaoh-necho   *FEHR oh-NEE koh*

Pharaoh-nechoh   *FEHR oh-NEE koh*

Pharaoh-neco   *FEHR oh-NEE koh*

Pharaoh Neco   *FEHR oh-NEE koh*

Pharathon   *FEHR uh thahn*

Pharathoni   *FEHR uh THOH nigh*

Phares   *FEHR iss*

Pharez   *FEHR iz*

Pharida   *FA rih duh, fa REE duh*

Pharisaic   *FEHR uh SAY ik*

Pharisee   *FEHR uh see*

Pharos   *FEH ruhss*

Pharosh   *FAY rahsh*

Pharpar   *FAHR pahr*

Pharzite   *FAHR zight*

Phasael   *FAY see uhl*

Phasaelis   *fuh SEE luhs*

Phasaelus   *fuh SEE luhs*

Phaseah   *fuh SEE uh*

Phaselis   *fuh SEE liss*

Phasiron   *FASS uh rahn*

Phassaron   *FASS uh rahn*

Phebe   *FEE bih*

Phelet   *FEE lit*

Phenice   *fih NIGH sih*

Phenicia   *fuh NISH ih uh*

phi (Greek letter)   *FIGH*

Phibeseth   *FIGH buh seth*

Phichol   *FIGH kahl*

Phicol   *FIGH kahl*

Philadelphia   *FIL uh DEL fih uh*

Philadelphian   *FIL uh DEL fih uhn*

Philarches   *fil AHR keez*

Philemon   *figh LEE muhn*

Philetus   *fih LEE tuhs*

Philip   *FIL ip*

Philippi   *FIH lih pigh*

Philippians   *fih LIP ih uhnz*

Philistia   *fih LISS tih uh*

Philistim   *fih LISS tim*

Philistine   *fih LISS teen*

Philo   *FIGH loh*

Philologus   *fih LAHL oh guhs*

Philometor   *FIL uh MEE tawr*

Philopator   *FIL uh PAY tawr*

P

a-HAT; ah-far FAHR; aw-call KAWL; ay-name NAYM; B-BAD; ch-CHEW; d-DAD; e,eh-met MET; ee-sea SEE; ew-truth TREWTH; f-FOOT, enough ee NUHF; g-GET; h-HIM; hw-whether HWEH thuhr; i, ih-city SI ti, or SIH tih; igh sign SIGHN, eye IGH; igh LIGHT; j-jack JAK, germ JUHRM; k-KISS, chorus KOH ruhss, ks-(for x) ox AHKS; kw-quail KWAYL; l-live LIHV, LIGHV; m-more MOHR; ng-ring RING; oh-go GOH; row ROH (a boat); oo-LOOK; oo-boot BOOT

Philoteria   *FIL uh TEHR ih uh*

Phineas   *FIN ih uhs*

Phinees   *FIN ih uhs*

Phinehas   *FIN ih huhs*

Phinoi   *FIN oy*

Phison   *FIGH sahn*

Phlegon   *FLEE gahn*

Phoebe   *FEE bih*

Phoenicia   *fih NISH ih uh*

Phoenix   *FEE niks*

Phogor   *FOH gawr*

Phoros   *FAHR ahs*

Phrygia   *FRIJ ih uh*

Phrygian   *FRIJ ih uhn*

Phud   *FUHD*

Phurah   *FYOO ruh*

Phurim   *FYOO rim*

Phut   *FUHT*

Phuvah   *FYOO vuh*

Phygellus   *fih JEL uhs*

Phygelus   *fih JEL uhs*

phylactery   *FIH LAK tuh rih*

phylarch   *FIGH lahrk*

pi (Greek letter)   *PIGH*

Pibeseth   *pigh-BEE seth*

Pi-beseth   *pigh-BEE seth*

Pi Beseth   *pigh-BEE seth*

Pihahiroth   *PIGH-huh HIGH rahth*

Pi-hahiroth   *PIGH-huh HIGH rahth*

Pi Hahiroth   *PIGH-huh HIGH rahth*

Pilate   *PIGH luht*

Pildash   *PIL dash*

Pileha   *PIL ih ha (a as in cat)*

Pileser   *pih LEE suhr*

Pilha   *PIL huh*

Pilneser   *pil NEE zuhr*

Piltai   *PIL tigh*

pim   *PIM*

Pinon   *PIGH nahn*

Pira   *PIGH ruh*

Piram   *PIGH ram*

Pirathon   *pigh RAY thahn*

Pirathonite   *PIHR uh thuh night*

piriform   *PIHR ih fohrm*

Pisgah   *PIZ guh*

Pishon   *PIGH shahn*

Pisidia   *pih SID ih uh*

Pisidian   *pih SID ih uhn*

Pisidian Antioch   *pih SID ih uhn-AN tih ahk*

Pison   *PIGH sahn*

Pispa   *PIS puh*

ow-cow KOW, out OWT; oy-boil BOYL; p-PAT; r-RAN; s-star STAHR, tsetse SET see; sh-show SHOH, action AK shuhn, mission MIH shuhn, vicious VIH shuhss; t-tie TIGH, Thomas TAH muhss; th-thin THIN or THIHN; th-there THEHR; tw-TWIN; u, uh-tub TUB or TUHB, Joshua JAHSH yew uh, term TUHRM; v-veil VAYL, of AHV; w-WAY; wh (whether) see hw; y-year YEER; z-xerox ZIHR ahks, ZEE rahks, his HIZ or HIHZ, zebra ZEE bruh; zh-version VUHR zhuhn

P

Pispah   *PIS puh*

pithoi (pl.)   *PITH oy (oy as in boy)*

Pithom   *PIGH thahm*

Pithon   *PIGH thahn*

pithos   *PITH ahss*

Plato   *PLAY toh*

Platonic   *pluh TAHN ik*

Platonism   *PLAY tuh* NIZ *uhm*

Pleiades   *PLEE uh deez*

pleroma   *plih ROH muh*

Pliny   *PLIN ee, PLIGH nee*

Plutarch   *PLOO tahrk*

pneumatic   *nyoo MAT ik*

Pochereth   *PAHK uh reth*

Pocherethhazzebaim   *PAHK uh reth-haz uh BAY im*

Pochereth-hazzebaim   *PAHK uh reth-haz uh BAY im*

Pokereth-hazzebaim   *PAHK uh reth-haz uh BAY im*

Pollux   *PAHL uhks*

Polycarp   *PAH lih kahrp*

Polyglot   *PAH lih glaht*

polytheism   *PAH lee thee* IHZ *uhm (th as in thin)*

polytheistic   *PAH lee thee ISS tik (th as in thin)*

Pompeii   *pahm PAY*

Pontius   *PAHN shuhs*

Pontius Pilate   *PAHN chuhss PIGH luht*

Pontus   *PAHN tuhs*

Poratha   *poh RAY thuh*

Porathai   *poh RAY thigh*

Porcius   *PAWR shuhs*

Porcius Festus   *PAWR shuss FESS tuhss*

Posidonius   *PAHS ih DOH nih uhs*

Poti   *POH tigh*

Potiphar   *PAHT ih fuhr*

Potiphera   *poh TIH-fih ruh*

Poti-pherah   *poh TIH-fih ruh*

potsherd   *PAHT shuhrd*

praetor   *PREE tawr*

Praetorian   *pri TAWR ih uhn*

Praetorium   *pri TAWR ih uhm*

Preacher   *PREE chuhr*

prefect   *PREE fekt*

presbyter   *PREZ buh tuhr, PRESS buh tuhr*

presbytery   *PREZ buh* TEHR *ih*

Pretorium   *pree TOHR ee uhm*

Prisca   *PRISS kuh*

Priscilla   *prih SIL uh*

P

---

a-HAT; ah-far FAHR; aw-call KAWL; ay-name NAYM; B-BAD; ch-CHEW; d-DAD; e,eh-met MET; ee-sea SEE; ew-truth TREWTH; f-FOOT, enough ee NUHF; g-GET; h-HIM; hw-whether HWEH thuhr; i, ih-city SI ti, or SIH tih; igh sign SIGHN, eye IGH; igh LIGHT; j-jack JAK, germ JUHRM; k-KISS, chorus KOH ruhss; ks-(for x) ox AHKS; kw-quail KWAYL; l-live LIHV, LIGHV; m-more MOHR; ng-ring RING; oh-go GOH, row ROH (a boat); oo-LOOK; oo-boot BOOT .

Prochorus *PRAHK uh ruhs*

proconsul *proh KAHN suhl*

proconsular *proh KAHN suh luhr*

Procorus *PRAHK uh ruhs*

procurator *PRAHK yuh RAY tuhr*

prophet *PRAHF it*

proselyte *PRAHS uh light*

proverb *PRAHV uhrb*

Proverbs *PRAHV uhrbs*

psalm *SAHLM*

Psalms *SAHLMZ*

Psalter *SAWL tuhr*

psaltery *SAWL tuh rih*

Psammethichus *sahm MITH ih kuhs*

Psephinus Tower *sih FIN ih uhs-TOW wehr (OW as in cow)*

pseudepigrapha *soo dih PIH gruh fuh*

Pseudepigrapha *soo dih PIH gruh fuh*

pseudepigraphy *soo dih PIH gruh fih*

pseudo *SOO doh*

pseudonym *SOO duhn im*

psi (Greek letter) *puh SIGH*

Ptolemaic *TAHL uh MAY ihk*

Ptolemais *TAHL uh MAY uhs*

Ptolemy *TAHL uh mih*

Pua *PYOO uh*

Puah *PYOO uh*

publican *PUHB lih kuhn*

Publius *PUHB lih uhs*

Pudens *PYOO denz*

Puhite *PYOO hight*

Puite *PYOO ight*

Pul *PUHL*

Punic *PEW nik*

Punite *PYOO night*

Punon *PYOO nahn*

Pur *PUHR*

Purah *PYOO ruh*

Purim *PYOO rim*

Put *PUHT*

Puteoli *pyoo TEE oh ligh*

Puthite *PYOO thight*

Putiel *PYOO tih el*

Puvah *PYOO vuh*

Puvahite *PYOO vuh hight*

Puvvah *PYOO vuh*

pygarg *PIGH gahrg*

Pyrrhus *PIHR uhs*

pyxis *PIK siss*

P

---

ow-cow KOW, out OWT; oy-boil BOYL; p-PAT; r-RAN; s-star STAHR, tsetse SET see; sh-show SHOH, action AK shuhn, mission MIH shuhn, vicious VIH shuhss; t-tie TIGH, Thomas TAH muhss; th-thin THIN or THIHN; th-there THEHR; tw-TWIN; u, uh-tub TUB or TUHB, Joshua JAHSH yew uh, term TUHRM; v-veil VAYL, of AHV; w-WAY; wh (whether) see hw; y-year YEER; z-xerox ZIHR ahks, ZEE rahks, his HIZ or HIHZ, zebra ZEE bruh; zh-version VUHR zhuhn

133

Q

Qadesh   *KAY desh, KAH desh*

Qarqar   *KAHR kahr*

Qere   *kuh RAY*

qof (Hebrew letter)   *QOHF*

Qoheleth   *koh HEL eth*

quadrans   *KWAD ruhns*

quadrat   *KWAH drat*

Quadratus   *KWAHD ruh tuhs*

Quartus   *KWAHR tuhs*

quaternion   *kwah TUHR nih uhn*

Quintus   *KWIN tuhs*

Quirinius   *kwih RIN ih uhs*

Qumran   *KOOM rahn*

R

Ra   *RAH*

Raama   *RAY uh muh*

Raamah   *RAY uh muh*

Raamiah   *RAY uh MIGH uh*

Raamses   *ray AM seez*

Rab   *RAB*

Rabbah   *RAB uh*

Rabbat Ammon   *rah BAHT-ah MOHN*

Rabbath   *RAB uhth*

Rabbath-ammon   *rah BAHTH-ah MOHN*

rabbi   *RAB igh (eye)*

Rabbim   *RAB im*

rabbinic   *ruh BIH nik*

Rabbith   *RAB ith*

rabboni   *ra BOH nigh*

rabbouni   *ra BOO nigh*

Rab-mag   *RAB-mag*

Rabmag   *RAB-mag*

Rabsaces   *RAB suh seez*

Rab-saris   *RAB-suh riss*

Rabsaris   *RAB-suh riss*

Rabshakeh   *RAB-shuh keh*

Rab-shakeh   *RAB-shuh keh*

raca   *RAH kuh*

Racal   *RAY kuhl*

Rachab   *RAY kab*

Rachal   *RAY kuhl*

Rachel   *RAY chuhl*

Raddai   *RAD ay igh, RAD igh (eye)*

Ragaba   *rah GAH buh*

Ragae   *RAY ghee*

---

a-HAT; ah-far FAHR; aw-call KAWL; ay-name NAYM; B-BAD; ch-CHEW; d-DAD; e,eh-met MET; ee-sea SEE; ew-truth TREWTH; f-FOOT, enough ee NUHF; g-GET; h-HIM; hw-whether HWEH thuhr; i, ih-city SI ti, or SIH tih; igh sign SIGHN, eye IGH; j-jack JAK, germ JUHRM; k-KISS, chorus KOH ruhss; ks-(for x) ox AHKS; kw-quail KWAYL; l-live LIHV, LIGHV; m-more MOHR; ng-ring RING; oh-go GOH, row ROH (a boat); oo-LOOK; oo-boot BOOT

Ragau   *RAY gaw*

Rages   *RAH guhs, RA gehz*

Raguel   *ruh GYOO el*

Rahab   *RAY hab*

Rahab-hem-shebeth   *RAY hab-hem-SHEE beth*

Raham   *RAY ham*

Rahel   *RAY hel*

Rakem   *RAY kem*

Rakkath   *RAK uhth*

Rakkon   *RAK ahn*

Ram   *RAM*

Rama   *RAY muh*

Ramah   *RAY muh*

Ramath   *RAY math*

Ramathaim   *RAY muh THAY im (TH as in thin)*

Ramathaim-zophim   *RAY muh THAY im-ZOH fim*

Ramathaimzophim   *RAY muh THAY im-ZOH fim*

Ramathaim Zophim   *RAY muh THAY im-ZOH fim*

Ramathem   *RAM uh them (th as in thin)*

Ramathite   *RAY math ight*

Ramath-lehi   *RAY math-LEE high*

Ramathlehi   *RAY math-LEE high*

Ramath Lehi   *RAY math-LEE high*

Ramath-mizpah   *RAY math-MIZ pah*

Ramath Mizpah   *RAY math-MIZ pah*

Ramath-mizpeh   *RAY math-MIZ peh*

Ramathmizpeh   *RAY math-MIZ peh*

Ramat Madred   *rah MAT-MAH dred*

Ramat Negev   *rah MAT-NEH gehv*

Ramat Rahel   *rah MAT-rah HAYL*

Rameses   *RAM uh seez*

Ramesses   *RAM uh seez*

Ramiah   *ruh MIGH uh*

Ramoth   *RAY mahth*

Ramothgilead   *RAY mahth-GIL ih uhd*

Ramoth Gilead   *RAY mahth-GIL ih uhd*

Ramoth Gilead   *RAY mahth-GIL ih uhd*

Ramoth-negeb   *RAY mahth-NEH gehv*

Ramoth Negev   *RAY mahth-NEH gehv*

rampart   *RAM part*

R

ow-cow KOW, out OWT; oy-boil BOYL; p-PAT; r-RAN; s-star STAHR, tsetse SET see; sh-show SHOH, action AK shuhn, mission MIH shuhn, vicious VIH shuhss; t-tie TIGH, Thomas TAH muhss; th-thin THIN or THIHN; th-there THEHR; tw-TWIN; u, uh-tub TUB or TUHB, Joshua JAHSH yew uh, term TUHRM; v-veil VAYL, of AHV; w-WAY; wh (whether) see hw; y-year YEER; z-xerox ZIHR ahks, ZEE rahks, his HIZ or HIHZ, zebra ZEE bruh; zh-version VUHR zhuhn

Ramses   *RAM seez*

Rapha   *RAY fah*

Raphael   *RAF ay el*

Raphah   *RAY fuh*

Raphaim   *RAF ay im*

Raphain   *RAF ay in*

Raphia   *ruh FIGH uh*

Raphon   *RAY fahn*

Raphu   *RAY fyoo*

Ras el-Ain   *RAHS-el-IGHN*

Rasses   *RASS eez*

Ras-shamra   *rah-SHAM rah,*
  rahs-SHAHM ruh

Ras Shamra   *rah-SHAM rah*

Rassis   *RASS iss*

Rassisite   *RASS ih sight*

Rathamin   *RATH uh min*

Rathumus   *ruh THYOO muhs*

Razis   *RAY ziss*

Re   *RAY*

Reaia   *rih AY yuh*

Reaiah   *rih IGH (eye) uh*

Reba   *REE buh*

Rebecca   *reh BEK uh*

Rebekah   *reh BEK uh*

Recab   *REE kab*

Recabite   *REK uh bight*

Recah   *REE kuh*

recension   *rih SEN shuhn*

Rechab   *REE kab*

Rechabite   *REK uh bight*

Rechah   *REE kuh*

Rechokim   *REK oh kim*

redact   *rih DAKT*

redaction   *rih DAK shuhn*

redactor   *rih DAK tuhr*

Red-sea   *RED-SEE*

Red Sea   *RED-SEE*

Reed Sea   *REED-see*

Reelaiah   *REE el IGH uh*

Reeliah   *REE uh LIGH uh*

Reelius   *REE uh LIGH uhs*

Reesaias   *REE uh SAY yuhs*

Regem   *REE ghem*

Regem-melech   *REE*
  ghem-MEE lek

Regemmelech   *REE*
  ghem-MEE lek

Rehabiah   *REE huh BIGH uh*

Rehob   *REE hahb*

Rehoboam   *REE huh BOH*
  uhm

Rehoboth   *rih HOH bahth*

Rehoboth-han-nahar   *rih*
  HOH bahth-hahn-NAY hahr

Rehoboth-ir   *rih HOH*
  bahth-IHR

---

a-HAT; ah-far FAHR; aw-call KAWL; ay-name NAYM; B-BAD; ch-CHEW; d-DAD; e,eh-met
MET; ee-sea SEE; ew-truth TREWTH; f-FOOT, enough ee NUHF; g-GET; h-HIM; hw-whether
HWEH thuhr; i, ih-city SI ti, or SIH tih; igh sign SIGHN, eye IGH; igh LIGHT; j-jack JAK, germ
JUHRM; k-KISS, chorus KOH ruhss, ks-(for x) ox AHKS; kw-quail KWAYL; l-live LIHV, LIGHV;
m-more MOHR; ng-ring RING; oh-go GOH, row ROH (a boat); oo-LOOK; oo-boot BOOT

Rehoboth Ir   *rih HOH bahth-IHR*

Rchum   *REE huhm*

Rei   *REE igh (eye)*

Rekem   *REE kem*

Remaliah   *REM uh LIGH uh*

Remeth   *REE meth*

Remmon   *REM ahn*

Remmon-methoar   *REM ahn-meh THOH ahr*

Remphan   *REM fan*

Rephael   *REF ay el*

Rephah   *REE fuh*

Rephaiah   *rih FAY yuh, rih FIGH uh*

Rephaim   *REF ay im*

Rephaite   *REF ay ight*

Rephan   *REE fan*

Rephidim   *REF ih dim*

Resaiah   *rih SAY yuh*

Resen   *REE sin*

resh (Hebrew letter)   *RAYSH*

Resheph   *REE shef*

Resin   *REE zihn*

Reu   *REE yoo*

Reuben   *RHOO ben*

Reubenite   *RHOO ben ight*

Reuel   *RHOO el*

Reumah   *RHOO muh*

Revelation   *REV uh LAY shuhn*

Rezeph   *REE zef*

Rezia   *ree ZIGH uh*

Rezin   *REE zin*

Rezon   *REE zahn*

Rhegium   *REE jih uhm*

Rheims   *REEMZ*

Rheims-Douay   *reemz-DOO ay*

Rhesa   *REE suh*

rho (Greek letter)   *ROH*

Rhoda   *ROH duh*

Rhodanite   *ROH duh night*

Rhodes   *ROHDZ*

Rhodocus   *RAHD uh kuhs*

rib   *REEB*

Ribai   *RIGH bigh, RIGH bay igh (eye)*

ribh   *REEV*

Riblah   *RIB luh*

Rimmon   *RIM uhn*

Rimmono   *rih MOH noh*

Rimmon-parez   *RIM uhn-PAY reez*

Rimmon-perez   *RIM uhn-PEE reez*

Rimmonperez   *RIM uhn-PEE reez*

Rinnah   *RIN nuh*

R

ow-cow KOW, out OWT; oy-boil BOYL; p-PAT; r-RAN; s-star STAHR, tsetse SET see; sh-show SHOH, action AK shuhn, mission MIH shuhn, vicious VIH shuhss; t-tie TIGH, Thomas TAH muhss; th-thin THIN or THIHN; th-there THEHR; tw-TWIN; u, uh-tub TUB or TUHB, Joshua JAHSH yew uh, term TUHRM; v-veil VAYL, of AHV; w-WAY; wh (whether) see hw; y-year YEER; z-xerox ZIHR ahks, ZEE rahks, his HIZ or HIHZ, zebra ZEE bruh; zh-version VUHR zhuhn

Riphath   *RIGH fath*

Rishathaim   *RISH uh THAY*
   im

Rissah   *RISS uh*

Rithmah   *RITH muh*

riv   *REEV*

Rizia   *RIZ ih uh, rih ZIGH uh*

Rizpah   *RIZ puh*

Roboam   *roh BOH uhm*

Rodanim   *RAHD uh nim*

Rogel   *ROH gehl*

Rogelim   *ROH guh lim*

Rohgah   *ROH guh*

Roi   *ROH ih*

Roimus   *ROH ih muhs*

Romamti-ezer   *roh MAM*
   tigh-EE zuhr

Romamtiezer   *roh MAM*
   tigh-EE zuhr

Roman   *ROH muhn*

Romans   *ROH muhnz*

Rome   *ROHM*

Rompha   *ROHM fuh*

Rosetta   *roh ZET uh*

Rosh   *RAHSH*

Rosh Hashannah   *RAHSH-huh*
   SHAH nuh

Ruben   *ROO ben*

rue   *ROO*

Rufus   *ROO fuhs*

Ruhama   *roo HAY muh*

Ruhamah   *roo HAY muh*

Rumah   *ROO muh*

Ruth   *ROOTH, REWTH*

S

Saba   *SAY buh*

sabachthani   *sah BAK thuh*
   nigh

Sabaean   *sah BEE uhn*

Sabaoth   *SAB ay ahth*

Sabat   *SAB uht*

Sabateas   *sab uh TEE uhs*

Sabatus   *SAB uh tuhs*

Sabbaias   *suh BAY uhs*

Sabban   *SAB an*

Sabbath   *SAB uhth*

Sabbatheus   *SAB uh THEE uhs*
   (TH as in thin)

sabbatical   *suh BAT ih kuhl*

Sabbeus   *sa BEE uhs*

Sabean   *suh BEE uhn*

Sabi   *SAY bigh*

Sabta   *SAB tuh*

Sabtah   *SAB tuh*

Sabteca   *SAB tee kuh*

Sabtecah   *SAB tee kuh*

Sabtecha   *SAB tee kuh*

Sabtechah   *SAB tee kuh*

Sacar   *SAY kahr*

Sachar   *SAY kawr*

Sachia   *suh KIGH uh*

Sadamias   *SAD uh MIGH uhs*

Sadas   *SAY duhs*

Saddeus   *SAD ih uhs*

Sadduc   *SAD uhk*

Sadducee   *SAD joo see*

Sadduk   *SAD uhk*

sadhe   *SAH deh*

Sadoc   *SAY dahk*

Safed   *SAH fed*

Sage   *ZAH geh*

Sahar   *SAY hahr*

Sahara   *sah HAHR uh*

Saida   *SAY duh*

Sais   *SISS*

Sakia   *suh KIGH uh*

Sakkuth   *SAK uhth*

Sala   *SAY luh*

Salah   *SAY luh*

Salamiel   *suh LAY mih el*

Salamis   *SAL uh miss*

Salasadai   *SAL uh SAD igh (eye)*

Salathiel   *suh LAY thih el*

Salcah   *SAL kuh*

Salchah   *SAL kuh*

Salecah   *SAL ih kuh*

Salem   *SAY luhm*

Salim   *SAY lim*

Sallai   *SAL ay igh, SAL igh (eye)*

Sallu   *SAL oo*

Sallumus   *SAL uh muhs*

Salma   *SAL muh*

Salmai   *SAL migh*

Salman   *SAL man*

Salmon   *SAL mahn*

Salmone   *sal MOH nih*

Salom   *SAY lahm*

Salome   *suh LOH mih*

Salt-city   *SAWLT-SIT ih*

Salt-sea   *SAWLT-SEE*

Salt Sea   *SAWLT-SEE*

Salu   *SAY lyoo*

Salum   *SAY luhm*

Sam'al   *sahm AHL*

Samael   *SAM ay uhl*

Samaias   *suh MAY yuhs*

Samaria   *suh MEHR ih uh*

S

---

ow-cow KOW, out OWT; oy-boil BOYL; p-PAT; r-RAN; s-star STAHR, tsetse SET see; sh-show SHOH, action AK shuhn, mission MIH shuhn, vicious VIH shuhss; t-tie TIGH, Thomas TAH muhss; th-thin THIN or THIHN; th-there THEHR; tw-TWIN; u, uh-tub TUB or TUHB, Joshua JAHSH yew uh, term TUHRM; v-veil VAYL, of AHV; w-WAY; wh (whether) see hw; y-year YEER; z-xerox ZIHR ahks, ZEE rahks, his HIZ or HIHZ, zebra ZEE bruh; zh-version VUHR zhuhn

Samarian *suh MEHR ih uhn*

Samaritan *suh MEHR ih tuhn*

Samarra *suh MAH ruh*

Samatus *suh MAY tuhs*

samech *SAH mek*

Sameius *suh MEE yuhs*

samekh (Hebrew letter) *SAH mek*

Samgar *SAM gahr*

Samgarnebo *SAM gahr-NEE boh*

Samgar-nebo *SAM gahr-NEE boh*

Samgar-nebu *SAM gahr-NEE buh*

Sami *SAY migh*

Samis *SAY miss*

Samlah *SAM luh*

Sammus *SAM uhs*

Samos *SAY mahs*

Samothrace *SA muh thrays*

Samothracia *sa muh THRAY shuh (TH as in thin)*

Sampsames *SAMP suh meez*

Samson *SAM suhn*

Samuel *SAM yoo el, SAM yoo uhl*

Sanabassar *SAN uh BASS uhr*

Sanabassarus *SAN uh BASS uh ruhs*

Sanasib *SAN uh sib*

Sanballat *san BAL uht*

Sanhedrin *san HEE drihn, SAN hee druhn*

Sansannah *san SAN uh*

Saph *SAF*

Saphat *SAY fat*

Saphatias *SAF uh TIGH uhs*

Sapheth *SAY feth*

Saphir *SAY fuhr*

Saphon *SAY fahn*

Sapor *sa POOR*

Sapphira *suh FIGH ruh*

Saqqara *suh KAH ruh, SAK uh ruh*

Sara *SEHR uh*

Sarabias *SEHR uh BIGH uhs*

Sarah *SEHR uh*

Sarai *SEHR igh (eye)*

Saraias *suh RAY yuhs*

Saramel *SEHR uh mel*

Saraph *SAY raf*

Sarasadai *SEHR uh SAD igh (eye)*

Sarchedonus *SAHR kuh DOH nuhs*

---

a-HAT; ah-far FAHR; aw-call KAWL; ay-name NAYM; B-BAD; ch-CHEW; d-DAD; e,eh-met MET; ee-sea SEE; ew-truth TREWTH; f-FOOT, enough ee NUHF; g-GET; h-HIM; hw-whether HWEH thuhr; i, ih-city SI ti, or SIH tih; igh sign SIGHN, eye IGH; igh LIGHT; j-jack JAK, germ JUHRM; k-KISS, chorus KOH ruhss, ks-(for x) ox AHKS; kw-quail KWAYL; l-live LIHV, LIGHV; m-more MOHR; ng-ring RING; oh-go GOH, row ROH (a boat); oo-LOOK; oo-boot BOOT

sarcophagi *sahr KAHF uh gigh*

sarcophagus *sahr KAHF uh guhs*

Sardeus *sahr DEE uhs*

Sardinia *sahr DIN ih uh*

Sardis *SAHR diss*

Sardite *SAHR dight*

sardius *SAHR dih uhs*

Sarea *SEHR ee uh*

Sarepta *suh REP tuh*

Sargon *SAHR gahn*

Sarid *SAY rid*

Saron *SAY rahn*

Sarothie *suh ROH thee (th as in thin)*

Sarsechim *SAHR-sih kim*

Sar-sekim *SAHR-sih kim*

Saruch *SAY ruhk*

Satan *SAY tuhn*

Sathra-buzanes *SATH ruh-BYOO zuh neez*

Sathrabuzanes *SATH ruh-BYOO zuh neez*

satrap *SAY trap, SA trap*

satrapy *SAY truh pih, SA truh pih*

Saul *SAWL, SAHL*

Savaran *SAV uh ran*

Savias *suh VIGH uhs*

Savior *SAY vih'awr*

Saviour *SAY vih'awr*

scarab *SKA ruhb*

Sceva *SEE vuh*

Schedia *shuh DIGH uh*

schin *SHIN*

schism *SIZ uhm*

schismatic *siz MAT ik*

scribe *SKRIGHB*

Scripture *SKRIP chuhr*

Scythia *SITH ih uh*

Scythian *SITH ih uhn*

Scythopolis *sih THAHP oh liss*

Scythopolitan *SITH uh PAHL ih tuhn*

seah *SEE uh*

Seba *SEE buh*

Sebam *SEE bam*

Sebaste *see BASS tih*

Sebastiyeh *see BASS tee yuh*

Sebat *SEE bat*

Secacah *sih KAY kuh*

Sechenias *SEK uh NIGH uhs*

Sechu *SEE kyoo*

Secu *SEE kyoo*

Secundus *sih KUHN duhs*

Sedecias *SED uh KIGH uhs*

S

ow-cow KOW, out OWT; oy-boil BOYL; p-PAT; r-RAN; s-star STAHR, tsetse SET see; sh-show SHOH, action AK shuhn, mission MIH shuhn, vicious VIH shuhss; t-tie TIGH, Thomas TAH muhss; th-thin THIN or THIHN; th-there THEHR; tw-TWIN; u, uh-tub TUB or TUHB, Joshua JAHSH yew uh, term TUHRM; v-veil VAYL, of AHV; w-WAY; wh (whether) see hw; y-year YEER; z-xerox ZIHR ahks, ZEE rahks, his HIZ or HIHZ, zebra ZEE bruh; zh-version VUHR zhuhn

141

sedentarization *SEH dihn tehr ih ZAY shuhn*

Segub *SEE guhb*

Seir *SEE uhr*

Seira *SEE ih ruh*

Seirah *SEE ih ruh*

Seirath *SEE uh rath*

Sela *SEE luh*

selah *SEE luh*

Selah *SEE luh*

Sela-hammahlekoth *SEE luh–huh MAH lih kahth*

Sela Hammahlekoth *SEE luh–huh MAH lih kahth*

Seled *SEE led*

Selemia *SEL uh MIGH uh*

Selemias *SEL uh MIGH uhs*

Seleucia *sih LYOO shih uh*

Seleucid *sih LOO sid*

Seleucus *sih LOO kuhs*

Selinis *seh LIGH nuhs*

Sem *SEM*

Semachiah *SEM uh KIGH uh*

Semakiah *SEM uh KIGH uh*

Semei *SEM ih igh (eye)*

Semein *SEM ee ihn*

Semellius *sih MEL ih uhs*

Semis *SEE miss*

Semite *SEM ight*

Semitic *sih MIT ik*

Semiticizm *sih MIT uh SIZ uhm*

Semitism *SEM uh TIZ uhm*

Senaah *sih NAY uh*

Senate *SEN it*

Seneca *SEN uh kuh*

Seneh *SEE neh*

Senir *SEE nihr*

Sennacherib *suh NAK uh rib*

Senuah *sih NYOO uh*

Seorim *see OH rim*

Separvaim *SEF ahr-VAY im*

Sephar *SEE far*

Sepharad *SEF uh rad*

Sephar-vaim *SEF ahr-VAY im*

Sepharvite *SEF ahr vight*

Sephatiah *SEF uh TIGH uh*

Sephela *suh FEE luh*

Sepphoris *SEF uh riss*

Septuagint *sep TOO uh jint*

sepulcher *SEP uhl kuhr*

sepulchre *SEP uhl kuhr*

Serabit el-Khadim *SEHR uh bit-el-KUH deem*

Serah *SEE ruh*

Seraiah *sih RIGH uh, sih RAY yuh*

seraph *SEHR uhf*

---

a-HAT; ah-far FAHR; aw-call KAWL; ay-name NAYM; B-BAD; ch-CHEW; d-DAD; e,eh-met MET; ee-sea SEE; ew-truth TREWTH; f-FOOT, enough ee NUHF; g-GET; h-HIM; hw-whether HWEH thuhr; i, ih-city SI ti, or SIH tih; igh sign SIGHN, eye IGH; igh LIGHT; j-jack JAK, germ JUHRM; k-KISS, chorus KOH ruhss, ks-(for x) ox AHKS; kw-quail KWAYL; l-live LIHV, LIGHV; m-more MOHR; ng-ring RING; oh-go GOH, row ROH (a boat); oo-LOOK; oo-boot BOOT

seraphim *SEHR uh fim*

Serapis *sih RAH piss*

Sered *SEE red*

Seredite *SEE ruh dight*

Sergius *SUHR jih uhs*

Sergius Paulus *SUHR jih uhs–PAW luhs*

Seron *SEER ahn*

Serug *SEE ruhg*

Sesis *SEE siss*

Sesthel *SEHS thuhl*

Seth *SETH*

Sethur *SEE thuhr*

Seti *SEH tih*

Seveneh *sih VEN eh*

Sextus *SEKS toos (oo as in look)*

Shaalabbin *SHAY uh LAB in*

Shaalbim *shay AL bim*

Shaalbon *shay AL bahn*

Shaalbonite *SHAY AL boh night*

Shaalim *SHAY uh lim*

Shaaph *SHAY af*

Shaaraim *SHAY uh RAY im*

Shaashgaz *shay ASH gahz*

Shabbethai *SHAB ih thigh*

Shachia *shuh KIGH uh*

Shaddai *SHAD igh (eye)*

Shadday *SHAD igh (eye)*

Shadrach *SHAD rak*

Shage *SHAY gih*

Shagee *SHAY ghee*

Shageh *SHAY geh*

Shahar *SHAY hahr*

Shaharaim *SHAY huh RAY im*

Shahazimah *SHAY huh ZIGH muh*

Shahazumah *SHAY huh ZOO muh*

Shakeh *SHAY keh*

Shalal *SHAY lal*

Shalem *SHAY luhm*

Shalim *SHAY lim*

Shalisha *SHAL uh shah*

Shalishah *SHAL ih shah*

Shallecheth *SHAL ih keth*

Shalleketh *SHAL ih keth*

Shallum *SHAL uhm*

Shallun *SHAL uhn*

Shalmai *SHAL migh, SHAL may igh (eye)*

Shalman *SHAL man*

Shalmaneser *SHAL muh NEE zuhr*

Shalom *shah LOHM*

Shama *SHAY muh*

Shamariah *SHAM uh RIGH uh*

S

ow-cow KOW, out OWT; oy-boil BOYL; p-PAT; r-RAN; s-star STAHR, tsetse SET see; sh-show SHOH, action AK shuhn, mission MIH shuhn, vicious VIH shuhss; t-tie TIGH, Thomas TAH muhss; th-thin THIN or THIHN; th-there THEHR; tw-TWIN; u, uh-tub TUB or TUHB, Joshua JAHSH yew uh, term TUHRM; v-veil VAYL, of AHV; w-WAY; wh (whether) see hw; y-year YEER; z-xerox ZIHR ahks, ZEE rahks, his HIZ or HIHZ, zebra ZEE bruh; zh-version VUHR zhuhn

143

Shamed *SHAY med*	Shashai *SHAY shigh*
Shamer *SHAY muhr*	Shashak *SHAY shak*
Shamgar *SHAM gahr*	Shaul *SHAWL, SHAH ool*
Shamhuth *SHAM huhth*	*(Hebrew)*
Shamir *SHAY muhr*	Shaulite *SHAW light, SHAH ool ight*
Shamlai *SHAM ligh*	Shaveh *SHAY veh*
Shamma *SHAM uh*	Shavehkiriathaim *SHAY veh-kihr ih uh THAY im*
Shammah *SHAM uh*	Shaveh-kiriathaim *SHAY veh-kihr ih uh THAY im*
Shammai *SHAM ay igh, SHAM igh (eye)*	Shaveh Kiriathaim *SHAY veh-kihr ih uh THAY im*
Shammoth *SHAM ahth*	Shavsha *SHAV shuh*
Shammua *SHAM yoo uh*	Shawsha *SHAW shuh*
Shammuah *SHAM yoo uh*	Sheal *SHEE al*
Shamsherai *SHAM shuh righ*	Shealtiel *shih AL tih el*
Shan *SHAN*	Shean *SHEE uhn*
Shapham *SHAY fam*	Shear *SHEE uhr*
Shaphan *SHAY fan*	Sheariah *SHEE uh RIGH uh*
Shaphat *SHAY fat*	Shearjashub *SHEE ahr-JAY shuhb*
Shapher *SHAY fuhr*	Shear-jashub *SHEE ahr-JAY shuhb*
Shaphir *SHAY fuhr*	Shear Jashub *SHEE ahr-JAY shuhb*
Sharai *SHAY righ*	
Sharaim *shuh RAY im*	Sheba *SHEE buh*
Sharar *SHAY ruhr*	Shebah *SHEE buh*
Sharezer *shuh REE zuhr*	Shebam *SHEE bam*
Sharon *SHEHR uhn*	Shebaniah *SHEB uh NIGH uh*
Sharonite *SHEHR uh night*	
Sharuhen *shuh ROO hen*	
Sharuhen *sheh ROO hen*	

S

a-HAT; ah-far FAHR; aw-call KAWL; ay-name NAYM; B-BAD; ch-CHEW; d-DAD; e,eh-met MET; ee-sea SEE; ew-truth TREWTH; f-FOOT, enough ee NUHF; g-GET; h-HIM; hw-whether HWEH thuhr; i, ih-city SI ti, or SIH tih; igh sign SIGHN, eye IGH; igh LIGHT; j-jack JAK, germ JUHRM; k-KISS, chorus KOH ruhss, ks-(for x) ox AHKS; kw-quail KWAYL; l-live LIHV, LIGHV; m-more MOHR; ng-ring RING; oh-go GOH, row ROH (a boat); oo-LOOK; oo-boot BOOT

144

Shebarim   *SHEB uh rim*

Shebat   *SHEE bat*

Sheber   *SHEE buhr*

Shebna   *SHEB nuh*

Shebnah   *SHEB nuh*

Shebuel   *shi BYOO uhl*

Shecaniah   *SHEK uh NIGH uh*

Shechaniah   *SHEK uh NIGH uh*

Shechem   *SHEK uhm*

Shechemite   *SHEK uhm ight*

Shedeur   *SHED ih uhr*

Sheerah   *SHEE uh ruh*

Shehariah   *SHEE huh RIGH uh*

shekel   *SHEK uhl*

Shekinah   *shuh KIGH nuh*

Shelah   *SHEE luh*

Shelahite   *SHEE luh hight*

Shelanite   *SHEE luhn ight*

Shelemiah   *SHEL uh MIGH uh*

Sheleph   *SHEE lef*

Shelesh   *SHEE lesh*

Shelomi   *shih LOH migh*

Shelomith   *shih LOH mith*

Shelomoth   *shih LOH mahth*

Shelumiel   *shih LOO mih el*

Shem   *SHEM*

Shema   *SHEE mah, shuh MAH*

Shemaah   *shih MAY uh*

Shemaiah   *shih MAY yuh*

Shemariah   *SHEM uh RIGH uh*

Shemeber   *shem EE buhr*

Shemed   *SHEE mid*

Shemei   *SHEM ih igh (eye)*

Shemer   *SHEE muhr*

Shemesh   *SHEM ish*

Shemiah   *shih MIGH uh*

Shemida   *shih MIGH duh*

Shemidah   *shih MIGH duh*

Shemidaite   *shih MIGH duh ight*

Sheminith   *SHEM uh nith*

Shemiramoth   *shih MIHR uh mahth*

Shemite   *SHEM ight*

Shemoth   *SHEE mahth*

Shemuel   *SHEM yoo el*

Shen   *SHEN*

Shenazar   *shih NAY zuhr*

Shenazzar   *shih NAY zuhr*

Shenir   *SHEE nuhr*

Sheol   *SHEE ohl*

Shepham   *SHEE fam*

Shephathiah   *SHEF uh THIGH uh*

S

ow-cow KOW, out OWT; oy-boil BOYL; p-PAT; r-RAN; s-star STAHR, tsetse SET see; sh-show SHOH, action AK shuhn, mission MIH shuhn, vicious VIH shuhss; t-tie TIGH, Thomas TAH muhss; th-thin THIN or THIHN; th-there THEHR; tw-TWIN; u, uh-tub TUB or TUHB, Joshua JAHSH yew uh, term TUHRM; v-veil VAYL, of AHV; w-WAY; wh (whether) see hw; y-year YEER; z-xerox ZIHR ahks, ZEE rahks, his HIZ or HIHZ, zebra ZEE bruh; zh-version VUHR zhuhn

145

Shephatiah   *SHEF uh TIGH uh*

Shephelah   *SHEF fih lah*

Shepher   *SHEE fuhr*

Shephi   *SHEE figh*

Shepho   *SHEE foh*

Shephupham   *shih FYOO fam*
(few)

Shephuphan   *shih FYOO fan*
(few)

Sherah   *SHEE ruh*

Sherebiah   *SHER uh BIGH uh*

Sheresh   *SHEE resh*

Sherezer   *shih REE zuhr*

Sheshach   *SHEE shak*

Sheshai   *SHEE shigh*

Sheshak   *SHEE shak*

Sheshan   *SHEE shan*

Sheshbazzar   *shesh BAZ uhr*

Sheth   *SHETH*

Shetha-boznai   *SHEE
thahr-BAHZ nigh*

Shethar   *SHEE thahr*

Shethar-baznai   *SHEE
thahr-BAHZ nigh*

Shethar-bozenai   *SHEE
thahr-BAHZ ih nigh*

Shethar-bozenai   *SHEE
thahr-BAHZ ih nigh*

Sheva   *SHEE vuh*

Shibah   *SHIB uh*

shibboleth   *SHIB oh leth*

Shibmah   *SHIB muh*

Shicron   *SHIK rahn*

Shiggaion   *shih GAY ahn*

Shiggionoth   *SHIG ih OH
nahth*

Shigionoth   *SHIG ih OH nahth*

Shihon   *SHIGH hahn*

Shihor   *SHIGH hawr*

Shihor-libnath   *SHIGH
hawr-LIB nath*

Shihorlibnath   *SHIGH
hawr-LIB nath*

Shihor Libnath   *SHIGH
hawr-LIB nath*

Shikkeron   *SHIK uhr rahn*

Shilhi   *SHIL high*

Shilhim   *SHIL him*

Shillem   *SHIL em*

Shillemite   *SHIL em might*

Shiloah   *shigh LOH uh*

Shiloh   *SHIGH loh*

Shiloni   *shigh LOH nigh*

Shilonite   *SHIGH loh night*

Shilshah   *SHIL shah*

Shimea   *SHIM ih uh*

Shimeah   *SHIM ih uh*

Shimeam   *SHIM ih am*

a-HAT; ah-far FAHR; aw-call KAWL; ay-name NAYM; B-BAD; ch-CHEW; d-DAD; e,eh-met
MET; ee-sea SEE; ew-truth TREWTH; f-FOOT, enough ee NUHF; g-GET; h-HIM; hw-whether
HWEH thuhr; i, ih-city SI ti, or SIH tih; igh sign SIGHN, eye IGH; igh LIGHT; j-jack JAK, germ
JUHRM; k-KISS, chorus KOH ruhss, ks-(for x) ox AHKS; kw-quail KWAYL; l-live LIHV, LIGHV;
m-more MOHR; ng-ring RING; oh-go GOH, row ROH (a boat); oo-LOOK; oo-boot BOOT

Shimeath *SHIM ih ath*

Shimeathite *SHIM ih uh thight*

Shimei *SHIM ih igh (eye)*

Shimeite *SHIM ee ight*

Shimeon *SHIM ih uhn*

Shimhi *SHIM high*

Shimi *SHIM igh (eye)*

Shimite *SHIM ight*

Shimma *SHIM uh*

Shimon *SHIGH mahn*

Shimrath *SHIM rath*

Shimri *SHIM righ*

Shimrith *SHIM rith*

Shimrom *SHIM rahm*

Shimron *SHIM rahn*

Shimronite *SHIM rahn ight*

Shimronmeron *SHIM rahn-MEE rahn*

Shimron-meron *SHIM rahn-MEE rahn*

Shimron Meron *SHIM rahn-MEE rahn*

Shimshai *SHIM shigh*

shin (Hebrew letter) *SHEEN*

Shinab *SHIGH nab*

Shinar *SHIGH nahr*

Shion *SHIGH ahn*

Shiphi *SHIGH figh*

Shiphmite *SHIF might*

Shiphrah *SHIF ruh*

Shiphtan *SHIF tuhn*

Shiqmona *sheek MOH nuh*

Shir Hashirim *SHIHR-HAH shuh rim*

Shisha *SHIGH shuh*

Shishak *SHIGH shak*

Shitrai *SHIT ray igh, SHIT righ*

shittah *SHIT uh*

Shittah *SHIT uh*

shittim *SHIT im*

Shittim *SHIT im*

Shiza *SHIGH zuh*

Shoa *SHOH uh*

Shobab *SHOH bab*

Shobach *SHOH bak*

Shobai *SHOH bay igh, SHOH bigh*

Shobal *SHOH bal*

Shobek *SHOH bek*

Shobi *SHOH bigh*

Shocho *SHOH koh*

Shochoh *SHOH koh*

Shoco *SHOH koh*

shofar *SHOH fahr*

Shofetim *SHOH fuh tim*

Shoham *SHOH ham*

S

ow-cow KOW, out OWT; oy-boil BOYL; p-PAT; r-RAN; s-star STAHR, tsetse SET see; sh-show SHOH, action AK shuhn, mission MIH shuhn, vicious VIH shuhss; t-tie TIGH, Thomas TAH muhss; th-thin THIN or THIHN; th-there THEHR; tw-TWIN; u, uh-tub TUB or TUHB, Joshua JAHSH yew uh, term TUHRM; v-veil VAYL, of AHV; w-WAY; wh (whether) see hw; y-year YEER; z-xerox ZIHR ahks, ZEE rahks, his HIZ or HIHZ, zebra ZEE bruh; zh-version VUHR zhuhn

147

Shomer *SHOH muhr*

Shomron *SHOHM rahn*

Shophach *SHOH fak*

Shophan *SHOH fan*

shophar *SHOH fahr*

Shoshanim *shoh SHAN im*

Shoshannim *shoh SHAN im*

Shoshannim-eduth *shoh SHAN im-EE duhth*

Shoshannim Eduth *shoh SHAN im-EE duhth*

Shua *SHOO uh*

Shuah *SHOO uh*

Shual *SHOO uhl*

Shubael *SHOO bay el*

Shuh *SHOO*

Shuhah *SHOO ha*

Shuham *SHOO ham*

Shuhamite *SHOO ham ight*

Shuhite *SHOO hight*

Shulamite *SHOO lam ight*

Shulammite *SHOO lam ight*

Shumathite *SHOO math ight*

Shunamite *SHOO nuhm ight*

Shunammite *SHOO nuhm ight*

Shunem *SHOO nem*

Shuni *SHOO nigh*

Shunite *SHOO night*

Shupham *SHOO fam*

Shuphamite *SHOO fam ight*

Shuppim *SHUHP im*

Shuppite *SHUH pight*

Shur *SHOOR (OO as in look), SHOOR*

Shuruppak *shuh ROO puhk*

Shushan *SHOO shan*

Shushanchite *SHOO shan kight*

Shushan-eduth *SHOO shan-EE duhth*

Shushan Eduth *SHOO shan-EE duhth*

Shuthalhite *shoo THAL hight*

Shuthelah *SHOO thuh luh*

Shuthelahite *shoo THEE luh hight*

Shuthelaite *shoo THEE luh ight*

Shuthite *SHOO thight*

Sia *SIGH uh*

Siaha *SIGH uh huh*

Sibbecai *SIB uh kigh*

Sibbechai *SIB uh kigh*

sibboleth *SIB oh leth*

Sibmah *SIB muh*

Sibraim *SIB ray im*

Sibylline *SIB uh leen*

---

a-HAT; ah-far FAHR; aw-call KAWL; ay-name NAYM; B-BAD; ch-CHEW; d-DAD; e,eh-met MET; ee-sea SEE; ew-truth TREWTH; f-FOOT, enough ee NUHF; g-GET; h-HIM; hw-whether HWEH thuhr; i, ih-city SI ti, or SIH tih; igh sign SIGHN, eye IGH; igh LIGHT; j-jack JAK, germ JUHRM; k-KISS, chorus KOH ruhss, ks-(for x) ox AHKS; kw-quail KWAYL; l-live LIHV, LIGHV; m-more MOHR; ng-ring RING; oh-go GOH, row ROH (a boat); oo-LOOK; oo-boot BOOT

Sicarii *sih KAHR ee igh*

Sichem *SIGH kem*

Sicyon *SISH ih uhn*

Siddim *SID im*

Side *SIGH dee*

Sidon *SIGH duhn*

Sidonian *sigh DOH nih uhn*

Sidrach *SID rak*

sigma (Greek letter) *SIHG muh*

Sihon *SIGH hahn*

Sihor *SIGH hawr*

Sikkuth *SIK uhth*

Silas *SIGH luhs*

Silla *SIL uh*

Silo *SIGH loh*

Siloah *sigh LOH uh*

Siloam *sigh LOH uhm*

Silvanus *sil VAY nuhs*

Silwan *SIHL wahn*

Simalcue *sih MAL kyoo ee*

Simeon *SIM ih uhn*

Simeonite *SIM ih uh night*

Simmagir *SIM uh guhr*

Simon *SIGH muhn*

Simon-Peter *SIGH muhn-PEE tuhr*

Simri *SIM righ*

Sin *SIN*

sin (Hebrew letter) *SEEN*

Sina *SIGH nuh*

Sinai *SIGH nigh, SIGH nay igh (eye)*

Sinaitic *SIGHN ih IT ik*

Sinaiticus *SIGHN ih IT uh kuhs*

Sinim *SIGH nim*

Sinite *SIGH night*

Sion *SIGH uhn*

Siphmoth *SIF mahth*

Sippai *SIP ay igh, SIP igh (eye)*

Sippar *sih PAHR*

Sira *SIGH ruh*

Sirach *SIGH rahk*

Sirah *SIGH ruh*

Sirion *SIHR ih ahn*

Sisera *SIS uh ruh*

Sisinnes *sih SIN ess*

Sisamai *SIS uh migh*

Sismai *SIS migh*

sistrum *SIS troom (oo as in look)*

Sithri *SITH righ*

Sitnah *SIT nuh*

Sivan *SIGH van*

Siyon *SIGH yahn*

Smyrna *SMUHR nuh*

S

ow-cow KOW, out OWT; oy-boil BOYL; p-PAT; r-RAN; s-star STAHR, tsetse SET see; sh-show SHOH, action AK shuhn, mission MIH shuhn, vicious VIH shuhss; t-tie TIGH, Thomas TAH muhss; th-thin THIN or THIHN; th-there THEHR; tw-TWIN; u, uh-tub TUB or TUHB, Joshua JAHSH yew uh, term TUHRM; v-veil VAYL; of AHV; w-WAY; wh (whether) see hw; y-year YEER; z-xerox ZIHR ahks, ZEE rahks, his HIZ or HIHZ, zebra ZEE bruh; zh-version VUHR zhuhn

So *SOH*

Socho *SOH koh*

Sochoh *SOH koh*

Soco *SOH koh*

Socoh *SOH koh*

Sodi *SOH digh*

Sodom *SAHD uhm*

Sodoma *SAHD oh muh*

Sodomite *SAHD uhm <u>ight</u>*

Sohar *SOH hahr*

Soharite *SOH huh <u>right</u>*

Solomon *SAHL uh muhn*

Solomonic *SAHL uh MAHN ik*

Song of Solomon
  SAHNG-ahv–SAHL uh muhn

Sopater *SAHP uh tuhr, SOH puh tuhr*

Sophar *SOH fahr*

Sophereth *SAHF uh reth*

Sopherim *SAHF uh rim*

Sophia *soh FEE uh*

Sophonias *SAHF uh NIGH uhs*

Sorek *SOH rek*

Sores *SOH rees*

Sorites *SOH rih tayss*

Sosipater *soh SIP uh tuhr*

Sosthenes *SAHS thuh neez*

Sostratus *SAHS truh tuhs*

Sotai *SOH tay igh, SOH tigh*

Soter *SOH tehr*

soteriological *soh TIHR ee uh LAHJ ih kuhl*

soteriology *soh TIHR ee AHL uh jee*

Spain *SPAYN*

Sparta *SPAHR tuh*

Spartan *SPAHR tuhn*

Spirit *SPIHR it*

Stachys *STAY kiss*

stacte *STAK tee*

stadia *STAY dih uh*

stater *STAY tuhr*

stela *STEE luh*

stelae *STEE lee*

stele *STEE lee*

Stephanas *STEF uh nuhs*

Stephen *STEE vuhn*

steppe *STEP*

stoa *STOH uh*

Stoic *STOH ihk*

Stoicism *STOH ih SIZ uhm*

Stoick *STOH ihk*

storax *STOHR aks*

Strabo *STRAY boh*

strata (pl.) *STRA tuh*

stratigraphy *struh TIH gruh fih*

---

a-HAT; ah-far FAHR; aw-call KAWL; ay-name NAYM; B-BAD; ch-CHEW; d-DAD; e,eh-met MET; ee-sea SEE; ew-truth TREWTH; f-FOOT, enough ee NUHF; g-GET; h-HIM; hw-whether HWEH thuhr; i, ih-city SI ti, or SIH tih; igh sign SIGHN, eye IGH; <u>igh</u> LIGHT; j-jack JAK, germ JUHRM; k-KISS, chorus KOH ruhss, ks-(for x) ox AHKS; kw-quail KWAYL; l-live LIHV, LIGHV; m-more MOHR; ng-ring RING; oh-go GOH; row ROH (a boat); oo-LOOK; <u>oo</u>-boot B<u>OO</u>T

stratum *STRA tuhm*

strophe *STROH fee*

Stygian *STIH jih uhn*

Sua *SOO uh*

Suah *SOO uh*

Suba *SOO buh*

Subai *SOO bigh*

Subas *SOO buhs*

Sucathite *SOO kuh thight*

Succoth *SUHK ahth*

Succoth-benoth *SUHK ahth-BEE nahth*

Succothbenoth *SUHK ahth-BEE nahth*

Succoth Benoth *SUHK ahth-BEE nahth*

Suchathite *SOO kuh thight*

Sud *SUHD*

Sudan *SOO dan*

Sudanese *SOO duh neez*

Sudias *SOO dih uhs*

Suetonius *swee TOH nih uhs*

Suez *SOO ehz*

Sukkiim *SUHK ih im*

Sukkite *SUHK kight*

Sukkoth *SUHK ahth*

Sumer *SOO muhr*

Sumeria *soo MEHR ih uh*

Sumerian *soo MEHR ih uhn*

Suph *SOOF*

Suphah *SOO fuh*

Sur *SUHR*

Susa *SOO suh*

Susah *SOO suh*

Susanchite *SOO san kight*

Susanna *soo ZAN uh*

Susi *SOO sigh*

Susian *SOO sih uhn*

Susim *SOO sim*

Susitha *soo SIGH thuh*

suzerain *soo zuh rehn*

suzerainty *SOO zuh RUHN tee*

sycamine *SIK uh meen*

Sychar *SIGH kahr*

Sychem *SIGH kem*

Syelus *suh EE luhs*

Syene *sigh EE nih*

Symeon *SIM ih uhn*

Symmachus *SIM uh kuhs*

synagogue *SIN uh gahg*

syncretism *SIN kruh TIHZ uhm*

synopsis *sih NAHP siss*

synoptic *sih NAHP tik*

Syntyche *SIN tih kee*

Syracuse *SIHR uh kyooz*

Syria *SIHR ih uh*

S

---

ow-cow KOW, out OWT; oy-boil BOYL; p-PAT; r-RAN; s-star STAHR, tsetse SET see; sh-show SHOH, action AK shuhn, mission MIH shuhn, vicious VIH shuhss; t-tie TIGH, Thomas TAH muhss; th-thin THIN or THIHN; th-there THEHR; tw-TWIN; u, uh-tub TUB or TUHB, Joshua JAHSH yew uh, term TUHRM; v-veil VAYL, of AHV; w-WAY; wh (whether) see hw; y-year YEER; z-xerox ZIHR ahks, ZEE rahks, his HIZ or HIHZ, zebra ZEE bruh; zh-version VUHR zhuhn

Syriac *SIHR ih ak*

Syriack *SIHR ih ak*

Syria-damascus *SIHR ih uh-duh MASS kuhs*

Syria-maachah *SIHR ih uh-MAY uh kah*

Syrian *SIHR ih uhn*

Syro-Ephraimite *SIGH roh-EE fray uh might*

Syro-Israelite *SIGH roh-IZ ray uh light*

Syrophenecian *SIGH roh-fih NEE shuhn*

Syrophoenician *SIGH roh-fih NEE shuhn*

Syro-phoenician *SIGH roh-fih NEE shuhn*

Syrtis *SUHR tiss*

T

Taanach *TAY uh nak*

Taanathshiloh *TAY uh nath-SHIGH loh*

Taanath-shiloh *TAY uh nath-SHIGH loh*

Taanath Shiloh *TAY uh nath-SHIGH loh*

Tabaliah *TAB uh LIGH uh*

Tabaoth *TA ba ohth*

Tabbaoth *TAB ay ahth*

Tabbath *TAB uhth*

Tabbur-haares *TAB uhr-hay AHR ess*

Tabeal *TAY bih uhl*

Tabeel *TAB ih uhl*

Tabellius *tuh BEL ih uhs*

Taberah *TAB uh ruh*

Tabernacle *TAB uhr NAK uhl*

Tabitha *TAB ih thuh*

Tabor *TAY bawr*

tabret *TAB ret*

Tabrimmon *tab RIM uhn*

Tabrimon *tab RIM uhn*

tache *TAK*

Tachemon *TAK ee muhn*

Tachmonite *TAK muh night*

Tacitus *TASS uh tuhs*

Tadmor *TAD mawr*

Tahan *TAY han*

Tahanite *TAY han ight*

Tahapanes *tuh HAP uh neez*

Tahash *TAY hash*

Tahath *TAY hath*

Tahchemonite *tah KEE muh night*

Tahkemonite *tah KEE muh
night*

Tahpanhes *TA puhn heez*

Tahpannes *TA pih neez*

Tahpenes *TA pih neez*

Tahrea *TA ree uh*

Tahtim-hodshi *TA
tim–HAHD shigh*

Tahtim Hodshi *TA
tim–HAHD shigh*

talent *TAL uhnt*

talitha-cumi *TAL ih
thuh–KOO mih*

talitha cumi *TAL ih thuh–KOO
mih*

talitha-koum *TAL ih thuh
KOOM*

Talmai *TAL migh*

Talmon *TAL mahn*

Talmud *TAL mood (oo as in
look)*

Talmudic *tal MOOD ik (OO
as in look)*

Talsas *TAL suhs*

Tamah *TAY muh*

Tamar *TAY mahr*

tamarisk *TAM uh risk*

Tammuz *TAM uhz*

Tanach *TAY nahk, TAH nahk*

Tanak *TAY nak, TAH nahk*

Tanakh *TAY nak*

Tanhumeth *tan HYOO meth*

Tanis *TAN iss*

Taphath *TAY fath*

Taphnes *TAF neez*

Taphnez *TAF neez*

Taphon *TAY fahn*

Tappuah *TA pyoo uh*

Tarah *TAY ruh*

Taralah *TAHR uh lah*

Tarea *TAY rih uh*

Targum *TAHR guhm*

Tarpelite *TAHR puh light*

Tarshish *TAHR shish*

Tarshishah *TAHR shuh shah*

Tarsus *TAHR suhs*

Tartak *TAHR tak*

Tartan *TAHR tan*

Tartarus *TAHR tuh ruhs*

Taschith *TASS kith*

Tatam *TAY tuhm*

Tatnai *TAT nigh, TAT nay
igh (eye)*

Tattenai *TAT ih nigh*

tau (Greek letter) *TAW*

Taurus *TAW ruhs*

taw (Hebrew letter) *TAW*

Tebah *TEE buh*

T

ow-cow KOW, out OWT; oy-boil BOYL; p-PAT; r-RAN; s-star STAHR, tsetse SET see; sh-show SHOH, action AK shuhn, mission MIH shuhn, vicious VIH shuhss; t-tie TIGH, Thomas TAH muhss; th-thin THIN or THIHN; th-there THEHR; tw-TWIN; u, uh-tub TUB or TUHB, Joshua JAHSH yew uh, term TUHRM; v-veil VAYL, of AHV; w-WAY; wh (whether) see hw; y-year YEER; z-xerox ZIHR ahks, ZEE rahks, his HIZ or HIHZ, zebra ZEE bruh; zh-version VUHR zhuhn

153

Tebaliah   *TEB uh ligh uh*

Tebeth   *TEE beth*

Tehaphnehes   *tih HAF nuh heez*

Tehillim   *tih HIL im*

Tehinnah   *tih HIN uh*

teil   *TEEL*

tekel   *TEE kel, TEK uhl*

Tekoa   *tih KOH uh*

Tekoah   *tih KOH uh*

Tekoite   *tih KOH ight*

tel   *TELL*

Tel   *TEHL (tell)*

Telabib   *TEL-AY bib, uh BEEB*

Tel-abib   *TEL-AY bib, uh BEEB*

Tel Abib   *TEL-AY bib, uh BEEB*

Telah   *TEE luh*

Telaim   *tih LAY im*

Telam   *TEE luhm*

Tel-assar   *tel-ASS uhr*

Telassar   *tih LASS uhr*

Tel Assar   *tel-ASS uhr*

Tel Aviv   *TEL-uh VEEV*

Tel Balata   *TELL-buh LAH tuh*

Tel Batash   *TELL-bah TAHSH*

Teleilat Ghassul   *TELL ih laht-gah SOOL*

Telem   *TEE lehm*

Tel Erani   *TELL-ee RAHN ee*

Tel-haresha   *TEL-huh REE shuh*

Tel Haror   *TELL-hah ROHR*

Tel-harsa   *tel-HAHR suh*

Tel-harsha   *tel-HAHR shuh*

Telharsha   *tel-HAHR shuh*

Tel Harsha   *tel-HAHR shuh*

tell   *TEL*

Tell Abu Hawam   *tell-ah BOO-hah WAHN*

Tell Abu Matar   *tell-ah BOO-muh TAHR*

Tell Atchana   *tell-aht KAH nuh*

Tell Beit Mirsim   *tell-bayt-mihr SEEM, MIHR sim*

Tell Brak   *tell-BRAK*

Tell Deir' Alla   *tell-deer-AH lah*

Tell ed-Duweir   *tell-ed-doo WEER*

Tell el-Ajjul   *tell-el-ah JUHL*

Tell el-Amarna   *TEL-el-uh MAHR nuh*

---

a-HAT; ah-far FAHR; aw-call KAWL; ay-name NAYM; B-BAD; ch-CHEW; d-DAD; e,eh-met MET; ee-sea SEE; ew-truth TREWTH; f-FOOT, enough ee NUHF; g-GET; h-HIM; hw-whether HWEH thuhr; i, ih-city SI ti, or SIH tih; igh sign SIGHN, eye IGH; igh LIGHT; j-jack JAK, germ JUHRM; k-KISS, chorus KOH ruhss, ks-(for x) ox AHKS; kw-quail KWAYL; l-live LIHV, LIGHV; m-more MOHR; ng-ring RING; oh-go GOH, row ROH (a boat); oo-LOOK; oo-boot BOOT

Tell el-Farah   *tell-el-FEHR uh*

Tell el-FUL   *tell-el-FULL*

Tell el-Harari   *tell-el-hah RAHR ee*

Tell el-Hesi   *tell-el-HEH sih*

Tell el-Husn   *tell-el-HOO suhn*

Tell el-Kheleifeh   *tell-el-keh LEE feh*

Tell el-Mutesellim   *tell-el-muh TESS uh leem*

Tell el-Qasileh   *tell-el-kuh SEE leh*

Tell el-Qedah   *tell-el-KEH duh*

Tell el-Yahudiyeh   *tell-el-yeh HOO dih yay*

Tell en-Nasbeh   *tell-en-NAZ beh*

Tell es-Sa'ideyeh   *tell-ess-suh DEE yuh*

Tell es-Sultan   *tell-ess-sool TAHN*

Tell ez-Zakariyet   *tell-ez-zak uh REE uh*

Tell Fekheriyeh   *tell-fek uh REE uh*

Tell Halif   *tell-hah LEEF*

Tell Hesban   *tell-HESS ban*

Tell Hesban   *tell-HESS bahn*

Tell Jemmeh   *tell-JIM uh*

Tell Judaiyideh   *tell-joo DIGH yuh deh*

Tell Keisan   *tell-kee SAHN*

Tell Mardikh   *tell-mahr DEEK*

Telloh   *TEHL oh*

Tell Qasile   *tell-kah SEE leh*

Tell Sandahannah   *tell-san duh HAN uh*

Tell Siran   *tell-see RAHN*

Tell Zakariyeh   *tell-zak uh REE yuh*

Tel Masos   *TELL-mah SOHSS*

Tel-melah   *tel-MEE luh*

Telmelah   *tel-MEE luh*

Tel Melah   *tel-MEE luh*

Tel Miqne   *TELL-MIK nay*

Tel Sera'   *TELL-SEH ruh*

Tema   *TEE muh*

Temah   *TEE muh*

Teman   *TEE man*

Temani   *TEE muh nigh*

Temanite   *TEE muhn ight*

Temeni   *TEE muh nigh, TEM uh nigh*

Temenite   *TEM uh night*

tenon   *TEN uhn*

tepe   *TEH peh*

Tepe Gawra   *TEH peh-GAH ruh*

Tepe Hissar   *TEH peh-HISS ahr*

Tephon   *TEE fahn*

Terah   *TEE ruh, TEHR uh*

teraphim   *TEHR uh fim*

terebinth   *TEHR uh binth*

Teresh   *TEE resh*

Tertius   *TUHR shih uhs, TUHR shuhss*

Tertullian   *TUHR TUHL ih uhn*

Tertullus   *tuhr TUHL uhs*

Testament   *TESS tuh muhnt*

Teta   *TAY tuh*

teth (Hebrew letter)   *TAYTH*

tetrarch   *TET rahrk*

Tetrateuch   *TET truh tyook*

tetter   *TET uhr*

Textus Receptus   *TEKS tuhs-ree SEP tuhs*

Thaddaeus   *THAD ih uhs*

Thaddeus   *THAD ih uhs*

Thahash   *THAY hash (TH as in thin)*

Thamah   *THAY muh (TH as in thin)*

Thamar   *THAY mahr (TH as in thin)*

Thammuz   *THAM uhz (TH as in thin)*

Thamnatha   *THAM nuh thuh (TH as in thin)*

Thara   *THAY ruh (TH as in thin)*

Thares   *THAY ress (TH as in thin)*

Tharra   *THAY rah (TH as in thin)*

Tharshish   *THAHR shish (TH as in thin)*

Thassi   *THASS igh (eye) (TH as in thin)*

Thebes   *THEEBS, THEEBZ (TH as in thin)*

Thebez   *THEE bez (TH as in thin)*

Thecoe   *thuh KOH ee (th as in thin)*

Thelasar   *thih LAY sahr*

Thelersas   *thih LUHR suhs (th as in thin)*

Theman   *THEE muhn (TH as in thin)*

Theocanus   *thee AHK uh nuhs (th as in thin)*

theocracy   *thee AHK ruh sih*

theocratic   *THEE oh KRAT ik*

Theodotion   *THEE oh DOH shuhn*

---

a-HAT; ah-far FAHR; aw-call KAWL; ay-name NAYM; B-BAD; ch-CHEW; d-DAD; e,eh-met MET; ee-sea SEE; ew-truth TREWTH; f-FOOT, enough ee NUHF; g-GET; h-HIM; hw-whether HWEH thuhr; i, ih-city SI ti, or SIH tih; igh sign SIGHN, eye IGH; <u>igh</u> <u>LIGHT</u>; j-jack JAK, germ JUHRM; k-KISS, chorus KOH ruhss; ks-(for x) ox AHKS; kw-quail KWAYL; l-live LIHV, LIGHV; m-more MOHR; ng-ring RING; oh-go GOH, row ROH (a boat); oo-LOOK; <u>oo</u>-boot B<u>OO</u>T

Theodotus   *thee AHD uh tuhs*
(th as in thin)

theological   THEE *uh LAHJ ih*
kuhl

theology   *thee AHL uh jih*

theophany   *thee AHF uh nih*

Theophilus   *thee AHF ih luhs*
(th as in thin)

Thera   THIHR *uh*

Theras   THEE *ruhs (TH as in*
thin)

Thermeleth   *thuhr MEE leth*
(th as in thin)

Thermopylae   *thuhr MAH*
puh lee (th as in thin)

Thessalonian   THESS *uh LOH*
nih uhn (th as in thin)

Thessalonica   THESS *uh loh*
NIGH *kuh*

theta (Greek letter)   THAY
tuh (TH as in thin)

Theudas   THOO *duhs*

Thimnathah   THIM *nuh tha*
(a as in cat)

Thisbe   THIS *bee (TH as in*
thin)

Thomas   TAHM *uhs*

Thomoi   THAHM *oy (TH as*
in thin)

Thrace   THRAYSS

Thracian   THRAY *shih uhn*
(TH as in thin)

Thraseas   *thray SEE uhs (th as*
in thin)

Three Taverns   THREE-TAV
uhrns

Thummim   THUHM *im*

Thutmose   THUT *mohss suh,*
THUT *mohss*

Thyatira   THIGH *uh* TIGH *ruh*

thyine   THIGH *in*

Tiamat   *tee AH maht*

Tiber   TIGH *buhr*

Tiberia   *tigh BIHR ih uh*

Tiberias   *tigh BIHR ih uhs*

Tiberius   *tigh BIHR ih uhs*

Tibhath   TIB *hath*

Tibni   TIB *nigh*

Ticon   TIGH *kuhn*

Tidal   TIGH *dal*

Tiglath-pileser   TIG *lath-pih*
LEE *zuhr*

Tiglathpileser   TIG *lath-pih*
LEE *zuhr*

Tigris   TIGH *griss*

Tikvah   TIK *vah*

Tikvath   TIK *vath*

Tilgath-pilneser   TIL *gath-pil*
NEE *zuhr*

T

ow-cow KOW, out OWT; oy-boil BOYL; p-PAT; r-RAN; s-star STAHR, tsetse SET see; sh-show
SHOH, action AK shuhn, mission MIH shuhn, vicious VIH shuhss; t-tie TIGH, Thomas TAH muhss;
th-thin THIN or THIHN; th-there THEHR; tw-TWIN; u, uh-tub TUB or TUHB, Joshua JAHSH yew
uh, term TUHRM; v-veil VAYL, of AHV; w-WAY; wh (whether) see hw; y-year YEER; z-xerox ZIHR
ahks, ZEE rahks, his HIZ or HIHZ, zebra ZEE bruh; zh-version VUHR zhuhn

157

Tilgathpilneser *TIL gath-pil*
  NEE zuhr

Tilon *TIGH lahn*

Timaeus *tigh MEE uhs*

Timna *TIM nuh*

Timnah *TIM nuh*

Timnah-serah *TIM*
  nuh-SIHR uh

Timnat *TIM nat*

Timnath *TIM nath*

Timnath-heres *TIM*
  nath-HEE reez

Timnathheres *TIM*
  nath-HEE reez

Timnath Heres *TIM*
  nath-HEE reez

Timnath-serah *TIM*
  nath-SEE ruh

Timnathserah *TIM nath-SEE*
  ruh

Timnath Serah *TIM*
  nath-SEE ruh

Timnite *TIM night*

Timon *TIGH mahn*

Timotheus *tih MOH thih*
  uhs

Timothy *TIM uh thih*

Tindale *TIN duhl, TIN dayl*

Tiphsah *TIF suh*

Tiras *TIGH ruhs*

Tirathite *TIGH rath ight*

Tirhakah *tuhr HAY kuh*

Tirhanah *tuhr HAY nuh*

Tiria *TIHR ih uh*

Tirshatha *tuhr SHAH thuh*

Tirzah *TUHR zah, TIHR*
  zuh

Tishbe *TISH bee*

Tishbite *TISH bight*

Tishri *TISH ree*

Titan *TIGH tuhn*

Titius *TIT ih uhs (Greek),*
  TIH shuhs (Roman)

Titius Justus *TIT ih*
  uhs-JUHS tuhs, TIH shuhs
  (Roman)

tittle *TIT uhl*

Titus *TIGH tuhs*

Tiz *TIHZ*

Tizite *TIGH zight, TIZ ight*

Toah *TOH uh*

Tob *TAHB*

Tobadonijah *TAHB-ad uh*
  NIGH juh

Tob-adonijah *TAHB-ad uh*
  NIGH juh

Tobiad *toh BIGH uhd*

Tobiads *toh BIGH ads*

Tobiah *toh BIGH uh*

---

a-HAT; ah-far FAHR; aw-call KAWL; ay-name NAYM; B-BAD; ch-CHEW; d-DAD; e,eh-met
MET; ee-sea SEE; ew-truth TREWTH; f-FOOT, enough ee NUHF; g-GET; h-HIM; hw-whether
HWEH thuhr; i, ih-city SI ti, or SIH tih; igh sign SIGHN, eye IGH; igh LIGHT; j-jack JAK, germ
JUHRM; k-KISS, chorus KOH ruhss, ks-(for x) ox AHKS; kw-quail KWAYL; l-live LIHV, LIGHV;
m-more MOHR; ng-ring RING; oh-go GOH, row ROH (a boat); oo-LOOK; oo-boot BOOT

Tobias   *toh BIGH uhs*

Tobie   *TOH bee*

Tobiel   *TOH bee el*

Tobijah   *toh BIGH juh*

Tobit   *TOH bit*

Tochen   *TOH ken*

Togarmah   *toh GAHR muh*

Tohu   *TOH hyoo*

Toi   *TOH igh (eye)*

token   *TOH ken*

Tokhath   *TAHK hath*

Tola   *TOH luh*

Tolad   *TOH lad*

Tolaite   *TOH lay ight*

Tolbanes   *TAHL buh neez*

Tophel   *TOH fel*

Tophet   *TOH fet*

Topheth   *TOH feth*

topography   *tuh PAH gruh fih*

toponym   *TAH puh nim*

Torah   *TOH rah*

Tormah   *TAWR muh*

Tou   *TOH oo*

Toubiani   *TOO bih AY nih*

Trachonitis   *TRAK uh NIGH tiss*

Traconitis   *TRAK uh NIGH tiss*

Trajan   *TRAY juhn*

Trans-euphrates   *TRANS-yoo FRAY teez*

Transeuphrates   *TRANS-yoo FRAY teez*

transfiguration   *trans FIG yuh RAY shuhn*

transfigure   *trans FIG yuhr*

Trans-jordan   *TRANS-JAWR duhn*

Transjordan   *TRANS-JAWR duhn*

tribunal   *trigh BYOO nuhl*

tribune   *TRIB yoon*

trigon   *TRIGH gahn*

Tripolis   *TRIH puh liss*

Troas   *TROH az*

Trogyllium   *troh JIL ih uhm*

Trophimus   *TRAHF ih muhs*

Troy   *TROY*

Tryphaena   *trigh FEE nuh*

Tryphena   *trigh FEE nuh*

Trypho   *TRIGH foh*

Tryphon   *TRIGH fahn*

Tryphosa   *trigh FOH suh*

tsidkenu   *sih KEN oo*

Tubal   *TYOO buhl*

Tubal-cain   *TYOO buhl-KAYN*

Tubalcain   *TYOO buhl-KAYN*

T

ow-cow KOW, out OWT; oy-boil BOYL; p-PAT; r-RAN; s-star STAHR, tsetse SET see; sh-show SHOH, action AK shuhn, mission MIH shuhn, vicious VIH shuhss; t-tie TIGH, Thomas TAH muhss; th-thin THIN or THIHN; th-there THEHR; tw-TWIN; u, uh-tub TUB or TUHB, Joshua JAHSH yew uh, term TUHRM; v-veil VAYL, of AHV; w-WAY; wh (whether) see hw; y-year YEER; z-xerox ZIHR ahks, ZEE rahks, his HIZ or HIHZ, zebra ZEE bruh; zh-version VUHR zhuhn

Tubieni   *TOO bih EE nih*

Tuleilat el-Ghassul   *TOO lih laht–el–gah SOOL*

tumuli (pl.)   *TOO moo ligh*

tumulus   *TOO moo luhs*

Twin Brothers   *TWIN-BRUH thuhrz*

Tychicus   *TIK ih kuhs*

Tyndale   *TIN duhl, TIN dayl*

typology   *tigh PAHL uh jih*

Tyrannus   *tigh RAN uhs*

Tyre   *TIGHR*

Tyrian   *TIHR ih uhn*

Tyropean   *tigh roh PEE uhn, tuh ROH pih uhn*

Tyropoeon   *tigh ROH pee uhn*

Tyrus   *TIGH ruhs*

tz(s)ade (Hebrew letter)   *SAH deh*

U

Ucal   *YOO kal*

Uel   *YOO el*

Ugarit   *yoo GA rit*

Ugaritic   *yoo guh RIT ik*

Uknaz   *UHK naz*

Ulai   *YOO ligh, YOO lay igh (eye)*

Ulam   *YOO lam*

Ulla   *UHL uh*

Umayyad   *yoo MAH ad*

Ummah   *UHM uh*

uncial   *UHN shuhl*

unction   *UHNK shuhn*

Unleavened Bread   *uhn LEV uhnd-BRED*

Unni   *UHN igh (eye)*

Unno   *UHN oh*

upharsin   *yoo FAHR sin*

Uphaz   *YOO faz*

upsilon (Greek letter)   *OOP sih lahn*

Ur   *UHR*

Urartu   *yoo RAHR too*

Urbane   *UHR bayn*

Urbanus   *uhr BAY nuhs*

Uri   *yoo RIGH*

Uriah   *yoo RIGH uh*

Urias   *yoo RIGH uhs*

Uriel   *YOO rih el*

Urijah   *yoo RIGH juh*

Urim   *YOO rim*

Uruk   *YUHR uhk, OO ruhk*

Urukian   *yoo ROOK ih ahn (oo as in look)*

---

a-HAT; ah-far FAHR; aw-call KAWL; ay-name NAYM; B-BAD; ch-CHEW; d-DAD; e,eh-met MET; ee-sea SEE; ew-truth TREWTH; f-FOOT, enough ee NUHF; g-GET; h-HIM; hw-whether HWEH thuhr; i, ih-city SI ti, or SIH tih; igh sign SIGHN, eye IGH; igh LIGHT; j-jack JAK, germ JUHRM; k-KISS, chorus KOH ruhss, ks-(for x) ox AHKS; kw-quail KWAYL; l-live LIHV, LIGHV; m-more MOHR; ng-ring RING; oh-go GOH, row ROH (a boat); oo-LOOK; oo-boot BOOT

V

Urushalem   *yoo ROO shah
lehm*

Uthai   *YOO thigh*

Utica   *YOO tih kuh*

Utnapishtim   *yoot NAHF ish
tuhn*

Uz   *UHZ*

Uzai   *YOO zigh*

Uzal   *YOO zal*

Uzza   *UHZ uh*

Uzzah   *UHZ uh*

Uzzen-sheerah   *UH
zihn-SHEE ih ruh*

Uzzensheerah   *UH zihn-
SHEE ih ruh*

Uzzen Sheerah   *UH zihn-
SHEE ih ruh*

Uzzen-sherah   *UH zihn-
SHEE ruh*

Uzzen Sherah   *UH zihn-
SHEE ruh*

Uzzi   *UHZ igh (eye)*

Uzzia   *uh ZIGH uh*

Uzziah   *uh ZIGH uh*

Uzziel   *UHZ ih uhl*

Uzzielite   *uhz ih EE light*

Vaheb   *VAY heb*

Vaizatha   *VIGH zuh thuh*

Vajezatha   *vuh JEZ uh thuh*

Vaniah   *vuh NIGH uh*

Vashni   *VASH nigh*

Vashti   *VASH tigh*

vassal   *VASS uhl*

Vaticanus   *VAT ih KAN uhs*

vau   *VOO (OO as in look)*

Vedan   *VEE duhn*

vellum   *VEL uhm*

Veronica   *vuh RAHN ih kuh*

Vespasian   *vess PAY zhuhn*

Vesuvius   *veh SOO vih uhs*

Via Appia   *VEE ah-A(a) pee uh*

Via Dolorosa   *VEE ah-doh luh
ROH suh*

Via Egnatia   *VEE ah-eg NAY
shuh*

Via Maris   *VEE uh-MAH riss*

Victorinus   *vik tahr RIGH nuhs*

vizier   *vih ZEER, vuh ZEER*

Vophsi   *VAHF sigh*

votive   *VOH tihv*

Vulgate   *VUHL gayt*

---

ow-cow KOW, out OWT; oy-boil BOYL; p-PAT; r-RAN; s-star STAHR, tsetse SET see; sh-show
SHOH, action AK shuhn, mission MIH shuhn, vicious VIH shuhss; t-tie TIGH, Thomas TAH muhss;
th-thin THIN or THIHN; th-there THEHR; tw-TWIN; u, uh-tub TUB or TUHB, Joshua JAHSH yew
uh, term TUHRM; v-veil VAYL, of AHV; w-WAY; wh (whether) see hw; y-year YEER; z-xerox ZIHR
ahks, ZEE rahks, his HIZ or HIHZ, zebra ZEE bruh; zh-version VUHR zhuhn

W

Wadi   *WAH dih*

Wadi al'Arish   *WAH dih-al-ah REESH*

Wadi ed-Daliyah   *WAH dih-ed-DAHL yuh*

Wadi el-Hasi   *WAH dih-el-HAH sih*

Wadi el-Hesi   *WAH dih-el-HEH sih*

Wadi ez-Zarqa   *WAH dih-ez-ZAHR kuh*

Wadi Mujib   *WAH dih-moo JEEB*

Wadi Murabba'at   *WAH dih-MUHR uh baht*

Wadi Qelt   *WAH dih-KEHLT*

Wadi Qilt   *WAH dih-KIHLT*

Wadi Tumilat   *WAH dih-TOO muh laht*

Wadi Zerqa   *WAH dih-ZEHR kah*

Waheb   *WA heb (A as in cat)*

Warka   *WAR kah*

waw (Hebrew letter)   *WAW.*

Wayiqra   *wah YIK ruh*

Weeks   *WEEKS*

wen   *WEN*

Whitsuntide   *WHIT suhn tighd*

Wisdom   *WIZ duhm*

Wisdom of Sirach   *WIZ duhm-ahv-SIGH ruhk*

Wisdom of Solomon   *WIZ duhm-ahv-SAHL uh muhn*

Wyclif   *WIK lif*

Wycliffe   *WIK lif*

X

Xanthicus   *ZAN thih kuhs*

Xanthus   *ZAN thoos*

Xenophon   *ZEH nuh fuhn*

Xerxes   *ZUHRK seez*

xi (Greek letter)   *ZEE*

Y

Ya'udi   *yah OO dih*

Yad-abshalom   *yahd-AB shuh luhm*

Yah   *YAH*

W

Yahveh   *YAH weh*

Yahvist   *YAH wist*

Yahweh   *YAH weh*

Yahweh-nissi   *YAH weh-NISS igh (eye)*

Yahweh-shalom   *YAH weh-shah LOHM*

Yahweh-yireh   *YAH weh-YIHR eh*

Yahwist   *YAH wist*

Yam Suph   *yahm-SOOF*

Yarkon   *YAHR kahn*

Yarmuk   *YAHR muhk*

yarmulke   *YAH muhl kuh*

Yaudi   *YAW dih*

Yavan   *YAY van*

Yavne-yam   *YAHV neh-yahm*

Yeb   *YEHB*

Yehezqel   *yuh HEZ kuhl*

Yehoshua   *yuh HAHSH yoo uh*

Yenoam   *YIH noh ahm*

Yeshayahu   *YEE shah YAH hoo*

Yirmeyahu   *YIHR muh YAH hoo*

Yiron   *YIGH rahn*

yodh (Hebrew letter)   *YOHD*

Yom Kippur   *YAHM-kih POOR, KIH puhr*

Yoqneam   *YAK nee ahm*

Yurza   *YURT sah*

Z

Zaanaim   *ZAY uh NAY im*

Zaanan   *ZAY uh nan*

Zaanannim   *zay uh NAN im*

Zaavan   *ZAY uh van*

Zab   *ZAB*

Zabad   *ZAY bad*

Zabadaeans   *ZA buh DEE uhnz*

Zabadaius   *ZAB uh DAY yuhs*

Zabadean   *ZAB uh DEE uhn*

Zabbai   *ZAB igh, ZAB ay igh (eye)*

Zabbud   *ZAB uhd*

Zabdeus   *ZAB dee uhs*

Zabdi   *ZAB digh*

Zabdiel   *ZAB dih el*

Zabud   *ZAY buhd*

Zabulon   *ZAB yoo lahn*

Zaccai   *ZAK igh, ZAK ay igh (eye)*

Zacchaeus   *za KEE uhs*

Zaccheus   *za KEE uhs*

Zacchur   *ZAK uhr*

Zaccur   *ZAK uhr*

Zachai   *ZAK igh (eye)*

ow-cow KOW, out OWT; oy-boil BOYL; p-PAT; r-RAN; s-star STAHR, tsetse SET see; sh-show SHOH, action AK shuhn, mission MIH shuhn, vicious VIH shuhss; t-tie TIGH, Thomas TAH muhss; th-thin THIN or THIHN; th-there THEHR; tw-TWIN; u, uh-tub TUB or TUHB, Joshua JAHSH yew uh, term TUHRM; v-veil VAYL, of AHV; w-WAY; wh (whether) see hw; y-year YEER; z-xerox ZIHR ahks, ZEE rahks, his HIZ or HIHZ, zebra ZEE bruh; zh-version VUHR zhuhn

163

Zachariah   *ZAK uh RIGH uh*

Zacharias   *ZAK uh RIGH uhs*

Zacher   *ZAY kuhr*

Zadok   *ZAY dahk*

Zadokite   *ZAY dahk ight*

Zafed   *ZAH fed*

Zagros   *ZAY grahs, ZAG rahss*

Zaham   *ZAY ham*

Zahar   *ZAY hahr*

zain   *ZA yin*

Zair   *ZAY ihr*

Zakir   *zah KIHR*

Zakkur   *ZAK uhr*

Zalaph   *ZAY laf*

Zalmon   *ZAL muhn*

Zalmonah   *zal MOH nuh*

Zalmunna   *zal MUHN uh*

Zambri   *ZAM brigh*

Zamoth   *ZAY mahth*

Zamzummim   *zam ZUHM im*

Zamzummin   *zam ZUHM in*

Zamzummite   *zam ZUHM ight*

Zannanim   *zuh NAN im*

Zanoah   *za NOH uh*

Zaphaniah   *ZAF uh NIGH uh*

Zaphenath-paneah   *ZAF ee nath-pan EE uh*

Zaphenathpaneah   *ZAF ee nath-pan EE uh*

Zaphnath-paaneah   *ZAF nath-pay uh NEE uh*

Zaphon   *ZAY fahn*

Zara   *ZAY ruh*

Zaraces   *ZEHR uh seez*

Zarah   *ZEHR uh*

Zaraias   *zuh RAY yuhs*

Zarathushtra   *ZEHR uh THOOSH truh*

Zarathustra   *ZEHR uh THOOS truh*

Zardeus   *ZAR dee oos*

Zareah   *ZAY rih uh*

Zareathite   *ZAY rih uh thight*

Zared   *ZAY red*

Zarephath   *ZAR ih fath (A,a as in cat)*

Zaretan   *ZEHR ih tan (a as in cat)*

Zarethan   *ZEHR ih than (th as in thin)*

Zarethshahar   *ZAY reth SHAY hahr*

Zareth-shahar   *ZAY reth-SHAY hahr*

Zarhite   *ZAHR hight*

Zarius   *ZAHR ih uhs*

Zartanah   *ZAHR tuh nuh*

a-HAT; ah-far FAHR; aw-call KAWL; ay-name NAYM; B-BAD; ch-CHEW; d-DAD; e,eh-met
MET; ee-sea SEE; ew-truth TREWTH; f-FOOT, enough ee NUHF; g-GET; h-HIM; hw-whether
HWEH thuhr; i, ih-city SI ti, or SIH tih; igh sign SIGHN, eye IGH; igh LIGHT; j-jack JAK, germ
JUHRM; k-KISS, chorus KOH ruhss; ks-(for x) ox AHKS; kw-quail KWAYL; l-live LIHV, LIGHV;
m-more MOHR; ng-ring RING; oh-go GOH, row ROH (a boat); oo-LOOK; oo-boot BOOT

164

Zarthan   *ZAHR than (th as in thin)*

Zathoe   *ZATH oh ee*

Zathui   *ZATH oo ee*

Zatthu   *ZAT thoo*

Zattu   *ZAT oo*

Zavan   *ZAY van*

zayin (Hebrew letter)   *ZA yihn (A as in cat)*

Zaza   *ZAY zuh*

zealot   *ZEH luht*

Zealot   *ZEHL uht*

Zealotism   *ZEL aht IHZ uhm*

Zebadiah   *ZEB uh DIGH uh*

Zebah   *ZEE buh*

Zebaim   *zih BAY im*

Zebedee   *ZEB uh dee*

Zebidah   *zih BIGH duh*

Zebina   *zih BIGH nuh*

Zeboiim   *zih BOY im*

Zeboim   *zih BOH im*

Zebub   *ZEE buhb*

Zebudah   *zih BYOO duh*

Zebul   *ZEE buhl*

Zebulonite   *ZEB yoo luh night*

Zebulun   *ZEB yoo luhn*

Zebulunite   *ZEB yoo luh night*

Zechariah   *ZEK uh RIGH uh*

Zecher   *ZEE kuhr*

Zedad   *ZEE dad*

Zedechias   *ZED uh KIGH uhs*

Zedekiah   *ZED uh KIGH uh*

Zeeb   *ZEE eb*

Zeguma   *zeh GOO muh*

Zeker   *ZEE kuhr*

Zela   *ZEE luh*

Zelah   *ZEE luh*

Zelek   *ZEE lek*

Zelophehad   *zih LOH fih had*

Zelotes   *zih LOH teez*

Zelzah   *ZEL zuh*

Zemaraim   *ZEM uh RAY im*

Zemarite   *ZEM uh right*

Zemer   *ZEE muhr*

Zemira   *zih MIGH ruh*

Zemirah   *zih MIGH ruh*

Zenan   *ZEE nan*

Zenas   *ZEE nuhs*

Zephaniah   *ZEF uh NIGH uh*

Zephath   *ZEE fath*

Zephathah   *ZEF uh thuh*

Zephi   *ZEE figh*

Zepho   *ZEE foh*

Zephon   *ZEE fahn*

Zephonite   *ZEE fahn ight*

Zer   *ZUHR*

Zerah   *ZEE ruh*

Zerahiah   *ZER uh HIGH uh*

---

ow-cow KOW, out OWT; oy-boil BOYL; p-PAT; r-RAN; s-star STAHR, tsetse SET see; sh-show SHOH, action AK shuhn, mission MIH shuhn, vicious VIH shuhss; t-tie TIGH, Thomas TAH muhss; th-thin THIN or THIHN; th-there THEHR; tw-TWIN; u, uh-tub TUB or TUHB, Joshua JAHSH yew uh, term TUHRM; v-veil VAYL, of AHV; w-WAY; wh (whether) see hw; y-year YEER; z-xerox ZIHR ahks, ZEE rahks, his HIZ or HIHZ, zebra ZEE bruh; zh-version VUHR zhuhn

165

Zerahite   *ZEE ruh hight*

Zeraiah   *zuh RAY yuh*

Zerdaiah   *zuhr DAY yuh*

Zered   *ZEE red*

Zereda   *ZER ih duh*

Zeredah   *ZER ih duh*

Zeredatha   *ZER uh DAY thuh*

Zererah   *ZER uh ruh*

Zererath   *ZER ih rath*

Zeresh   *ZEE resh*

Zereth   *ZEE reth*

Zerethshahar   *ZEE reth-SHAY hahr*

Zereth-shahar   *ZEE reth-SHAY hahr*

Zereth Shahar   *ZEE reth-SHAY hahr*

Zeri   *ZEE righ*

Zeror   *ZEE rawr*

Zeruah   *zeh ROO uh*

Zerubbabel   *zuh RUHB uh buhl*

Zeruiah   *ZER uh IGH (eye) uh*

zeta (Greek letter)   *ZAY tuh*

Zetham   *ZEE tham (th as in thin)*

Zethan   *ZEE than   (th as in thin)*

Zethar   *ZEE thahr (th as in thin)*

Zeus   *ZOOS*

Zia   *ZIGH uh*

Ziba   *ZIGH buh*

Zibeon   *ZIB ih uhn*

Zibia   *ZIB ih uh*

Zibiah   *ZIB ih uh*

Ziboiim   *zih BOY im (OY as in boy)*

Zichri   *ZIK righ*

Zicri   *ZIK righ*

Ziddim   *ZID im*

Zidkijah   *zid KIGH juh*

Zidon   *ZIGH duhn*

Zidonian   *zigh DOH nih uhn*

Zif   *ZIF*

ziggurat   *ZIH guh rat*

Ziha   *ZIGH huh*

Ziklag   *ZIK lag*

Zillah   *ZIL uh*

Zillethai   *ZIL uh thigh*

Zilpah   *ZIL puh*

Zilthai   *ZIL thigh*

Zimmah   *ZIM uh*

Zimnah   *ZIM nuh*

Zimran   *ZIM ran*

Zimri   *ZIM righ*

Z

a-HAT; ah-far FAHR; aw-call KAWL; ay-name NAYM; B-BAD; ch-CHEW; d-DAD; e,eh-met MET; ee-sea SEE; ew-truth TREWTH; f-FOOT, enough ee NUHF; g-GET; h-HIM; hw-whether HWEH thuhr; i, ih-city SI ti, or SIH tih; igh sign SIGHN, eye IGH; igh LIGHT; j-jack JAK, germ JUHRM; k-KISS, chorus KOH ruhss; ks-(for x) ox AHKS; kw-quail KWAYL; l-live LIHV, LIGHV; m-more MOHR; ng-ring RING; oh-go GOH, row ROH (a boat); oo-LOOK; oo-boot BOOT

Zin   *ZIN*

Zina   *ZIGH nuh*

Zinjirli   *ZIN juhr lih*

Zion   *ZIGH uhn*

Zior   *ZIGH awr*

Ziph   *ZIF*

Ziphah   *ZIGH fuh*

Ziphim   *ZIF im*

Ziphion   *ZIF ih ahn*

Ziphite   *ZIF ight*

Ziphron   *ZIF rahn*

Zippor   *ZIP awr*

Zipporah   *zi POH ruh*

Zithri   *ZITH righ*

Ziv   *ZIV*

Ziz   *ZIZ*

Ziza   *ZIGH zuh*

Zizah   *ZIGH zuh*

Zoan   *ZOH an*

Zoar   *ZOH uhr*

Zoba   *ZOH buh*

Zobah   *ZOH buh*

Zobebah   *zoh BEE buh*

Zodiac   *ZOH dih ak*

Zohar   *ZOH hahr*

Zoheleth   *ZOH huh leth*

Zoheth   *ZOH heth*

Zophah   *ZOH fuh*

Zophai   *ZOH figh*

Zophar   *ZOH fahr*

Zophim   *ZOH fim*

Zorah   *ZOH ruh*

Zorathite   *ZOH rath ight*

Zoreah   *zoh REE uh*

Zores   *ZOH reez*

Zorite   *ZOH right*

Zoroaster   *ZOH roh ASS tuhr*

Zoroastrianism   *ZOH roh ASS trih uhn IHZ uhm*

Zorobabel   *zoh RAHB uh buhl*

Zostrianos   *ZOHS trih AH nahs*

Zostrianus   *ZOHS trih AH nahs*

Zuar   *ZOO uhr*

Zuph   *ZUHF*

Zuphite   *ZOO fight*

Zur   *ZUHR*

Zuriel   *ZOO rih el*

Zurishaddai   *ZOO rih SHAD igh (eye)*

Zuth   *ZOOTH*

Zuzim   *ZOO zim*

Zuzite   *ZOO zight*

---

ow-cow KOW, out OWT; oy-boil BOYL; p-PAT; r-RAN; s-star STAHR, tsetse SET see; sh-show SHOH, action AK shuhn, mission MIH shuhn, vicious VIH shuhss; t-tie TIGH, Thomas TAH muhss; th-thin THIN or THIHN; th-there THEHR; tw-TWIN; u, uh-tub TUB or TUHB, Joshua JAHSH yew uh, term TUHRM; v-veil VAYL, of AHV; w-WAY; wh (whether) see hw; y-year YEER; z-xerox ZIHR ahks, ZEE rahks, his HIZ or HIHZ, zebra ZEE bruh; zh-version VUHR zhuhn

Z

Biblical Names and Meanings

NAMES OF GOD

Adoni title of honor meaning "lord" or "Lord"

El short form of Elohim or name of a Canaanite deity

Elohim generic Hebrew word for "God" or "gods"

El-Berith "God of the Covenant"

El-Bethel "God of Bethel" or "God of the house of God" or "El of Bethel"

El-Elohe-Israel "El is the God of Israel" or "God is the God of Israel"

El-Elyon "God most high"

El-Gibbor "God the warrior" or "mighty God"

El-Olam "God the everlasting One"

El-Roi "God who sees"

El-Shaddai "God almighty"

Jehovah or YHWH or Yahweh or Jahweh "I am"; often translated "LORD"

Jehovah-Jirah "Yahweh will provide"

Jehovah-Mekaddesh "Yahweh sanctifies"

Jehovah-Nissi "Yahweh is my banner"

Jehovah-Sabaoth "Yahweh of hosts"

Jehovah-Shalom "Yahweh is peace"

Jehovah-Shamma "Yahweh is there"

Jehovah-Tsidkenu "Yahweh our righteousness"

NAMES OF PEOPLE AND PLACES

Aaron perhaps "mountaineer" or "enlightened" or "rich, fluent"

Abaddon "to perish" or "destruction"

Abda "servant"

Abdeel "servant of God"

Abdi "my servant"

Abdiel "servant of God"

Abdon "service" or "servile"

Abednego "servant of Nabu"

Abel "breath, vapor, meadow"

Abel-Cheramim or Abel-Keramim "brook of the vineyards"

Abel-Meholah "brook of the round dancing"

Abel-Mizraim "brook of the Egyptians" or "mourning of the Egyptians"

Abi-Albon "my father is overpowering"

Abiathar "father of abundance"

Abida or Abidah "my father knows"

Abidan "my father judged"

Abiel "my father is God"

Abiezer "my father is help"

Abigail "my father rejoiced"

Abihail "my father is terror"

Abihu "my father is he"

Abihud or Abiud "my father is glorious"

Abijah or Abijam "my father is Yahweh"

Abimael "God is my father"

Abimelech "my father is king"

Abinadab "my father is generous"

Abinoam "my father is gracious"

Abiram "my father is exalted"

Abishag "my father strayed" or "my father is a wanderer"

Abishai or Abshai "father exists"

Abishur "my father is a wall"

Abital "my father is dew"

Abner "father is a lamp"

Abraham "father of a multitude"

Abram "father is exalted"

Absalom or Abishalom "father of peace"

Achan perhaps "man of trouble"

Achbor "mouse"

Achor "trouble, affliction," or "taboo"

Achsa or Achsah or Acsah "bangle, ankle ornament"

Achshaph or Acshaph "place of sorcery"

Achzib or Aczib "deceitful"

Adah "adornment, ornament"

Adaiah "Yahweh has adorned"

Adam "mankind"

Adamah "soil, farmland"

Addar "threshing floor"

Addi "adornment"

Adiel "an ornament is God"

Adina "delightful, luxuriant"

Admah "red soil"

Admatha "unconquered"

Adoni-Bezek "lord of Bezek"

Adonijah "Yahweh is Lord"

Adonikam "the Lord has arisen"

Adoni-Zedek "the Lord is righteous" or "Zedek is righteous"

Adoraim "double strength"

Adrammelech "Adra is king"

Adriel "God is my help"

Adullam "sealed off place"

Adummim "red ones"

Aenon "double spring"

Agabus "locust"

Agag "fiery one"

Agee perhaps "camel thorn"

Agur "hired hand"

Ahab "father's brother"

Ahasai or Ahzai "property"

Ahaz "he has grasped"

Ahaziah "Yahweh has grasped"

Ahban "the brother is wise"

Ahiah or Ahijah or Ahio "Yahweh is my brother"

Ahian "little brother"

Ahiezer "my brother is help"

Ahihud "my brother is splendid or majestic"

Ahikam "my brother stood up"

Ahilud "a brother is born"

Ahimaaz perhaps "brother of anger" or "my brother is counselor"

Ahimelech "my brother is king"

Ahinoam "my brother is gracious"

Ahio "my brother is Yahweh"

Ahira "my brother is a friend"

Ahithophel "brother of folly"

Ahitub "my brother is good"

Ahumai "a brother is it"

Ai or Aiath "ruin"

Aiah or Ajah "hawk"

Aijalon or Ajalon "place of the deer"

Akkub perhaps "protector" or "protected one"

Akrabbim "scorpions"

Alemeth or Allemeth "concealed" or "dark"

Aliah "height"

Alian "high one"

Allamelech "king's oak" or "royal holy tree"

Almon-Diblathaim "road sign of the two figs"

Aloth "the height"

Amariah "Yahweh has spoken"

Amasa "burden" or "bear a burden"

Amasai "burden bearer"

Amasiah "Yahweh has borne"

Amaziah "Yahweh is mighty"

Amittai "loyal, true"

Ammi "my people"

Ammiel "people of God" or "God is of my people"

Ammihud "my people is splendid"

Amminadab "my people give freely"

Ammishaddai "people of the Almighty"

Ammizabad "my people give"

Amnon "trustworthy, faithful"

Amok "deep"

Amon "faithful"

Amos "a load"

Amoz "strong"

Amram "exalted people"

Amraphel perhaps "the God Amurru paid back" or "mouth of God has spoken"

Amzi "my strong one"

Anah "answer"

Anaharath "gorge"

Anaiah "Yahweh answered"

Anak or Anakim "long-necked" or "strong-necked"

Anam Melech "Anu is king"

Anan "cloud"

Ananias "Yahweh has dealt graciously"

Anath "answer" or the name of a Canaanite deity

Anem "fountains"

Anna "grace"

Annas "merciful"

Antipatris "in place of father"

Anub "grape" or "with a mustache"

Aphek or Aphik "bed of brook or river" or "fortress"

Aphiah "forehead"

Apollonia "belonging to Apollo"

Apollos "destroyer"

Appaim "nostrils"

Ar "city"

Arabah "dry, infertile area"

Arah "ox" or "traveler"

Aram-Naharaim "Aram of the two rivers"

Aran "ibex"

Arba "four"

Archippus "first among horsemen"

Ard "hunchbacked"

Aretas "moral excellence, power"

Argob "mound of earth"

Arieh "lion"

Ariel "God's lion"

Arioch "servant of the moon god"

Aristarchus perhaps "best ruler"

Armageddon or **Har-Mage-don** "mountain of Megiddo"

Armoni "born in Armon"

Arnon "rushing river" or "river flooded with berries"

Arod or Arodi "hump-backed"

Aroer "juniper"

Artaxerxes "kingdom of righteousness"

Arubboth "smoke hole" or "chimney"

Arumah "exalted" or "height"

Arza "wooden worm" or "earthiness"

Asa "doctor" or "healing"

Asahel "God acted" or "God made"

Asaiah "Yahweh made"

Asaph "he collected"

Asarel "God has sworn" or "God rejoiced"

Asenath "belonging to Neith"

Ashan "smoke"

Ashbel "having a long upper lip"

Asher or Aser "happiness, fortune"

Ashhur or Ashur "to be black" or "belonging to Ishara"

Ashima "guilt"

Ashvath "that which has been worked"

Asriel or Ashriel "God has made happy"

Assir "prisoner"

Atarah "crown" or "wreath"

Ater "crippled" or "left-handed"

Athach "attack"

Athaliah "Yahweh has announced his exalted nature" or "Yahweh is righteous"

Athlai "Yahweh is exalted"

Attai "timely"

Augustus "reverend"

Aven "wickedness"

Avith "ruin"

Azarael or Azareel or Azarel "God helped"

Azariah "Yahweh has helped"

Azaz "he is strong"

Azaziah "Yahweh is strong"

Azekah "cultivated ground"

Azel "noble"

Azgad "Gad is strong"

Aziza "strong one"

Azmaveth "strong as death" or "death is strong"

Azmon "bones"

Aznoth-Tabor "ears of Tabor"

Azriel "God is my help"

Azrikam "my help stood up"

Azubah "forsaken"

Azzan "he has proven to be strong"

Azzur or Azur "one who has been helped"

Ballah "wife, lady" or "residence of Baal"

Baalath "feminine Baal"

Baalath-Beer "the baal of the well"

Baal-Berith "lord of covenant"

Baal-Hamon "lord of abundance"

Baal-Meon "lord of the residence"

Baal-Peor "Baal of Peor" or "lord of Peor"

Baal-Perazim "lord of the breakthroughs" or "Baal of the breeches"

Baal-Shalishah "Baal of Shalishah" or "lord of Shalishah"

Baal-Tamar "Baal of the palm tree" or "lord of the palm tree"

Baal-Zebub "lord of the flies"

Baal-Zephon "lord of the north" or "Baal of the north"

Baara "burning"

Bahurim "young men"

Bakbuk "bottle"

Balaam perhaps "the clan brings forth"

Baladan "God gave a son"

Balak "devastator"

Bamoth-Baal "high places of Baal"

Bani "built"

Barabbas "son of father"

Barachel "God blessed"

Barak "lightning"

Bar-Jona "son of John"

Barnabas "son of prophecy" or "son of exhortation"

Barsabas "son of the Sabbath"

Bartholomew "son of Talmai"

Bartimaeus or Bartimeus "son of Timai" or "son of the unclean"

Baruch "blessed"

Barzillai "made of iron"

Basemath or Bashemath or Basmath "balsam"

Bath-Rabbim "daughter of many"

Bathsheba "daughter of completeness" or "daughter of Sheba" or "daughter of oath"

Bathshua "daughter of nobility"

Bazlith "in the shadow" or "onions"

Bealoth "feminine Baals" or "ladies"

Bebai "child"

Becher or Beker "firstborn" or "young male camel"

Beeliada "Baal knows" or "the Lord knows"

Beelzebub or Beelzebul or Baal-Zebub "lord of the flies"

Beer "well"

Beer-Elim "well of the rams,

the heros, the terebinths, or the mighty trees"

Beeri "well"

Beer-Lahairoi "well of the living one who sees me"

Beeroth "wells"

Beer-Sheba or Beersheva "well of the oath" or "well of the seven"

Beeshterah "in Ashtaroth"

Bela or Belah "he swallowed"

Belshazzar "Bel, protect the king"

Belteshazzar "protect the king's life"

Ben-Abinadab "son of Abinadab"

Benaiah "Yahweh has built"

Ben-Ammi "son of my people"

Bene-Berak "sons of Barak" or "sons of lightning"

Ben-Hadad "son of Hadad"

Ben-Hail "son of strength"

Ben-Hinnom "son of Hinnom"

Ben-Hur "son of a camel" or "son of Horus"

Beninu "our son"

Benjamin "son of the right

hand" or "son of the south"

Beno "his son"

Benoni "son of my sorrow"

Ben-Zoheth "son of Zoheth"

Beor "burning"

Beracah or Berachah "blessing"

Berakiah or Berechiah "Yahweh blessed"

Bered "cool"

Beriah "Yahweh created"

Berothai "wells"

Besodeiah "in Yahweh's counsel"

Betah "security"

Beten "womb"

Beth-Abara "house of crossing"

Bethany perhaps "house of the poor"

Beth-Arbel "house of Arbel"

Beth-Aven "house of deception" or "house of idolatry"

Beth-Barah "house of God"

Bethcar "house of sheep"

Beth-Dagon "house of Dagon"

Beth-Diblathaim "house of the two fig cakes"

Beth-Eden "house of bliss"

Beth-Eked "house of shearing"

Bethel "house of God" or "house of El"

Beth-Emek "house of the valley"

Bether "division"

Bethesda "house of mercy"

Beth-Ezel "house of the leader" or "house at the side"

Beth-Gamul "house of retaliation"

Beth-Haccerem or Beth-Haccherem "house of the vineyard"

Beth-Haggan "house of the garden"

Beth-Hoglah "house of the partridge"

Beth-Horon "house of the caves" or "house of anger" or "house of the hollow" or "house of Hauron"

Beth-Jeshimoth or Beth Jesimoth "house of deserts"

Beth-Lebaoth "house of lionesses"

Bethlehem "house of bread" or "house of fighting"

Beth-Maacah or Beth-Maachah "house of Maacah" or "house of pleasure"

Beth-Marcaboth "house of chariots"

Beth-Meon "house of residence"

Beth-Millo "house of fulness"

Beth-Pelet "house of deliverance"

Beth-Peor "house of Peor"

Bethphage "house of unripe figs"

Beth-Rapha "house of a giant"

Bethsaida "house of fish"

Beth-Shan or Bethshan or Beth-Shean "house of quiet"

Beth-Shemesh "house of the sun"

Beth-Shittah "house of Accacia"

Beth-Togarmah "house of Togarmah"

Bethuel or Bethul "house of God"

Beth-Zur "house of the rock"

Betonim "pistachios"

Bezek "lightning"

Bezer "inaccessible"

Bichri or Bicri or Bikri "firstborn" or "of the clan of Becher"

Bigvai "god" or "fortune"

Bildad "the Lord loved"

Bilgah "brightness"

Bilhah "unworried, unconcerned"

Bilshan "their lord"

Binnui "built"

Bishlam "in peace"

Bithron "ravine"

Biziothiah or Bizjothjah "scorns of Yahweh"

Blastus "sprout"

Boanerges "sons of thunder"

Boaz perhaps "lively" or "quickness" or "agile"

Bocheru or Bokeru "firstborn"

Bochim or Bokim "weepers"

Bohan "thumb" or "big toe"

Bor-Ashan "well of smoke" or "pit of smoke"

Boscath or Bozkath "swelling"

Bozrah "inaccessible"

Bukki or Bukkiah "Yahweh proved" or "Yahweh has emptied"

Bunah "understanding"

Bunni "built"

Buz "scorn"

Buzi "scorn"

Cabul "fettered" or "braided"

Caiaphas "rock" or "depression"

Cain "acquisition" or "spear"

Caleb "dog"

Cana "the nest"

Capernaum "village of Nahum"

Carcas or Carkas "hawk"

Carmi "my vineyard"

Carpus "fruit"

Casiphia "silversmith"

Cephas "rock"

Chedor-Laomer "son of La'gamal"

Chemosh "subdue"

Chenaanah "tradeswoman"

Chenani "one born in the month of Kanunu"

Chenaniah "Yahweh empowers"

Chephar-Ammoni or Chephar-Ha-Ammoni "open village of the Ammonites"

Chephirah "queen of the lions"

Cherith or Kerith "cutting" or "ditch"

Chesalon "on the hip"

Chesed "one of the Chaldeans"

Chesil "foolish"

Chileab or Kileab "everything of the father"

Chilion or Kilion "sickly"

Chilmad or Kilmad "marketplace"

Chimham or Kimham "paleface"

Chinnereth or Chinneroth or Cinneroth "harp-shaped"

Chislon or Kislon "clumsy"

Chiun or Kaiwan or Kiyyun "the constant, unchanging one"

Chloe "verdant"

Christ "the anointed one" or "Messiah"

Chuza "seer"

Cleopas or Cleophas "renowned father"

Cosam "diviner"

Conaniah "Yahweh has established"

Cozbi "my falsehood"

Cozeba "deceptive"

Crescens "growing"

Crispus "curly"

Cushan-Rishathaim "dark one of double evil"

Dabbasheth or Dabbesheth "hump"

Dagon "little fish" or "dear"

Damaris "heifer"

Dan "judge"

Daniel "God is judge" or "God's judge"

Dannah "fortress"

Darda "pearl of knowledge"

Darkon perhaps "hard"

Dathan "fountain" or "warring"

David "favorite" or "beloved"

Debir "back, behind"

Deborah "bee"

Decapolis "ten cities"

Delilah "with long hair hanging down"

Demetrius "belonging to Demeter"

Deuel "God knows"

Diblah or Diblath "cake of figs"

Diblaim "two fig cakes"

Dibon perhaps "pining away" or "fence of tubes"

Dibri "talkative" or "gossip"

Didymus "twin"

Diklah "date palm"

Dimnah "manure"

Dimon perhaps "blood"

Dinah "justice" or "artistically formed"

Diotrephes "nurtured by Jove"

Dishan "bison" or "antelope"

Dizahab "place of gold"

Dodai "favorite" or "beloved"

Dodavah "beloved of Yahweh"

Dor "dwelling"

Dorcas "gazelle"

Dumah "silence" or "permanent settlement"

Dura "circuit wall"

Ebal "bare" or "baldy"

Ebed "servant"

Ebed-Melech "servant of the king"

Ebenezer "stone of help"

Eber "the opposite side"

Ebiasaph "my father has collected or taken in"

Eden "flatland" or "wilderness" or "delight" or "pleasure"

Eder "water puddle" or "herd"

Edom "red" or "ruddy"

Eglah "heifer, young cow"

Eglaim "two cisterns"

Eglath-Shelishiyah "the third heifer"

Eglon perhaps "young bull"

Ehi "my brother"

Ehud "unity, powerful"

Eker "root" or "offspring"

Elah "oak" or "mighty tree" or "terebinth"

Elam "highland"

Elasah "God has made"

Elath or Eloth "ram" or "mighty trees" or "terebinth"

Eldaah "God has called" or "God has sought" or "God of wisdom"

Eldad "God loved"

Elead "God is a witness"

Eleadah or Eladah "God adorned himself"

Elealeh "God went up" or "high ground"

Eleasah "God acted" or "God made"

Eleazar "God helps"

El-Hanan "God is gracious"

Eli "high"

Eliab "God is father"

Eliada or Eliadah "God has known"

Eliahba "God hides in safety" or "my god is Chiba"

Eliakim "God will raise up"

Eliam "God is an uncle or relative" or "God of the people"

Eliasaph "God has added"

Eliashib "God repays or leads back"

Eliathah "my God has come"

Eliel "my God is God" or "my god is El"

Eliezer "God helps"

Elihoreph "my God repays" or "my God is giver of the autumn harvest" or "Apis is my God"

Elihu "he is God"

Elijah "my God is Yahweh"

Elika "my God has arisen" or "my God has vomited"

Elim "trees"

Elimelech "my God is king"

Elioenai "to Yahweh are my eyes"

Eliphal "God has judged"

Eliphaz "my God is gold"

Elipheleh or Eliphelehu "God treated him with distinction"

Eliphelet or Elpalet or Elpelet "God is deliverance"

Elisabeth or Elizabeth "my God is good fortune"

Elisha "my God is salvation"

Elishama "God heard"

Elishaphat "God had judged"

Elisheba "God is good fortune"

Elishua "God is salvation"

Eliud "God is high and mighty"

Elizaphan or Elzaphan "God has hidden or treasured up"

Elizur "God is a rock"

Elkanah "God created"

Elnaam "God is a delight"

Elnathan "God has given"

Elon "great tree" or "tree of god" or "terebinth"

Elpaal "God has made"

Elteke or Eltekeh "place of meeting" or "place of hearing" or "plea for rain"

Eltekon "securing advice"

Elymas perhaps "wise" or "magician"

Elzabad "God made a gift"

Emek-Keziz "the cut off valley" or "the valley of gravel"

Emim "frightening ones"

Emmanuel or Immanuel "God with us"

Emmaus "hot baths"

Enaim or Enam "two eyes or springs"

Endor "spring of Dor" or "spring of settlement"

En-Eglaim "spring of two calves"

En-Gannim "the spring of gardens"

Engedi "spring of the young goat"

En-Hakkore "spring of the partridge" or "spring of the caller"

En-Hakkore "spring of the partridge" or "spring of the caller"

En-Mishpat "spring of judgment"

Enoch or Henoch "dedicated"

Enos "humanity" or "a man"

En-Rimmon "spring of the pomegranate"

En-Rogel "spring of the fuller" or "spring of the foot"

En-Tappuah "spring of apple"

Epaenetus "praise"

Epaphras "lovely"

Epaphroditus "favored by Aphrodite or Venus"

Ephah "darkness"

Ephai "bird"

Ephes-Dammin or Pas-dammin "end of blood-shed"

Ephlal "notched" or "cracked"

Ephraim "two fruit land" or "two pasture lands"

Ephratah or Ephrath "fruit-ful"

Ephron "dusty"

Er "protector" or "watchful"

Eran "of the city" or "watch-ful"

Erastus "beloved"

Eri "of the city of" or "watchful"

Esarhaddon "Ashur has given a brother"

Esau "hairy"

Esek "strife"

Eshan or Eshean "I lean on"

Esh-Baal "man of Baal"

Eshcol "valley of grapes" or "cluster"

Eshek "oppression" or "strong"

Eshtaol "asking"

Eshtemoa or Eshtemoh "being heard"

Esther "Ishtar"

Etham "fort"

Ethan "long-lived"

Eth-Baal "with him is Baal"

Ether "smoke of incense"

Ethnan "gift"

Eubulus "good counsel"

Eunice "victorious"

Euodia or Euodias "good journey" or "success"

Eutychus "good fortune"

Eve "life"

Evi perhaps "desire"

Evil-Merodach "worshiper of Marduk"

Ezekiel or Ezekias "God will strengthen"

Ezem "mighty" or "bone"

Ezer "gathering" or "pile" or "help" or "hero"

Ezra or Ezrah "Yahweh helps"

Ezri "my help"

Felix "happy"

Gaal "abhorrence, neglect" or "dung-beetle"

Gaashi "rising and falling noisily"

Gabbatha "elevated"

Gabriel "strong man of God"

Gad "good fortune"

Gaddi or Gadi "my good fortune"

Gaddiel "God is my good fortune"

Gaham "flame"

Gadar "drought" or "small in spirit"

Gaius "I am glad, rejoice"

Galal "roll" or "turtle"

Galeed "pile for witness"

Galilee "circle" or "region"

Gallim "piles"

Gamaliel "God rewards with good"

Gamul "receiver of good deeds"

Gareb "scabby"

Gath "winepress"

Gath-Hepher "winepress on the watering hole"

Gath-Rimmon "winepress on the pomegranate tree"

Gaza "strong"

Gazez "sheepshearing"

Geba "hill"

Gebal "mountain"

Geber "young man" or "hero"

Gedaliah "Yahweh has done great things"

Geder "stone wall"

Gederah "sheepfold" or "stone wall"

Gederoth "walls"

Gederothaim "two walls"

Gedor "wall"

Geharashim "valley of the handcraft workers"

Gehazi "valley of vision" or "goggled-eyed"

Gehenna "valley of lamentation" or "valley of whining"

Geliloth "circles" or "regions"

Gemalli "my camel" or "camel driver"

Gemariah "Yahweh has completed or carried out"

Genubath "theft" or "foreign guests"

Gera "stranger, alien, or sojourner"

Gerar perhaps "drag away"

Gerizim "cut off ones"

Gershom "sojourn there" or "expelled one" or "protected of the god Shom"

Gershon "expelled" or "bell"

Geshem "rain"

Geshur perhaps "bridge"

Geuel "pride of God"

Gezer or Gazer "isolated area"

Giah "bubbling"

Gibbethon "arched" or "hill" or "mound"

Gibeah "a hill"

Gibeath-Haaraloth "hill of foreskins"

Gibeon "hill place"

Gideon "one who cuts to pieces"

Gideoni "one who cuts down or cuts to pieces"

Gidom "cleared land"

Gihon "gushing fountain"

Gilboa perhaps "hill country" or "bubbling" or "fountain"

Gilead "raw" or "rugged"

Gilgal "circle"

Giloh "uncovered" or "revealed"

Gittaim "two winepresses"

Goah "low" or "bellow"

Gob "back" or "mountain crest"

Goiim "nation," particularly "a Gentile, foreign nation"

Golan "circle" or "enclosure"

Golgotha "skull"

Gomer "complete, enough" or "burning coal"

Gomorrah perhaps "enmity, malice"

Goshen perhaps "cultivated" or "inundated land"

Gur "foreign sojourner" or "young animal"

Gur-Baal "foreign sojourner of Baal" or "young animal of Baal"

Haahashtari "kingdom"

Habakkuk "plant" or "vegetable"

Habaziniah or Habazziniah "Yahweh inflated or caused to make merry"

Hadad "mighty"

Hadad-Ezer "Hadad helps"

Hadashah "new"

Hadassah "myrtle" or "bride"

Hadattah "new"

Hadoram "Hadad is exalted"

Haeleph "the ox"

Hagar "stranger"

Haggai "festive"

Haggi "my festival"

Haggiah "Yahweh is my festival"

Haggith "festival"

Hakkatan "the smaller one, the lesser"

Hali "jewel"

Hakkoz "the thorn"

Ham "hot" or "black"

Haman "magnificent"

Hamath "fortress" or "citadel"

Hamath-Zobah "hot place of Zobah" or "fortress of Zobah"

Hammath "hot spot" or "hot one" or "hot spring"

Hammedatha "given by the god"

Hamon-Gog "horde of Gog"

Hamonah "horde" or "nearby"

Hamor "donkey" or "ass"

Hamul "pitied, spared" or El is father-in-law" or "El is hot"

Hanameel or Hanamel "God is gracious"

Hanan "gracious"

Hananel or Hananeel "God is gracious"

Hanani "my grace"

Hananiah "Yahweh is gracious"

Haniel or Hanniel "God is gracious"

Hannah "grace"

Hanoch "dedicated" or "vassal"

Hanun "blessed" or "favored"

Haphraim or Hapharaim "two holes" or "two wells"

Haran "mountaineer" or "caravan route"

Harar perhaps "mountain"

Harim "dedicated"

Hariph "sharp" or "flesh"

Harod "quake" or "terror" or "intermittent spring"

Haroeh "the seer"

Harosheth "forest land"

Harsha "unable to talk, silent" or "magician, sorcerer"

Hashabiah "Yahweh has reckoned or imputed"

Hashabnah "reckoning"

Hashabneiah or Hashabniah "Yahweh has imputed to me"

Hashem "the name"

Hashum "flat-nosed"

Hassenuah "the hated one"

Havilah "sandy stretch"

Havoth-Jair or Havvoth-Jair "tents of Jair"

Hazael "El is seeing" or "God is seeing"

Hazaiah "Yahweh sees"

Hazazon-Tamar or Hazezon-Tamar "grave dump with palms"

Hazelelponi or Hazzelelponi "overshadow my face"

Hazeroth "villages" or "encampments"

Haziel or Hazo "God saw"

Hazor "enclosed settlement"

Hazor-Haddattah "new Hazor"

Heber "companion"

Hebron "association" or "league"

Helah "jewelry for the neck"

Helam "their army"

Helbah "forest"

Heldai "mole"

Heleb or Heled or Heldai "fat" or "the best"

Heliopolis "city of the sun"

Helkai "my portion"

Helkath-Hazzurim "field of flint stones" or "field of battle"

Heman "faithful"

Hemdan "beauty, charm"

Hephzibah "my delight is in her"

Heres "sun"

Heresh "unable to speak"

Hermogenes "born of Hermes"

Hermon "devoted mountain"

Herod "heroic"

Hesed "grace" or "steadfast love"

Heshbon "reckoning"

Heshmon "flat field"

Hezekiah "Yahweh is my strength"

Hezion "vision"

Hezron "camping place" or "reeds"

Hiddai "my majesty"

Hiel "God lives" or "brother of God"

Hierapolis "sacred city"

Hilkiah "Yahweh's portion"

Hillel "praise"

Hiram "brother of the lofty one" or "brother of the exalted one"

Hizkiah or Hizkijah "Yahweh is my strength"

Hizkiah or Hizkijah "Yahweh is my strength"

Hobab "beloved" or "cunning"

Hobah perhaps "guilt" or "land of reeds"

Hobiah or Hobaiah "Yahweh hides"

Hodaiah or Hodaviah or
  Hodevah "praise Yah-
  weh"

Hodiah or Hodijah "Yahweh
  is majestic"

Hodesh "new moon"

Hoglah "partridge"

Holon "sandy spot"

Hophni "tadpole"

Hophra "the heart of Re en-
  dures"

Hor "mountain"

Hor-Haggidgad or Hor-
  Hagidgad perhaps "hill
  of crickets"

Horeb "desolate region,
  desert, wilderness"

Horem "split rock"

Horesh "forest"

Hori "bleached" or "lesser"
  or "Horite"

Hormah "split rock" or
  "cursed for destruction"

Horonaim "twin caves"

Hosah "seeker of refuge"

Hosea or Hoshea "salvation"

Hoshaiah "Yahweh saved"

Hozai "seer"

Hukkok or Hukok "hewn
  out"

Huldah "mole"

Huppah "shelter" or "roof"
  or "bridal chamber"

Hur perhaps "white one" or
  "Horite" or "Horus"

Huram perhaps "exalted one"

Hushah "hurry"

Hushai "quick" or "from
  Hushah" or "gift of broth-
  erhood"

Husham "large-nosed" or
  "with haste"

Hushim "hurried ones"

Ibhar "he elected"

Ibleam "he swallowed the
  people"

Ibneiah "Yahweh builds"

Ichabod "where is the glory?"

Idbash "sweet as honey"

Idumea Greek term for
  Edom meaning "red" or
  "ruddy"

Iezer or Jeazer "where is
  help?" or "my father is
  help"

Igal or Igeal "he redeems"

Igdaliah "Yahweh is great"

Ijon "ruin"

Ikkesh "perverted, false"

Immanuel or Emmanuel
  "God with us"

Immer perhaps "lamb"

Imna or Imnah or Jimna or

Jimnah "he defends" or "he allots for" or "on the right hand, good fortune"

Imrah "he is obstinate"

Imri "Yahweh has spoken"

Iri "my city" or "my donkey's colt"

Ira "city" or "donkey's colt"

Irijah "Yahweh sees"

Irnahash "city of the snake" or "city of bronze"

Isaac "laughter"

Isaiah "Yahweh saves"

Iscah perhaps "they look"

Iscariot "man of Kerioth" or perhaps from Latin meaning "assassin" or "bandit"

Ish-Bosheth "man of shame"

Ishbah "he soothes"

Ishbak "come before, excel"

Ishbibenob "inhabitant of Nob"

Ishhod or Ishod "man of vigor and vitality"

Ishi "my deliverer or salvation"

Ishijah or Isshijah "let Yahweh forget"

Ishmael or Ishma "God hears"

Ishmaiah or Ismaiah "Yahweh hears"

Ishmerai "Yahweh protects"

Ishtob "man of good" or "man of Tob"

Ishuah or Ishvah or Isuah "he is equal" or "he satisfies"

Israel "God strives" or "God persists" or "let El persist" or "let El contend"

Issachar "man for hire" or "hireling"

Isshiah or Jesiah "let Yahweh forget"

Ithamar perhaps "island of palms" or "where is Tamar" or "Father of Tamar"

Ithiel "with me is God"

Ithlah "he hangs" or "hanging or lofty place"

Ithra or Ithran "remnant" or "abundance"

Ithream "remnant of the people"

Ittai "with God"

Ituraea or Iturea "related to Jetur"

Iye-Abarim or Ijeabarim "ruins of the crossings"

Izhar or Izehar "olive oil" or "he sparkles"

Izziah or Jeziah "Yahweh sprinkled"

Jaakan or Jakan   "to be fast"

Jaakobah   "may he protect"

Jaazaniah   "Yahweh hears"

Jaaziah or Jaaziel   "Yahweh nourishes"

Jabal   "stream"

Jabbok   "flowing"

Jabesh   "dry"

Jabesh-Gilead   "dry, rugged" or "dry place of Gilead"

Jabez   "hollow, depression" or "he hurries"

Jabin   "he understands"

Jabneel or Jabnah   "God builds"

Jachin or Jakin   "he establishes"

Jacob   "he grasps the heel" or "he cheats, supplants"

Jada   "he knew"

Jael   "mountain goat"

Jagur   "pile of stones"

Jahaz or Jahaza or Jahazah or Jahzah   perhaps "landsite"

Jahaziah or Jahzeiah   "Yahweh looked"

Jahaziel or Jehaziel   "God looks"

Jahmai   "he protects me"

Jair   "Yahweh shines forth"

Jairus   "Yahweh will enlighten"

Jakeh   "prudent"

Jakim   "he caused to stand"

Jalam or Jaalam   "their ibex or mountain goat" or "he is hidden or dark"

James   English form of Jacob

Jamin   "on the right" or "good luck"

Jamlech   "may he cause to be king"

Janoah or Janohah   "he rests"

Japheth   "may he have space" or "fair (skinned)"

Japhia   "place situated high above"

Japhlet   "he rescues"

Jareb   "the great one" or "he contends"

Jared or Jered   "slave"

Jarib   "he contends against" or "is legal opponent of"

Jarmuth   "height" or "swelling in the ground"

Jaroah   "smooth, gentle" or "shown mercy"

Jashobeam   "the uncle will return"

Jashub "He turns to" or "he returns"

Jashubilehem "Jashubites of bread" or "she returns for bread"

Jason perhaps "to heal" or Greek form of Hebrew Joshua meaning "Yahweh is salvation"

Jathniel "God gives"

Jattir "remainder"

Javan "Greece"

Jazer or Jaazer "may he help"

Jaziz "he goads"

Jearim "forests" or "parks"

Jeberechiah or Jeberekiah "Yahweh blesses"

Jebus "trodden under foot"

Jecamiah "Yahweh causes to stand"

Jedaiah "praise Yahweh" or "Yahweh has performed a merciful deed" or "Yahweh knows"

Jediael "the one whom God knows"

Jedidah "darling" or "beloved"

Jedidiah "Yahweh's darling"

Jeduthun "praise"

Jeezer "where is help?"

Jegar-Shadutha "stone marker"

Jehaleleel or Jehalelel or Jahallel "he praises God" or "God shines forth"

Jehdeiah "Yahweh rejoices"

Jehezekel "God strengthens"

Jehiah "may he live, Yahweh"

Jehiel "let him live, God"

Jehizkiah "Yahweh strengthens"

Jehoaddan or Jehoaddin "Yahweh is bliss"

Jehoahaz or Joahaz "Yahweh grasps hold"

Jehohanan or Johanan "Yahweh is gracious, merciful"

Jehoiachin or Jechoniah or Jeconiah "Yahweh establishes"

Jehoiada or Joiada "Yahweh knows" or "Yahweh concerns himself for"

Jehoiakim or Joiakim or Jokim "Yahweh caused to stand, established"

Jehoiarib or Joarib "Yahweh creates justice"

Jehonadab or Jonadab "Yahweh incites" or "Yahweh offers himself freely"

Jehonathan "Yahweh gave"

Jehoshaphat or Joshaphat "Yahweh judged" or "Yahweh established the right"

Jehosheba "Yahweh is fullness or fortune"

Jehozabad or Jozabad or Josabad "Yahweh bestowed" or "Yahweh gave"

Jehozadak or Jesedech "Yahweh deals righteously"

Jehu "Yahweh is he"

Jehucal "Yahweh proves to be mighty"

Jehud "praise"

Jehudi "Judean or Jewish"

Jehudijah "Jewess, Judean woman"

Jeiel or Jeuel perhaps "God is strong" or "God heals"

Jekabzeel "God assembled"

Jekamiah "Yahweh delivers"

Jekuthiel "God nourishes"

Jemima or Jemimah "turtle dove"

Jemuel "day of God" or "sea of God"

Jephthah "he will open"

Jephunneh "he will be turned" or "appeased"

Jerah "moon" or "month"

Jerahmeel "God shows compassion"

Jeremiah or Jeremai or Jeremias "may Yahweh lift up, throw, or found"

Jeremoth "swellings"

Jeriah "Yahweh saw"

Jericho "moon"

Jeriel "God sees"

Jerimoth perhaps "fat belly"

Jerioth "fearsome"

Jeroboam perhaps "he who contends for justice for people"

Jeroham "he found mercy"

Jerubbaal "Baal judges"

Jeruel "foundation of God" or "founded by El"

Jerusalem "founded by Shalem" or "city of Shalem" or "city of peace"

Jerusha or Jerushah "one taken in possession"

Jesaiah "Yahweh has saved"

Jeshanah "old city"

Jeshebeab "the father remains alive" or "he brings the father back"

Jeshimon "desert, wilderness"

Jeshishai "advanced in years"

Jeshurun or Jesurun "upright" or "straight"

Jesimiel "Yahweh places"

Jesse "man" or "manly"

Jesus Greek form of Joshua meaning "Yahweh is salvation"

Jether "remnant"

Jethlah "he or it hangs"

Jethro "excess" or "superiority"

Jetur "he set in courses or layers"

Jeush or Jehush "he helps"

Jeuz "he brought to safety"

Jezaniah "Yahweh gave ear"

Jezebel "where is the prince?" or Phoenician "Baal is the prince"

Jezer "he formed"

Jeziel "God sprinkled"

Jezoar "he was light-colored" or "reddish-yellow" or "tawny"

Jezrahiah "Yahweh shines forth"

Jezreel "God sows"

Jidlaph "he cries or is sleepless"

Joab "Yahweh is father"

Joah "Jah is brother" or "Yahweh is brother"

Joanna "Yahweh's gift"

Joash or Jehoash "Yahweh gives"

Job perhaps "enmity, hostility" or "penitent one"

Jobab perhaps "wilderness"

or "arm oneself for battle" or "howling"

Jochebed "Yahweh's glory"

Joed "Yahweh is witness"

Joel "Yahweh is God"

Joelah perhaps "female mountain goat" or "may he avail"

Joezer "Yahweh is help"

Jogbehah "height, little hill"

Jogli "he reveals"

Joha "Yahweh is merciful"

Johanan "Yahweh has been gracious"

John Greek form of Johanan meaning "Yahweh has been gracious"

Jokdeam "the people burned"

Jokmeam or Jokneam "he establishes the people" or "the kinsman establishes or delivers"

Jokshan "trap, snare"

Joktan "watchful" or "he is small"

Joktheel "God nourishes" or "destroys"

Jonah or Jona or Jonas "dove"

Jonan or Jonam "Yahweh is gracious"

Jonathan "Yahweh gave"

Joppa or Jaffa "beautiful"

Jorah "early or autumn rain"

Joram or Jehoram "Yahweh is exalted"

Jordan "descender, flowing downward"

Joseph "adding" or "may he add"

Joshaviah "Yahweh lets inhabit"

Joshua or Jeshua or Jeshuah "Yahweh is salvation"

Josiah or Josias "Yahweh heals"

Josiphiah "Yahweh adds to"

Jotbah "it is good"

Jotbathah "good"

Jotham "Yahweh has shown himself to be perfect"

Joachar "Yahweh thought of"

Jozadak "Yahweh acts in righteousness"

Jubal "a ram" or "a ram's horn"

Judah "praise Yahweh"

Judas Greek form of Judah meaning "praise Yahweh"

Judea or Judaea "Jewish"

Judith "Jewess"

Jushab-Hesed "mercy is brought back"

Kabzeel "may God gather"

Kadesh-Barnea "consecrated"

Kadmiel "God is of old" or "God goes before"

Kain "smith"

Kallai "swift" or "light"

Kareah or Careah "bald"

Karka "ground" or "floor"

Karkor "soft"

Karnaim "horns"

Kartah "city"

Kedar "mighty" or "swarthy" or "black"

Kedemah "eastward"

Kedemoth "ancient places" or "eastern places"

Kedesh "sacred place" or "sanctuary"

Kenelathah "assembly"

Kelita "crippled, dwarfed one" or "adopted one"

Kemuel perhaps "helper of God" or "assembly of God" or "God's mound"

Kerioth or Kirioth "cities"

Keros "bent"

Keturah "incense" or "perfumed one"

Keziah "cassia" or "cinnamon"

Kibroth-Hattaavah "graves of craving, lust, gluttony"

Kibzaim "double gathering" or "double heap"

Kidron "turbid, dusky, gloomy"

Kinah "lamentation"

Kir "wall"

Kir-Hareseth or Kir-Heres "city of pottery"

Kiriath or Kirjath "city"

Kiriathaim or Kirjathaim "double city" or "two cities"

Kiriath-Arba or Kirjath-Arba "city of Arba" or "city of four"

Kiriath-Huzoth or Kirjath-Huzoth "city of streets"

Kiriath-Jearim or Kiriath-Arim or Kirjath-Arim or Kirjath-Jearim "city of forests"

Kiriath-Sepher or Kirjath-Sepher "city of book"

Kish perhaps "gift" or "bow" or "power"

Kishion "hard ground"

Kishon or Kison "curving, winding"

Kolaiah "voice of Yahweh"

Korah "bald"

Kore "one who proclaims"

Koz or Coz "thorn"

Laadah "throat" or "double chin"

Laban "white"

Lachish "obstinate"

Lael "belonging to God"

Lahman "food" or "bread"

Lahmas perhaps "violence"

Laish "strong" or "lion"

Laishah "lioness" or "toward Laish"

Lakum or Lakkum "rising" or "fortification"

Lamech "powerful"

Lasharon "belonging to Sharon"

Lazarus "one whom God helps" or "God has helped"

Leah "wild cow" or "gazelle"

Lebana or Lebanah "white" or "full"

Lebanon "white" or "white mountain"

Lebo-Hamath "entrance to or come to Hamath"

Lebonah "the white one"

Lecah "go"

Lehem "bread"

Lehi "chin" or "jawbone"

Lemuel "devoted to God"

Leshem "lion"

Letushim "smiths"

Leummim "peoples"

Levi "a joining"

Leviathan "coiled one"

Libnah "white" or "storax tree"

Libni "white"

Linus "linen"

Lo-Ammi "not my people"

Lo-Debar "no word" or "to him a word" or "to speak"

Lois perhaps "more desirable" or "better"

Lo-Ruhamah "without love"

Lot "concealed"

Lucifer "day star"

Luhith "plateaus"

Luz "almond"

Maacah or Maacath or Maachah perhaps "dull" or "stupid"

Maarath "barren field"

Maasai or Maseiah or Maasiai "work of Yahweh"

Maaziah "Yahweh is a refuge"

Machi perhaps "reduced" or "bought"

Machir "sold"

Machnadebai or Macnadebai perhaps "possession of Nebo"

Machpelah "double cave"

Madai "middle land"

Madmannah "dung heap"

Madmen "dung pit"

Madmenah "dung hill"

Madon "site of justice"

Magbish "pile"

Magdala "the tower"

Magdiel "choice gift of God"

Magog "place of Gog"

Magor-Missabib "terror on every side"

Magpiash "moth exterminator"

Mahalaleel or Mahalalel "God shines forth" or "praise God"

Mahalath "dance" or "sickness"

Mahanaim "two camps"

Mahaneh-Dan "camp of Dan"

Maharai "hurried one"

Mahath "tough"

Mahazioth "visions"

Maher-Shalal-Hash-Baz "quick to the plunder, swift to the spoil"

Mahlah or Mahalah perhaps "weak one" or "sickness"

Mahli "shrewd" or "cunning" or "sick, weak one"

Mahlon "sickly"

Mahol "place of dancing"

Malachi "my messenger" or "my angel"

Malcam or Malcham "their king"

Malchiel "my God is king"

Malchijah or Malcijah or Malkijah or Melchiah "my king is Yahweh"

Malchiram "my king is exalted"

Malchishua or Melchishua "my king is salvation"

Malchus "king"

Mallothi "I spoke"

Malluch "being king"

Mamre "grazing land"

Manaen Greek form of Menaham meaning "comforter"

Manahath "resting place" or "settlement"

Manasseh "God has caused me to forget"

Manoah "rest"

Maoch "dumb, foolish"

Maon "dwelling"

Mara "bitter"

Marah "bitter"

Maralah or Mareal "site on mountain ledge"

Marcus Latin form of Mark meaning "large hammer"

Mareshah "place at the top"

Mark "large hammer"

Maroth "bitter" or "bitter fountain"

Martha "lady" or "mistress"

Mary Greek form of Miriam meaning "rebellious, bitter" or "beloved" or "God's gift"

Masrekah perhaps "vineyard"

Massa "burden"

Massah "to test, try"

Mattan "gift of God"

Mattanah "gift"

Mattaniah "gift of Yahweh"

Mattathias or Matthias "gift of Yahweh"

Mattattah "gift"

Mattenai "my gift"

Matthew "gift of Yahweh"

Mattithiah "gift of Yahweh"

Mebunnai "building of Yahweh"

Medad "beloved"

Medan "judgment"

Medeba "water of quiet"

Media perhaps "middle land"

Megiddo "place of troops"

Mehetabeel or Mehetabel "God does good"

Media perhaps "middle land"

Mehujael "struck by God" or "priest of God"

Mehuman "trusty"

Mejarkon "waters of Jarkon" or "pale-green waters"

Melatiah "Yahweh has set free"

Melchi "my king"

Melchizedek or Melchisedec "Zedek is my king" or "my king is righteousness"

Melech "king"

Memphis "the abode of the good one"

Menahem "consoler"

Menuhoth "resting places"

Mephaath "height"

Mephibosheth "shame destroyer" or "image breaker"

Merab "to become many"

Meraiah "Yahweh has promised" or "stubborn"

Meraioth "obstinate" or "rebellious"

Merari "bitterness" or "gall"

Merathaim "double bitterness" or "double rebellion"

Mered "rebel"

Meremoth "heights"

Meribbaal "opponent of Baal" or "obstinacy of Baal" or "beloved or hero of Baal"

Merodach-Baladan "Marduk gave an heir"

Merom "high place"

Mesha "safety"

Meshach "who is what Aku is?" or "the shadow of the prince"

Meshech or Meshek "sowing" or "possession"

Meshelemiah "Yahweh is recompense"

Meshezabeel or Meshezabel "God delivers"

Meshillemoth or Meshillemith "reconciliation"

Meshullam "allied" or "given as a replacement"

Meshullemeth "restitution"

Messiah "anointed one"

Methuselah "man of the javelin" or "worshiper of Selah"

Mezahab -- "waters of gold"

Micah or Mica "who is like Yahweh?"

Micaiah or Michah or Michaiah "who is like Yahweh?"

Michael "who is like God?" or "who is like El?"

Michal "who is like El?" or "who is like God?"

Michmash "hidden place"

Michmethah or Michmethath "hiding place" or "concealment"

Midian "strife"

Migron "precipice"

Milcah "queen"

Milcom "king" or "their king"

Millo "filling"

Miniamin "lucky, from the right hand"

Miriam perhaps "bitter" or God's gift" or "beloved" or "defiant"

Mishael perhaps "who is what God is?"

Misham perhaps "to inspect"

Mishma "fame"

Mishmannah "strength" or "tasty morsel"

Mithredath "gift of Mithra"

Mitylene "purity"

Mizar "littleness" or "little"

Mizpah or Mizpeh "watch-tower" or "lookout"

Mizpar or Mispar "writing"

Moab perhaps "from my father"

Moadiah "Yahweh promises" or "Yahweh's ornament"

Moladah "generation" or "kindred"

Molech or Moloch "king"

Mordecai "little man"

Moreh "instruction" or "archers"

Moresheth, Moresheth-Gath "inheritance of Gath"

Moriah perhaps "to see" or "to provide" or "Amorites"

Moses "drawn out of water" or Egyptian meaning "son, son of"

Moza "offspring"

Mozah "unleavened"

Mushi "draw out"

Naam "pleasantness"

Naamah "pleasant" or "delightful"

Naaman "pleasantness"

Naarah or Naarath "girl" or "mill"

Nabal "fool" or "rude, ill-bred"

Nabonidus "Nabu is awe-spiring"

Nabopolassar "Nabu, protect the son"

Naboth "sprout"

Nacon or Nachon "firm" or "prepared"

Nadab "willing" or "liberal"

Nahalal or Nahalol or Nahallal "pasture"

Nahaliel "palm grove of God" or "torrent valley of God" or "God is my inheritance"

Naham "consolation"

Nahash "serpent" or "magnificent"

Nahath "descent" or "rest" or "quietness" or "pure, clear"

Nahbi "hidden" or "timid"

Nahor or Nachor "snore, snort"

Nahshon or Naashon or Naason "serpent"

Nahum or Naum "comfort, encourage"

Nain "pleasant"

Naioth "dwelling"

Naomi "my pleasantness"

Naphish "refreshed"

Naphtali "wrestler"

Narcisus "daffodil"

Nathan "gift" or "he gives"

Nathan-Melech "the king has given" or "Molech has given"

Nathanael "giver of God"

Nazareth "branch"

Neah "settlement"

Neapolis "new city"

Neariah perhaps "Yahweh's young man"

Nebat "God has regarded"

Nebo "height"

Nebuchadnezzar or Nebuchadrezzar "Nabu protects"

Nebushasban or Nebushazban "Nabu save me"

Nebuzaradan "Nabu has given offspring"

Nedabiah "Yahweh is generous"

Negeb or Negev "dry" or "south"

Nehemiah "Yahweh comforts or encourages"

Nehushta "serpent" or "bronze"

Neiel "dwelling place"

Nepheg "boaster"

Nephtoah "opening"

Nergal "lord of the great city"

Nergal-Sharezer "Nergal, protect the king"

Neri "lamp"

Neriah "Yahweh is light"

Netaim "plantings"

Nethaneel or Nethanel "given by God"

Nethaniah "given of Yahweh"

Nethinim "those given"

Netophah "dropping"

Neziah "faithful" or "illustrious"

Nicanor "conqueror"

Nicodemus "conqueror of the people"

Nicolas or Nicolaus "conqueror of people"

Nicopolis "city of victory"

Niger "black"

Nimrah "clear"

Nimrim "leopards" or "basins of clear waters"

Nimrod "we shall rebel"

Nimshi "weasel"

No or No-Amon "best city" or "best city of Amon"

Noadiah "Yahweh has met"

Noah "rest"

Nobah "barking" or "howling"

Nod "wandering"

Nodab "nobility"

Obadiah "Yahweh's servant"

Obal "stout"

Obed "serving"

Obed-Edom "serving Edom"

Obil "camel driver" or "tender" or "mourner"

Oboth "fathers" or "water skins"

Ocran or Ochran "troubler"

Oded perhaps "counter" or "restorer" or "time-keeper"

Ohad "unity"

Oholah "tent dweller"

Oholiab "father's tent"

Oholibah "tent worshiper"

Oholibamah "tent of the high place"

Omar "talkative"

Omri "pilgrim" or "life"

On "city of the pillar"

Onam or Onan "power"

Onesimus "profitable" or "useful"

Onesiphorus "profit bearing"

Ono "grief"

Ophel "swelling, fat"

Ophir "dusty"

Ophni "high place"

Ophrah "fawn"

Oreb "raven"

Oren "cedar"

Orpah "neck" or "girl with a full mane" or "rain cloud"

Othniel "God is powerful"

Ozem "irritable" or "strength"

Paddan-Aram or Padan-Aram perhaps "way of Syria" or "field of Syria" or "plow of Syria"

Padon "redemption"

Pahath-Moab "governor of Moab"

Palal "God comes to judge"

Palti or Phalti "my deliverance"

Paltiel or Phaltiel "God is my deliverance" or "El is my deliverance"

Parah or Perath "heifer" or "young cow"

Parmenas "faithful" or "constant"

Parosh or Pharosh "flea"

Parri "revelation of Yahweh"

Paruah "blossoming" or "joyous" or "increase"

Pasdammin "boundary of blood"

Paseah or Phaseah "lame"

Pashur "son of Horus"

Patrobas "life of father"

Pau or Pai "they cry out"

Paul "little"

Pedahel "God delivers"

Pedaiah "Yahweh redeems"

Pekah "open-eyed"

Pekahiah "Yahweh has opened his eyes"

Pelaiah "Yahweh is wonderful or performs wonders"

Pelatiah "Yahweh delivers"

Peleg or Phalec "division" or "watercourse"

Pelet "escape"

Peleth "swift"

Peninnah perhaps "woman with rich hair" or "coral" or "pearl"

Penuel or Phanuel "face of God"

Peor "opening"

Peresh "separate"

Perez or Phares or Pharez "breach"

Perez-Uzzah or Perez-Uzza "breach of Uzzah"

Pergamum or Pergamos "citadel"

Perida "unique" or "separated"

Persis "Persian woman"

Peter "rock"

Pethahiah "Yahweh opens"

Pethor "sooth-sayer"

Pethuel "vision of God" or "youth of God"

Peullethai or Peulthai "recompense"

Pharaoh "great house"

Phibeseth "house of Bastet"

Phicol or Phichol "mighty"

Philadelphia "love of brother"

Philemon "affectionate"

Philetus "beloved"

Philip "fond of horses"

Philologus "lover of words"

Phinehas "dark-skinned one" or "mouth of brass"

Phlegon "burning"

Phoebe or Phebe "bright"

Phoenicia "purple" or "crimson"

Phoenix "date palm"

Phyrgia "parched"

Phygelus "fugitive"

Pihahiroth "house of Hathor"

Pilha or Pileha "millstone"

Piram perhaps "wild ass"

Pirathon "princely" or "height, summit"

Pisgah "the divided one"

Pishon "free-flowing"

Pitham "mansion or estate of Atom"

Pochereth-Hazzebaim or Pokereth-Hazzebaim "binder of gazelles"

Potiphar "belonging to the sun"

Prochorus or Procorus "leader of the chorus"

Puah "girl" or "red dye"

Publius "pertaining to the people"

Pudens "modest"

Punon "ore pit"

Purah or Phurah "beauty" or "fruitful"

Put or Phut "foreign bowman"

Putiel "he whom God gives" or "afflicted by God"

Pyrrhus "fiery red"

Quartus "fourth"

Rabbah or Rabbath "greatness"

Rabshakeh "chief cupbearer"

Rachel or Rahel "ewe"

Raddai "Yahweh rules"

Rahab "arrogant, raging, turbulent, afflicter"

Rahab or Rachab "broad"

Raham "mercy, love"

Ram "high, exalted"

Ramah or Rama "high"

Ramath "height, elevated place"

Ramiah "Yahweh is exalted"

Ramoth-Gilead "heights of Gilead"

Rapha or Raphah "he has healed"

Reaiah "Yahweh has seen"

Reba "lie down"

Rebekah or Rebecca perhaps "cow"

Rechab "rider" or "charioteer"

Regem "friend"

Rehob "broad or open place"

Rehoboam "he enlarges the people"

Rehoboth "broad places"

Rehum "merciful, compassionate"

Rei "friendly"

Rekem "maker of multicolored cloth"

Remaliah "may Yahweh be exalted" or "Yahweh adorned"

Remeth "height"

Rephaiah "God healed"

Rephaim "shades" or "dead"

Resen "fountain head"

Resheph "flame"

Reu "friend, companion"

Reuben "Look!, a son"

Reuel "friend of God"

Reumah "coral"

Rezeph "glowing coal"

Rezin "pleasant, agreeable"

Rezon "prince"

Rhoda "rose"

Ribai "Yahweh contends"

Rimmon or Remmon "pomegranate"

Rimmon-Perez "pomegranate of the pass"

Rimmono "his Rimmon"

Rissah perhaps "dewdrop" or "rain" or "ruins"

Rithmah "broom plant"

Rizia "delight"

Rizpah "glowing coals" or "bread heated over coals"

Rogelim "place of the fullers"

Romamti-Ezer "I have exalted help"

Rosh "head" or "chief"

Rufus "red-haired"

Ruhamah "pitied"

Rumah "elevated place"

Ruth "refresh" or "be satis-
fied" or "friend, compan-
ion"

Sacar or Sachar "salary"

Salim "peace"

Sallai perhaps "the restored
one"

Salome "pacific" or "peace,
well-being"

Salu "the restored one"

Samaria "mountain of watch-
ing"

Samos "height"

Samson "of the sun"

Samuel or Shemuel "Sumu is
God" or "his name is
God" or "his name is El"

Sanballat "Sin has healed"

Sansannah "branch of the
date palm"

Saph or Sippai "threshold"

Sapphira "beautiful" or "sap-
phire"

Sarah or Sara or Sarai
"princess"

Saraph "burning"

Sargon "the king is legiti-
mate"

Sarid "survivor"

Sarsechim or Sarsekim
"overseer of black slaves"
or "overseer of mercenary
troops"

Satan "adversary"

Saul or Shaul "asked for"

Sebam or Shebam "high" or
"cold"

Secacah "covered"

Sechu or Secu perhaps
"lookout"

Secundus "second"

Segub "he has revealed himself as exalted" or "he has
protected"

Seir "hairy" or "thicket"

Seirah or Seirath "toward
Seir"

Sela "rock"

Selah-Hammahlekoth "rock
of hiding, haunt, refuge"

Seled "jumping"

Seneh "shiny" or "slippery"

Senir "pointed"

Sennacherib "Sin has re-
placed my brother"

Seorim "the shaggy-haired"

Seraiah "Yahweh has proved
himself ruler"

Seraphim "burning ones"

Sered "baggage master"

Seth "he set, appointed" or "replaced"

Sethur "hidden"

Shaalabin or Shaalbim "places of foxes"

Shaalim or Shalim "caves, cavities"

Shaaraim "double doors"

Shabbethai "belonging to the Sabbath"

Shachia "Yahweh fenced in or protected"

Shadrach "circuit of the sun" or "servant of Sin"

Shaharaim "double dawns"

Shalem "peace, safety"

Shalisha or Shalishah "the third"

Shallum "replacer" or "the replaced"

Shalmai "coat"

Shalman "complete, peace"

Shalmaneser "Shalmanu is the highest ranking one"

Shama "he has heard"

Shamgar "Shimig has given"

Shamir "thorn" or "diamond"

Shammah or Shimeah perhaps "frightful" or "astonished" or "he heard"

Shammai "he heard"

Shammua or Shammuah "one who has heard"

Shaphan "coney"

Shaphat "he has established justice"

Sharai "he loosed or redeemed"

Sharezer "protect the king"

Sharon "flat land" or "wetlands"

Shaveh "valley, plain" or "ruler"

Sheal "ask"

Shealtiel "I have asked of God"

Sheariah "Yahweh has honored" or "Yahweh knows"

Sheba or Shibah "fullness, completeness"

Shebah "overflow" or "oath"

Shebaniah "Yahweh came near"

Shebarim "the breaking points"

Sheber perhaps "foolish one" or "lion" or "fracture"

Shebna or Shebnah "he came near"

Shebuel "return, O God"

Shecaniah or Shechaniah "Yahweh has taken up dwelling"

Shechem "shoulder, back"

Shedeur "Shaddai is light"

Shelah "please" or "be still, rest"

Shelemiah "Yahweh restored, replaced, repaid"

Shelomi "my peace"

Shelomoth or Shelomith "peaces"

Shelumiel "God is my wholeness or health"

Shem "name" or "dusky"

Shema "a hearing" or "hyena"

Shemaah "a hearing"

Shemaiah "Yahweh heard"

Shemariah "Yahweh protected"

Shemeber "powerful name"

Shemed or Shamed "destruction, ruin"

Shemer "protection, preservation"

Shemidah or Shemida "the Name has known" or "the Name troubles himself for"

Shen "tooth"

Shenazar or Shenazzar "Sin protects" or "may Sin protect"

Shephatiah "Yahweh has created justice"

Sheresh "sprout" or "sly, clever"

Sheshbazzar "may Shamash protect the father"

Sheva "similarity, like" or "vanity"

Shicron or Shikkeron "henbane"

Shihor or Sihor "pool of Horus"

Shilhi "he sent me" or "Salach has me" or "my offshoot"

Shiloah "being sent"

Shiloh perhaps "tranquil, secure"

Shilshah perhaps "little triplet"

Shimea or Shimeah "hearing"

Shimeath "hearing"

Shimei or Shimi or Shimhi "my being heard"

Shimrath "protection"

Shimri or Simri "my protection"

Shimshai "little sunshine"

Shinab "Sin is father"

Shiphi "my overflow"

Shiphrah "beauty"

Shiphtan "process of justice"

Shittim "accacia trees"

Shoa "help!"

Shobab "one brought back" or "fallen away, rebel"

Shobal "lion" or "basket" or "overflowing"

Shobek "victor"

Shuah "sunken" or "prosperity"

Shual "jackal"

Shur "wall"

Shushan "lily" or "lotus"

Sia or Siaha "helper"

Sibmah "cold" or "high"

Siddim "flats" or "fields"

Silas or Silvanus "asked"

Siloam "sending" or "the sender"

Simeon "hearing" or "little hyena beast"

Simon "flat-nosed"

Sinai perhaps "to shine"

Sirah "thorn"

Sisera "mediation"

Sitnah "hated, opponent"

Socoh or Soco or Shocho "thorns"

Sodi "my counsel"

Solomon "his peace" or "Salem"

Sopater "sound parentage"

Sophereth "learning"

Sorek "red grape"

Sosipater "to save one's father"

Sosthenes "of safe strength"

Stachys "head of grain"

Stephanas "crown"

Stephen "crown"

Succoth "booths"

Succoth Benoth "booths of daughters"

Suph "reed"

Susanna "lily"

Susi "my horse"

Sychar perhaps "falsehood"

Syntyche "pleasant acquaintance" or "good luck"

Taanath-Shiloh perhaps "approach to Shiloh"

Tabbath "sunken"

Tabeel "God is good"

Taberah "burning"

Tabitha "gazelle"

Tabor perhaps "height"

Tahan "gracious"

Tahash "porpoise" or "dugong"

Tahath "beneath, low" or "substitute, compensation"

Tahpanhes or Tehapanes "fortress of Penhase" or "house of the Nubian"

Talmai "plowman" or "big"

Talmon "brightness"

Tamar or Thamar "date palm"

Tanhumeth "comforting"

Taphath "droplet"

Tappuah "apple" or "quince"

Taralah "strength"

Tarshish or Tharshish "yellow jasper" or "smelting plant"

Tebah "slaughter"

Tebaliah "Yahweh has dipped, that is, purified" or "loved by Yahweh" or "good for Yahweh"

Tekoa "place of setting up a tent"

Tel-Abib or Tel-Aviv "mound of the flood" or "mound of grain"

Tel-Assar "mound of Asshur"

Tel-Harsha or Tel-Harsa or Tel-Haresha "mound of the forest" or "mound of magic"

Tel-Melah "mound of salt"

Telah "breech" or "fracture"

Telaim "young, speckled lambs"

Telem "brightness" or "lamb"

Tema "south country"

Teman "right side, southern"

Terah or Thara perhaps "ibex"

Teresh "firm, solid" or "desire"

Tertius "third"

Tertullus "third"

Thaddaeus perhaps "gift of God" or "breast nipple"

Theophilus "friend of God"

Theudas "gift of God"

Thomas "a twin"

Tibhath "place of slaughter"

Tibni "intelligent" or "straw"

Tiglath-Pileser or Tilgath-Peleser "my trust is the son of Esarra"

Tikvah or Tikvath or Tokhath "hope, expectation"

Timaeus "highly prized"

Timna "holding in check" or "she protects"

Timnah or Timnath "allotted portion"

Timon "honorable"

Timothy "honoring God"

Tiphsah "passage, ford"

Tiria "fear"

Tirzah "she is friendly"

Toah "humility"

Tob "good"

Tobadonijah "Yahweh, my Lord, is good"

Tobiah or Tobijah "Yahweh is good"

Tochen "measure"

Toi "error"

Tola "crimson worm"

Tophet or Topheth "fire-place"

Trachonitis "heap of stones"

Trophimus "nutritious"

Tryphaena or Tryphosa "dainty" or "delicate"

Tychicus "fortunate"

Ucal "I am strong" or "I am consumed"

Uel "will of God"

Unni "afflicted" or "answered"

Ur "fire oven"

Urbanus "of the city" as in "elegant, refined"

Uri "fiery"

Uriah "fire of Yahweh"

Uriel "God is light" or "flame of God"

Urijah "flame of Yahweh"

Uthai "Yahweh is help" or "he has shown himself supreme"

Uz or Huz "replacement"

Uzza or Uzzah "he is strong"

Uzai "hoped for" or "he has heard"

Uzzen-Sheerah "ear of Sheerah"

Uzzi "Yahweh is my strength"

Uzzia or Uzziah "Yahweh is strong, mighty"

Uzziel "God is strength"

Vaniah perhaps "worthy of love"

Vashti "the one desired, beloved"

Zaavan or Zavan "tremble" or "quake"

Zabad "he has given" or "gift"

Zabbud "gift"

Zabdi "my gift"

Zabdiel "God gives gifts" or "my gift is God"

Zabud "endowed"

Zaccai "pure" or "innocent"

Zaccheus "innocent"

Zaccur or Zacchur "well remembered"

Zadok "righteous"

Zaham "fatness" or "loathing"

Zair "small"

Zalaph "caper plant"

Zalmon "little dark one" or "small image"

Zalmonah "dark" or "shady"

Zalmunna "protection is withdrawn" or "Zelem rules"

Zanoah "broken district" or "stinking"

Zaphnath-Paneah or Zaphen-ath-Paaneah "the god has said, he will live"

Zaphon "north"

Zarephath "smelting, refining" or "to dye"

Zarethan or Zaretan or Zaranah or Zarthan perhaps "cooling"

Zebadiah "Yahweh has given"

Zebah "slaughter" or "sacrifice"

Zebedee "gift"

Zebidah or Zebudah "gift"

Zeboiim "hyenas"

Zeboim "hyenas" or "wild place"

Zebul "prince" or "captain"

Zebulun or Zabulon perhaps "elevated dwelling" or "honor, exalt"

Zechariah or Zachariah "Yahweh remembered"

Zedad "sloppy place" or "mountainous"

Zedekiah or Zidkijah "Yahweh is my righteousness" or "Yahweh is my salvation"

Zeeb "wolf"

Zelah or Zela "rib, side, slope"

Zelek "cleft, fissure"

Zelophehad "protection from terror"

Zemaraim "twin peaks"

Zemira or Zemirah "song"

Zenan "flocks"

Zenas "gift of Zeus"

Zephaniah "Yahweh sheltered or stored up" or "Zaphon is Yahweh"

Zephath "watchtower"

Zephathah "watchtower"

Zephi "purity" or "good fortune"

Zephon or Ziphion perhaps "north" or "lookout"

Zer "narrow" or "enemy"

Zerah or Zareah "sunrise"

Zerahiah "Yahweh has dawned"

Zeresh "shaggy head, disheveled"

Zerubbabel or Zorobabel "descendant of Babel"

Zeruiah "perfumed with mastix" or "bleed"

Zethan "olive tree" or "olive merchant"

Zibeon "little hyena"

Zibiah or Zibia "female gazelle"

Zichri "remembrance, mindful"

Ziddim "sides"

Ziha "the face of Horus has spoken"

Zillah "shadow"

Zillethai "Yahweh is a shadow"

Zilpah perhaps "short-nosed"

Zimmah or Zimnah "Yahweh has considered or resolved"

Zimran "celebrated in song, famous" or "mountain goat"

Zimri "Yahweh helped" or "Yahweh is my protection" or "Yahweh is my praise"

Zion "dry place" or "parched ground" or "hillcrest" or "mountainous ridge"

Zior "smallness"

Ziph perhaps "flowing"

Ziphah "flowing"

Zipporah "small bird" or "sparrow"

Ziz "blossom"

Ziza or Zizah "shining" or "brightness"

Zoar "small"

Zohar "witness" or "yellowish-red" or "tawny"

Zoheleth "creeping one"

Zophah "bellied jug"

Zophai perhaps "honeycomb"

Zophar perhaps "twittering bird" or "to leap"

Zophim "watchers"

Zorah or Zoreah "wasps" or "hornets"

Zuar "small" or "young"

Zuph "honeycomb"

Zur "rock"

Zuriel perhaps "God is a rock" or "my rock is God" or "rock is God"

Zurishaddai "Shaddai is a rock"